D0121701

Disclaimer: The opinions presented herein are solely those of the author except where specifically noted. Nothing in the book should be construed as investment advice or guidance, as it is not intended as investment advice or guidance, nor is it offered as such. Nothing in the book should be construed as a recommendation to buy or sell any financial or physical asset. It is solely the opinion of the writer, who is not an investment professional. The strategies presented in the book may be unsuitable for you, and you should consult a professional where such consultation is appropriate. The publisher/author disclaims any implied warranty or applicability of the contents for any particular purpose. The publisher/author shall not be liable for any commercial or incidental damages of any kind or nature.

First edition published April 2012

Oftwominds.com
P.O. Box 4727
Berkeley, California 94704

RESISTANCE
REVOLUTION
LIBERATION
A Model for Positive Change

Charles Hugh Smith

For my siblings Constance and Craig, who have always supported my writing.

Table of Contents

Introduction

When we see the word "revolution," the shared imagination conjures up images of violent political upheaval. I use the word not to denote the bloody overthrow of a political order, but to describe a blossoming of understanding so profound that it leads to peaceful transformation of our social order, economy and culture.

Concerted action flows from ideas that make sense of what no longer made sense in the old worldview. Thus a revolution in understanding leads to transformative action in the real world.

When a set of ideas share a coherent structure, we call it a philosophy. This book presents a unified philosophy of human nature and the transition of destabilizing social orders to new arrangements.

This book differs from other works of philosophy and political economy in three important ways. First, and perhaps most importantly, it is conscientiously limited in length. Contrary to popular supposition, it is far easier to write a long book than a short one. (I know, because I have written both.) Each chapter of this book could easily be expanded into a much longer work, but I have accepted the much more arduous task of composing a limited-length book that embraces a broad spectrum of ideas.

Second, it has long been a truism in the academic sector that produces the vast majority of books on philosophy and political economy that clarity and simplicity cannot possibly capture "serious thinking." As a result, only work that is intentionally "difficult," that is, linguistically codified for "academics only," passes muster.

This perverse inversion of insight—simplicity and clarity are rejected in favor of the intentionally opaque—results from the political structure of academia, which requires elaborate "gatekeeping" to conserve the existing order. Adding to the confusion is what we might term "hard-science envy," the social sciences' yearning for the rigor of the quantifying sciences. These two unspoken forces within academia have fostered a norm that substitutes technical jargon for readily accessible thinking.

Those seeking a secure position within the system self-select "data-driven" (i.e. mimicry of hard science) topics of inquiry. Simply put, broad speculation, especially the variety which subverts the Status Quo, has been selected out of academia. By devolving to career-driven signifiers recognizable only to other academics, "serious thought" has fully detached from the economy as we live it. Not coincidentally, in detaching from the real world, academia parallels the nation's tarnished financial sector, which has also unmoored from the real economy, and the Central State, which has abandoned the interests of the many to serve the interests of the few.

In effect, academia, government and the financial sector select out, corrupt or marginalize anyone challenging the Status Quo. What remain are trivialized speculations that threaten no power structure and superficial analyses that implicitly support a parasitical and predatory Status Quo by studiously ignoring the pathologies of our social order and economy.

As a result of these forces, "public intellectuals" from academia, government and the government-dependent private sector are incapable of critical thinking that threatens the intellectual foundations of the Status Quo. In the current system, their financial self-interest can only be served by joining the Upper Caste of the neofeudal social order and loyally serving powerful financial and political Elites (the modern-day equivalent of landed aristocracy and nobility).

The pool of leadership has thus been poisoned as potential leaders have been corrupted into complicity. Leadership of the peaceful transformation to a sustainable, just and free society thus falls to all who have opted out, been selected out or marginalized; the citizenry must lead, as their leadership has become hopelessly corrupted by the system that enriches and empowers the Upper Caste and the Elites it serves.

To understand the irrelevance of Status Quo "serious thought" to our situation, we might profitably turn to Buddha's Parable of the Poisoned Arrow, in which the Buddha differentiates between academic questions about a poisoned arrow lodged in one's chest—who shot it, what species of wood is the shaft made of, and so on—and the practical urgency to remove the arrow. If we pause to ponder all the possible technical and metaphysical questions raised by our colliding crises, we will expire—and without the answers we so distractedly sought. We are running out of time to parse irrelevancies.

Thus "serious thought" that implicitly supports the Status Quo via ritualistic appeals to social control myths, simulacra critiques and pseudo-realities becomes the opposite—trivial and superficial.

Those benefitting from our sociopathological, neofeudal Status Quo (as well as those who have been persuaded that their participation benefits them) will see no need for revolution. Indeed, they will view any transformation as a threat to their personal share of the Status Quo perquisites. But fundamental transformation is no longer a choice, whether you believe the Status Quo serves your self-interest or not. The unsustainable will crumble and another arrangement will take its place.

We cannot know when the Central State and financial system will destabilize, we only know they will destabilize. We cannot know which of the State's fast-rising debts and obligations will be renounced or written down; we only know the debts and obligations will be renounced in one fashion or another.

The process of the unsustainable collapsing under its own weight and being replaced with a new, more sustainable model is called revolution, and it combines cultural, technological, financial and political elements in a dynamic flux. Though these systemic transitions can be profitably understood as cycles, history only illuminates past transitions; what the new arrangement will be is our choice.

Given the entrenched nature of the neofeudal Elites and the Upper Caste that serves them, it is no surprise that revolution carries a negative connotation, as if any change that isn't instigated and directed by our corrupt leadership is considered illegitimate and dangerous to the social order. As noted above, that which is unsustainable will crumble regardless of the wishes of those benefitting from the Status Quo. Shall we call this inevitable crumbling "positive" because it is undirected by a coherent philosophy, and any coherently directed transformation "negative" because it places the interests of the many above those of the few?

Perhaps the Status Quo has it backward, and it is the uncontrollable dissolution of the unsustainable financialized State that we should fear, and the peaceful, transformative revolution we should welcome as a positive development for all—even those who cling to all that is unsustainable.

We will cover a great many ideas in the chapters ahead, and one that helps us understand our reluctance to embrace positive change is the social control myth. These myths are propagated and marketed by the Status Quo to maintain control of the social order so that it serves the interests of those in power at the expense of the non-Elites. If you control an individual's beliefs, you control his actions, habits and responses.

The key social control myth is that the system serves your self-interest. If you believe this, then you will defend an oppressive, exploitive, parasitical Status Quo in the misplaced belief it serves your personal interests.

The chief purpose of propaganda is to establish and renew various social control myths. Central States have long deployed powerful myths to solidify their control: "we are being threatened by outside forces, so rally round" remains popular due to its enduring success.

Another key social control myth is that individuals are powerless in the vast systems that dominate our society and economy. This is a very useful myth to the Status Quo, as it leads individuals to surrender their autonomy and liberty without coercion.

In the myth of top-down revolution, nothing can possibly change until the leadership has been replaced and vast, impersonal systems far beyond our individual influence have been reworked at the top of the pyramid.

In terms of directly influencing the centralized political and financial structures that dominate our lives, we are debt-serfs gazing upon the aristocracy's distant, inaccessible castle. But our remoteness from concentrations of wealth and power does not render us powerless.

The truth is that revolution and liberation are within our reach; when we liberate our minds from pathological illusions of self-interest, we have already achieved the first key step of liberation. We can do so without the permission of the aristocracy or the centralized State they control.

Rather than being powerless, we hold the fundamental building blocks of power. We need neither permission nor top-down political change to liberate ourselves. A powerless individual becomes powerful when he renounces the lies and complicity that enable the doomed Status Quo's dominance.

A single individual within a corrupt institution who reveals the truth can change history in a profoundly positive way, for the truth is always a positive force. Every individual who refuses to secure personal security at the expense of truth becomes powerful in ways that are beyond the reach of wealth and corruption.

This book challenges the conventional view of revolution and liberation. In the standard view, there are two basic types of revolution, one political and one spiritual. The political version involves the replacement of leadership and the reformation of State governance. In the mythology of political revolution, individuals participate in the transformation by joining public assemblies that often veer into destruction and violence.

In a spiritual revolution, participants eschew the political realm as either intrinsically polluted or simply irrelevant; they care not who or what ideology claims power, all are equal in spiritual terms. The resulting liberation is an essentially internal transformation of insight and faith.

The model of positive change I propose here is a synthesis of both internal and external liberation. In my view, political liberation is impossible if the mind and spirit are shackled by pathological conceptions of self-interest, and spiritual liberation is limited by the oppression and predation of corrupting, exploitive political-financial systems.

Peaceful transformation to a sustainable, non-pathological society and economy require both internal and external transformations—but the internal one must come first. That inner understanding then guides concerted action in the lived-in world toward positive goals that are not oppressive, exploitive or parasitical.

The mythology of political revolution is colored by chaos, violence and a disavowal of law. The revolution I describe here is legal and non-violent, for destruction and violence are counter-productive to positive transformation.

The mythology of spiritual revolution holds that political and economic systems are irrelevant to inner liberation. To the degree that political and financial systems limit freedom of faith, exchange, movement, expression, enterprise and association, then they limit the potential of all humans living under those systems. The lived-in world is the one we inhabit, and liberation is only partial if it is restricted to the mind and spirit.

Though it may seem as if we have no power in the current state of affairs, the reality is that our participation and complicity enable the Status Quo's pathologies and predation. Pathological systems dissolve when the citizens stop supporting the Status Quo with their participation, votes, resignation (i.e. "we have no choice") and complicity.

To fully understand the systems that dominate our lives and offer the false choice of either complicity or active support of the Status Quo, we must understand the dynamics of self-interest and the matrix of risk, gain, threat and loss that arises from both human nature and life itself.

We must also understand that our reason for supporting the Status Quo—to insure our own security and prosperity—is being invalidated by the changing nature of security and prosperity. The promises of financial security being made by the Central State are profoundly illusory, and the fundamental question "what is security?" is now an open one that demands new answers.

In all my work, I stress the importance of establishing an *integrated understanding* that clearly lays out the context and dynamics of our era. That is the first goal of this book.

The second goal is to irrevocably change your life in a positive fashion by changing the way you understand our world, and to do so via this one book.

Whether we like it or not, we are in an era of colliding crises that will culminate in a transition to a new social and economic system. Humanity always has burdens and troubles—that is the nature of a changeable world interacting with human nature—but there are decades in which little happens and years in which decades happen. We are in just such an era, and we will all be swept along by events that no longer respond to the Status Quo's financial magic.

It's easy to confuse faith and political ideology. We resist changing our understanding, as we experience this transition as instability and insecurity. But changing our minds does not require changing our faith; rather, the firmness of our faith—in our Creator, in truth, in our ability to help others and prevail—is the bedrock that gives us the discipline and resolve to confront the brutally unwelcome facts of our circumstances and make coherent plans accordingly.

You can now discern the third way in which this book differs from others on philosophy or political economy. It has long been apparent to me that no account of systemic transitions can make sense of our lived-in world unless it synthesizes an ethological understanding of human social order, an understanding of the Central State and modern capital's control of society, and perhaps most importantly, the experience of liberation. This may seem to describe a psychological state, but it actually describes a state of being in the lived-in world.

History is not fixed; it is in our hands. Revolutions spring not from history or abstract ideologies or street rebellions but from the transformed understanding of individuals. You cannot await a transition unfolding in a remote future or capitol to transform your life; that revolution begins in your internal understanding and reaches fruition in your coherently directed actions in the lived-in world.

Chapter One: Why the Financialized Economy and State Are Unsustainable

The Status Quo actively promotes the premise that it is both sustainable and eternal. Yet the system's demographic, financial and resource foundations are clearly unsustainable. The Status Quo's basic argument is the rear view mirror offers an excellent view of what lies ahead; those outside the Power Elites have looked through the windshield and discovered that the Status Quo's sustainability is illusory: past stability is no guarantee of future stability.

I have covered our systemic unsustainability in my books *Survival+: Structuring Prosperity for Yourself and the Nation* and *An Unconventional Guide to Investing in Troubled Times*, and many other authors have addressed the same issues in depth. Since there is no way to summarize entire books into a few lines, I will illustrate the unsustainability with a few examples.

The U.S. economy and Central State (in the U.S., the Federal government) both rely exclusively on creating vast quantities of money (i.e. increasing the money supply) and debt to sustain their operations. The Federal government borrows about 10% of the nation's entire output (GDP) each and every year ($1.5 trillion), or about 40% of its budget, if you include off-balance sheet supplemental borrowing.

Since the consumer no longer has the housing bubble to generate phantom assets that can be leveraged into more borrowing, consumer spending is now restrained to actual disposable income. Due to the rapid expansion of mortgage, student and consumer debt, much of this income is devoted to debt service, i.e. paying principal and interest.

Expanding debt is not cost-free; not only does it require paying interest, but as interest payments rise there is less money for consumption and investment. As a result, real (adjusted for inflation) disposable household income has been declining significantly in all income levels since 2008.

The solution offered by the Federal Reserve is to lower interest rates to zero so insolvent banks, local governments and consumers can all borrow more or mask their insolvency by refinancing old debt at lower rates. The debt does not disappear, but it becomes manageable over the short-term at near-zero rates of interest.

Due to a dynamic known as marginal return, it now takes $10 of new debt to generate $1 of economic activity. This requires debt to expand at fantastic rates to keep the economy expanding even modestly. (Back in the early 1960s when debt levels were modest and investment opportunities more abundant, a mere $1.50 in additional debt added $1 to the GDP.)

By some accounts, adding $10 in new debt actually causes a $1 decline in GDP as the costs of servicing that debt outweigh whatever thin shred of economic activity was added.

Rising debt has a consequence: rising interest. This consequence can be masked for a time by lowering interest rates, but unfortunately for the Federal Reserve's solution, interest rates cannot drop below zero.

The solution is for the Central Bank (the Federal Reserve) and Federal government to give banks and other insolvent enterprises hard cash to maintain the illusion of solvency. The Federal government borrows the money by selling Treasury bonds and then transfers it to its favored cartels via subsidies and bailouts. The Federal Reserve does so in a slightly less obvious fashion: it loans billions of dollars to banks at zero interest, then accepts this newly minted money back as deposits from the banks. It then pays interest to the banks on the free money they just received from the Federal Reserve. The banks receive interest on money that was given to them at zero interest.

Creating money out of thin air and borrowing immense sums have consequences. Once you expand the money supply at rates that far exceed the actual expansion of goods and services produced by the economy, then eventually money becomes so plentiful that it loses its value. When this dynamic reaches extremes, it is known as hyper-inflation.

If debt expands while the income that is leveraging the debt remains stagnant, eventually most of the income is diverted to servicing this debt, i.e. paying interest. That leaves little to no income for capital investment, and the economy starves itself to death. Only those collecting the interest, i.e. the financial sector, profit from this death spiral.

We can understand this death spiral by comparing a capital investment with debt. When an enterprise buys a machine tool or computer to increase productivity, that tool or computer eventually wears out or becomes obsolete. The productive life of the tool or computer is not only finite; it is relatively short—a few years at best. Debt, on the other hand, never expires. It is permanent and deathless until it is paid or renounced by default or bankruptcy.

Once the rising costs of servicing debt squeeze out new investment, the productivity from the aging equipment declines, as do profits (what I prefer to call surplus income). This sets up a positive feedback loop in which declining productivity lowers profits which means future investment is crimped, which further lowers productivity, and so on in a death spiral.

Once an entity has to borrow money to pay its expenses, then interest payments crowd out investment. Without new investment to replenish aging equipment, productivity and surpluses decline, reducing the pool of surplus available to pay the rising interest. When interest payments have crowded out all investment, then dwindling productivity can no longer generate the surplus needed to pay the interest, and the entity defaults on its debts.

Once this death spiral becomes undeniable, those with capital refuse to lend more money to the entity. Once it cannot borrow more, then it can no longer pay its expenses. This is scale-invariant, meaning that it holds true for households, companies and sovereign governments.

Lowering interest rates only masks this death spiral temporarily. It is much easier to create credit than it is to actually increase the production of goods and services in the real world. Debt can be added effortlessly even as the production of actual goods and services stagnates.

When an economy creates money and debt at rates far above the rate of expansion of its goods and services, then eventually the cost of servicing debt crimps investment, which then lowers productivity to the point that the economy starves itself to death as all surplus is devoted to paying interest on ballooning debt.

If a household's income is stagnant but its expenses rise by 6% a year, eventually the household will be unable to pay its expenses. If the household increases its debt 10% a year to pay its expenses, then eventually the principal and interest of the rising debt will crowd out all other expenses, and the household will no longer be able to meet its obligations.

Any nation that relies on expanding debt to pay its expenses, including the United States of America, is financially equivalent to that household.

Here is the primary point: creating debt and printing money do not create wealth. All they can create is a temporary illusion of wealth.

Nations have one trick they can use to extend the illusion of solvency: they can devalue their currency by creating vast quantities of it. In the short-run, this creates phantom "growth." Here is a real-world example: when a U.S.-based corporation earned 1 euro in profit in 2002, when it converted that profit into U.S. dollars it equaled $1. When the company earned 1 euro in 2008, after the Federal Reserve's relentless devaluation of America's currency, then that 1 euro magically became $1.60 in profit when converted to dollars.

The foul magic of currency devaluation created an illusory 60% rise in profits, which then boosted the stock market and tax revenues. Yet no more goods and services were created; the value of the item sold for 1 euro in profit was unchanged.

That illusory 60% rise in profits could then be leveraged into more debt: since income in dollars rose, then that income stream could support more debt. Yet the company did not create any more goods or services; the rise in profits was financial slight-of-hand, not an increase in efficiency or production.

Phantom assets created by devaluation or bubbles (in housing, stocks or tulip bulbs) can leverage new debt for only so long, and debt can expand faster than the real economy for only so long. The proverbial straw being loaded on the camel's back offers an excellent analogy: debt, like straw, appears light in small quantities, but in large enough quantities it will break the back of any economy, no matter how large.

Many people have boundless faith in technological solutions to all of humanity's troubles. Since current policies will lead to either the destruction of the purchasing power of money or the diversion of most surplus income generated by the economy to paying interest, then where will all the money come from to fund technological transformation? Private capital is not immune from these forces;

indeed, corporate debt has skyrocketed right alongside consumer and public debt.

The Status Quo policies are intended to produce the same solution that has worked for the past 300 years: economic expansion. Rising debt and interest payments both become lighter if the entire economy expands faster than the debt and interest. Thus in what we might call "the good old days" of high growth, $1 in capital is leveraged into $10 of new credit, which is then lent out and invested in fast-growing industries. This infusion of capital investment fuels rapid expansion of output, employment and profits large enough to handily pay the interest on the borrowed money and still fund further investment.

The past 300 years could be described as technology and capital moving from one tree's low hanging fruit to the next, all powered by higher energy-density fuels becoming cheaper and more widely available. Recently, the digital technology revolution has enabled dramatic increases in productivity and efficiency, creating more value with less energy, thus freeing up energy for recreational consumption.

We can understand the Status Quo's faith in this model of "growth conquers all problems, including indebtedness"—the model has shown remarkable resilience, making fools of all who doubted the notion that creating credit out of thin air was a dangerous way to fund growth.

There is a basic problem that these advances in energy and productivity have masked: it is much easier to create credit/money than it is to actually increase the production of goods and services in the real world. Put another way, the supply of trees bearing low-hanging fruit is not infinite. But since the creation of credit and loaning out money is so immensely profitable and low-cost, then borrowed capital is far more abundant than productive investment opportunities.

This is how mal-investment occurs: easily borrowed money seeks a high return, and the very abundance of such credit leads to investments being made in risky low-return investments. These mal-investments do not just fail to deliver returns, they collapse into stupendous losses.

A recent example is expensive luxury homes being built in the middle of nowhere during the housing bubble. At the time, it seemed as if any house built anywhere could be sold for a handsome profit, and so borrowed capital gushed like a mighty river into building homes far from jobs and other essentials.

This is one example of the financialization of the global economy: the process of creating credit from thin air and leveraging it into debt-based financial instruments is far more profitable than actually attempting to produce more goods and services in the real world. If all goes according to the "growth conquers all problems, including indebtedness" model, then there is no risk of losses ever becoming large enough to dent the pyramiding of debt and financial profits.

In other words, when the low-hanging fruit of investment opportunities become scarce, then the creation of debt and leverage become the dominant generators of profit. Thus financial profits have come to dominate the returns of the Standard & Poor's 500 corporations (the S&P 500).

Unfortunately, the growth model finally failed in 2007 because most of the capital being borrowed and invested was being invested in projects that did not yield an actual increase in goods or services. Building a luxury home in the middle of a field added to the nation's gross domestic product, but it didn't create any new goods or services; it was simply another form of consumption. Once the market discovered its real value was lower than its initial cost, then the illusion that building it created "growth" and "wealth" was shattered.

On the surface, the Internet boom of the 1990s and the housing bubble of the 2000s both generated strong increases in gross domestic product (GDP), employment and profits. But there were three fundamental differences between the two periods of growth.

In the Internet boom, capital flowed into companies that grew at spectacular rates building the infrastructure, both hardware and software, of the global Internet. It also flowed into companies that didn't grow and thus failed. Though some companies did borrow vast sums via corporate bonds, in general the money invested in technology companies was cash—what we call capital. If the company failed, that capital was lost. There was no debt to pay off.

The housing bubble, on the other hand, was fundamentally a credit bubble: vast sums of money were created out of thin air and invested in housing. Banks leveraged $1 in capital (cash) into $25 in new loans. When the bubble popped, the "wealth" vanished but the debt remained.

The second difference is that the Internet boom created an immensely productive technology that continues to lower costs via increasing efficiency in every sector of the global economy.

The housing bubble created no infrastructure or productive technologies; it was purely consumption. Once the homes were built then the increase in GDP, jobs and profits vanished, but the immense debts taken on remained to be paid. Mortgage debt roughly doubled in the bubble from $5 trillion to $10 trillion, and has barely declined in the five years since the 2007 bubble top.

This is the difference between productive investment and mal-investment: productive investment is based mostly on cash capital, and it creates assets that generate real value for years to come. Mal-investment is based on credit (borrowed money) and generates no productive technologies. It is essentially a financial event that briefly generates financial gains for banks from an explosive expansion of credit and speculation.

These mal-investments failed, and since the borrowed money was leveraged by phantom assets, then that failure led to the near-collapse of the global credit-creation machine. This is not difficult to understand: if we create a $10 loan with $1 of actual cash, then the moment the asset the borrower bought with the $10 is only worth $8.90, then the lender is bankrupt since the $1 of actual cash has been lost. The lender has a negative value and can no longer issue more credit.

Which type of growth generated the most profits for the financial sector, productive or mal-investment? The speculative, credit-bubble frenzy of the housing bubble was far more profitable, as it created more debt for the financialization machine to package and enabled a broader spectrum of "financial innovations" to sell for hefty upfront premiums.

There is another deeply pernicious dynamic in this financialization. As financial profits come to dominate an economy, then the economy (and the Central State that lives off tax revenues) becomes increasingly dependent on the creation of new leverage, new debt and new financial instruments to sell for its growth and profits. This need to issue new debt and debt instruments creates irresistible incentives for lenders to push newly borrowed money into increasingly risky and marginal investments; whether the investments fail or not no longer matters, because the profits are made by the origination and selling of the leveraged debt.

The interests of the financial sector and the Central State that depends on financial profits thus diverge from those of real-world, non-financial enterprises: the real-world enterprise is still constrained by the physical world of equipment and plant, by the costs of debt and the marketplace for goods and services. The financial sector makes money by creating debt and debt-based instruments from thin air and selling them for an immediate profit. When the debt goes bad, i.e. the borrower stops paying interest and principal, then the Central State steps in and transfers the losses from the private financial sector to the public. These enormous losses then burden the taxpayers for decades to come.

Put another way: financialization richly rewards all who originate vast quantities of debt and out-of-thin-air financial instruments that end up burdening the real-world economy. Financialization is thus a subtle but very real feedback loop of self-destruction.

Financialization did not unfold in a vacuum: Central State and central bank policies either enable or discourage leverage and mal-investment. At this point we might wonder why the Central State continues pursuing and enabling such visibly risky and ultimately destructive policies. The answer is profoundly obvious and thus profoundly dangerous: the rise of financialization created gargantuan concentrations of wealth, and since the political class requires huge sums of money to win re-election, these concentrations of wealth essentially bought control of the machinery of governance via unprecedented levels of campaign contributions and lobbying.

Such is their influence—or shall we be direct and call it a partnership of wealth and political power—that the Central Bank (the Federal Reserve) prints and distributes cash to the banking sector via the mechanism described above, and the Central State has injected trillions of dollars of direct cash subsidies and bailouts to the financial sector.

The self-serving apologists for this looting of the public coffers claim that this was necessary to maintain the "engine of growth that conquers all problems, including indebtedness." But this rationalization has failed to mask the reality that the Central State and bank's partnerships with extreme concentrations of financial wealth have broken the engine of growth by institutionalizing extremes of debt, leverage, fraud, misrepresentation of risk, mal-investment and devaluation of the nation's money.

As noted above, the expansive Central State requires an expanding economy and an expanding surplus that it can tax. It also requires a robust market for its own debt, Treasury bonds, so it can borrow virtually unlimited sums to fund its expansion.

Once the low-hanging fruit was all harvested, financial profits from the issuance of debt became the dominant source of growth and taxes. This is a key point: financialization serves the interests of the Central State even as it works against the interests of the citizenry. In other words, once a State becomes dependent on financialization for its own growth, the interests of the State diverge radically from those of its citizenry.

These financialization policies do not serve the interests of the citizens and taxpayers who now stagger under titanic burdens of public debt, but they do serve the interests of the political class devoted to maintaining their grasp on power and the financial sectors which have profited so immensely from the policies of the Central State they now control.

The Status Quo propaganda machine ceaselessly claims that the policies of the Central State and bank are aimed at restarting the "engine of growth conquers all problems, including indebtedness;" but the reality is the policies of the Central State and bank have crippled the engine of growth and put the nation into an economic death spiral.

As noted above, there are real-world limitations on the growth paradigm; there are not an infinite number of trees bearing low-hanging fruit awaiting capital investment to reap a windfall of productivity and profits. Indeed, the increasing visibility of marginal return suggests that windfalls have become few and far between, and that input costs are rising while output surplus is declining. In other words, more and more capital must be invested to reap less profit, and since surplus is declining, then the only way to get capital is to borrow money, which then increases the interest that must be paid out of the surplus. Once again we have a death spiral based on rising debt.

Surplus is simply what's left over after we subtract the total costs of the production from the value of the output. If all the investment capital was borrowed, then interest payments will make up a substantial portion of the production costs. If the surplus declines, then the cost of servicing the debt will eventually exceed the profit, and the enterprise will spend more than it takes in. Once its cash is devoured by losses, it becomes insolvent.

In other words, the financialization of the economy works admirably when the surpluses created by investing borrowed money grow faster than the interest payments. But once the surpluses decline, then the cost of servicing the monumental debt devours the enterprise from the inside.

Another way of describing this death spiral is depreciation outstrips new investment and rising interest outstrips increases in income.

There are two other reasons surpluses diminish in eras of concentrated financial and political power: Elites (aristocracy, oligarchy, theocracy, etc.) are fundamentally parasitical, contributing little if any productive value to the economy while absorbing a significant share of the surplus being generated. In our era, the parasitical classes include the financiers benefitting from financialization and the political class which feeds off the financial Elite's wealth.

In other eras, these parasitical classes might have been religious aristocracies constructing grandiose monuments to their order's glory or warlords bent on conquest. The nature of the parasitical Elite matters less than its size and burden on the economy. The more concentrated the wealth and power held by the Elite, the larger its consumption of the surplus. When the surplus shrinks below a critical threshold, the entire predatory, top-heavy social order collapses in a heap.

The second drain on surpluses in eras of self-serving financial and political power is what the Romans called "bread and circuses," the bribes offered to potentially restive classes of citizenry whose loyalty to the Status Quo is conditional. In the latter stages of Roman decline, some 40% of the population of Rome received free bread, and lavish, distracting entertainments (once held only on special occasions) were hosted by the Central State on a year-round basis. Both the free bread and free circus extravaganzas were horrendously costly, yet as the interests of the Elite diverged from those of the dwindling, overtaxed productive classes, these bribes to the lower classes were considered as vital to the survival of the Status Quo as the military legions—both of which eventually bankrupted an Empire ruled by an Elite obsessed with its own self-preservation.

Combine the heavy costs of supporting parasitical Elites with the ever-rising costs of bribing the non-Elite classes into sullen complicity and you soon have a deadly reduction of surplus to zero and the State implodes under its own weight.

The Elites ruling the Central State are left with only two ways to finance their dominance: devalue the currency, that is, steal purchasing power from every holder of the currency by creating new currency from thin air (i.e. the theft we know by the carefully benign term "inflation") or they borrow money from those with capital, and hope the lenders remain blind to the fact that their loan will never be paid back at full value.

Neither of these strategies works for long; rather, they hasten the collapse of an increasingly unsustainable social order dominated by predatory, parasitical self-serving Elites.

Creating credit only sparks productivity when the borrowed money is invested in high-value, high-profit enterprise so that the economy expands at a faster rate than the debt. Once credit is diverted to low-return mal-investments and debt skyrockets while the real economy stagnates, a financialized economy is revealed for what it truly is, a machine of self-destruction.

The Central State and bank have masked this self-destruction with three policies: zero interest rates that lower the short-term burden of monumental debts, bailouts of the politically protected financial sector, and perhaps most perniciously, the transfer of private financial-sector debts to the public via massive public borrowing. Rather than put an end to destructive leverage, indebtedness and financialization, the Federal government has embraced them as its core solution: borrow stupendous sums of money to prop up the Status Quo, all leveraged off future tax revenues, and hope future growth will somehow outrun the runaway debt train.

I have described the "magic solution" the Status Quo is relying on, "the engine of growth conquers all problems, including indebtedness," and explained why debt-based financialization necessarily leads to a death spiral of declining productivity, investment and profits. There is one other "magic solution" that many are counting on to erase the burdens of overleverage and over-indebtedness: inflation, i.e. the destruction of the currency.

This can be explained by a simple example. If there is $100 in the money supply, and $100 of goods and services to trade, then $1 will be exchanged for $1 of goods and services. If the money supply suddenly increases by $100, then the value of the existing $100 declines by half, as the money supply is now $200 and the supply of goods and services remains unchanged. Thus it now takes $2 to buy $1 in goods and services.

Holders of the currency have had half the value of their currency (what we call purchasing power) stolen by the central bank that issued the additional $100 in money supply.

The "magic" to this "solution" is that a $10 debt has effectively been reduced to $5: the debt can be repaid in full with the newly inflated currency, and the lender can only buy $5 worth of goods and services with the $10 he received in payment of the debt.

This is a very bad deal for holders of the currency, who have lost 50% of the value of their money, and for lenders, who also lost half the value of their loan. It is a good deal for borrowers, as their debt effectively declined by 50%.

The reason why this "magic solution" cannot possible work is equally simple. The interest rate charged on debt is sensitive to the devaluation of currency (i.e. inflation). If the currency is being devalued at 10% a year, then those with capital to lend will requires 13% interest in order to earn a real return of 3%, that is, they will add 3% to the rate of inflation/devaluation. This means the cost of new debt will always exceed the rate of inflation. This raises the cost of servicing debt and severely limits the issuance of new debt. Economies and households alike that depend on borrowing money to pay their expenses are quickly bankrupted by spiraling interest payments.

As interest costs rise, the surplus left for new investment is reduced, and once again we are back in a death spiral of rising interest payments and declining capital investment which leads to lower productivity and lower surpluses, and so on to the point of insolvency.

The Federal Reserve can manipulate the interest rate it charges banks, but it cannot set the interest rate private lenders demand. It can manipulate these rates by buying bonds, that is, artificially reducing the supply of debt, but its own balance sheet quickly explodes higher—by $2 trillion in the past few years. Ultimately, the Fed can only control interest rates by becoming the buyer of last resort. That will only succeed if the Fed's balance sheet expands to infinity and private lending ceases.

This is in effect what has happened in the home mortgage market: between the Fed buying $1 trillion of existing mortgages and the Federal government guaranteeing new mortgages, private mortgage lending has fallen to a mere 1% of the market. In other words, mortgage rates are only low because the entire mortgage market has been socialized by the Fed and the Central State. The "free market" in mortgages has ceased to exist, and all the stupendous risks of keeping the real estate bubble inflated have been transferred to the taxpayers.

There are two fundamental characteristics of capitalism: capital (cash savings) is put at risk in an investment to earn a return, and a transparent market discovers the price of debt, assets and risk. Once the market is no longer free to price the cost of money, assets and risk—i.e. when the State and central bank socialize the entire mortgage market—then we no longer have capitalism.

The term "moral hazard" describes the separation of risk and return, and the Federal Reserve and the Federal government have institutionalized moral hazard by guaranteeing all mortgage loans issued by private lenders, no matter how defective or risky they might be. This creates perverse incentives to further financialization, as banks and lenders know the State will transfer their losses to the public, while letting the banks and lenders keep the profits.

All that this socialization of risk accomplishes is that it transfers the death spiral of rising interest, declining surplus and marginal return to the Central State, i.e. the taxpayers. As the Central State attempts to collect enough tax revenues to fund its rising interest and other expenses, then it further squeezes private funds available for investment. This lowers the productivity of the private economy, which then generates fewer surpluses for the State to tax, and so on in another positive feedback death spiral.

The risk of ballooning debt cannot be extinguished, it can only be transferred; even the apparently all-powerful Federal Reserve and Federal government cannot rescind the consequences of runaway debt and financialization.

I have carefully described the dynamics of financialization, political corruption and moral hazard, and explained why financialization and reliance on debt for growth leads inevitably to a death spiral. There is no way out of this death spiral; there is no "magic." Either the currency is devalued to near-zero, wiping out the wealth of the citizens holding the currency, or the costs of servicing the ballooning debt bankrupt the nation by choking productivity and investment.

Debt cannot sustainably rise faster than the production of real goods and services. If your expenses rise by 6% a year and your income rises by 2% a year, then within a very few years your expenses will exceed your income and you will go broke: your debts will be repudiated and your other expenses will not be paid.

A third "magic solution" presents itself: taxing the Elites who own most of the nation's wealth and garner much of the national income. This is indeed a tempting solution, but it fails to grasp the point made above: it really doesn't matter who owns the economy if expenses expand by 6% a year and net income only rises by 2% a year; the system is in a death spiral of inevitable insolvency and bankruptcy. The Central State could expropriate the entire wealth of the financial Elite and absolutely nothing would change in the final outcome.

Indeed, many governments have tried this "magic" and found their economies implode anyway: if expenses and debt are rising while the actual surplus generated by the real economy is stagnant, then eventually the costs of servicing debt exceed the economy's net income. At that point, the debt is repudiated (default) and the expenses—State wages, pensions, entitlements, etc. —go unpaid.

The two options at the end of the death spiral, hyper-inflation or default, are not identical. If the Central State and bank choose to "solve" the problem of exponentially expanding debt by printing money to create inflation, then that inflation destroys all money. Everyone holding money (dollars) is wiped out.

Defaulting on debt, on the other hand, only wipes out debt-based assets. There is a key difference: destroying the value all money via high inflation wipes out people and enterprises who did not participate in the explosion of speculative debt—they held cash and cash assets. Since high inflation destroys all money, cash assets are wiped out and the innocent—those with cash capital—are wiped out even though they did not participate in the financialization.

Here is an example of how high inflation works. If inflation has been boosted to 30% a year to rid the Central State of its debts and obligations, then by year four, inflation has eroded $1 to a mere 24 cents. Any debt paying a fixed rate of low interest must be heavily discounted because no one wants a bond paying 5% when inflation is running 30% a year, so owners of debt-based assets have seen the value of their asset eroded just like cash. By year nine the value of the initial $1 has fallen to 4 cents, meaning that the debtor can pay off $1 in debt with 4 cents of purchasing power. Both cash and debt-based assets have been depreciated to near-zero.

This is excellent news for the Central State, which can then redeem fixed-rate bonds purchased for $1 with a mere 4 cents, even as its citizens' wealth is destroyed. This is why so many observers expect the State to pursue the path of high inflation, as it enables the central State to pay its debts for pennies on the dollar.

This works well if the Central State has ceased borrowing, but if its borrowing increases due to the death spiral described above, it must pay 33% interest on all new debt (3% real return plus the 30% inflation rate). Since inflation destroys capital and any incentive to invest over the long term, then high inflation causes productivity and investment to falter, leading to the same death spiral of lower productivity and higher interest payments.

Alternatively, if $1 in debt is written down to 4 cents in one fell swoop via default, then cash money retains its value and the incentives to invest capital for long-term gains in productivity remain in place. Those who hold cash are not punished for the sins of the debtor Central State, and those who bought debt-based assets (that is, they believed that extremes of leverage and debt posed no risk) suffered the loss when the risk was finally recognized. In other words, with default, risk and gain/loss are causally connected; in high inflation, everyone's wealth is destroyed to maintain the illusion of Central State solvency.

Wiping out debt strengthens the positive incentives of holding cash while exacting a cost for over-borrowing and speculating in debt-based financial "innovations." Wiping out debt via high inflation reinforces the incentives to borrow excessively and punishes anyone holding cash or investing capital in the real economy.

Default would wipe out those who depend on debt-based speculation, i.e. the "too big to fail" financial sector. This would be the equivalent of a vast swarm of crippling parasites suddenly dropping dead; the long-suffering organism (in this case, the real economy) would suddenly regain its vigor.

If we grasp even half the implications of the financialization death spirals described in this chapter, then our rational minds understand the Status Quo is unsustainable, and its various magic tricks to escape the death spiral are only actively speeding our approach to the cliff of insolvency.

Yet few of us are willing to entertain an exit from the belief system that supports the Status Quo.

I liken this to the state of mind on the "unsinkable" ocean liner, *Titanic*, moments after the ship's brief encounter with an iceberg on the night of April 14, 1912. In those first few moments, the ship seemed undamaged, and the possibility that the glancing collision with the iceberg had fatally wounded the great ship seemed not just remote but impossible.

Unbeknownst to everyone on board, the ship had fatal material and design flaws. The steel plates of the hull were brittle and did not deform when struck by the ice, they fractured much like shattered china. The ship was designed to survive four of its 16 watertight compartments being flooded, but the iceberg damaged six, dooming the great liner.

Shortly after the collision, simple calculations revealed that the ship would inevitably sink: as the first five watertight compartments flooded, water would eventually cascade over the top of the adjacent bulkheads in a domino-like effect.

The officers, though knowledgeable and experienced, had trouble grasping this fact, and this helps explain the confusing mix of reassurances given to passengers and half-measures to goad them into lifeboats when the ship's bow had only begun to settle slowly into the cold water of the Atlantic.

How many people would have acted on this knowledge had they been present at the briefing? We would like to think we would have acted appropriately by either boarding a lifeboat or if that was not possible, by lashing together deck chairs to form a makeshift raft, or some other method of remaining afloat after the great liner met its inevitable doom.

But few people acted on the inevitable until it became undeniable. By then, it was too late.

The financial system of the United States of America is like the *Titanic*. Hubris leads many to declare it financially unsinkable even as its fundamental design is riddled with fatal flaws and the human pilots in charge are running it straight into the ice field at top speed.

I have just explained in some detail how these flaws doom the financial system and government finances alike to either default or destruction of the nation's currency. There are no other end-points.

We could insist on changes to these policies, but we do not; why?

Some of our reluctance can be attributed to disbelief, as the gap between what we know is inevitable—the ship will sink beneath the waves—and what we currently see—a proud, mighty ship, apparently undamaged—is so wide.

But if we delve deeper, we discern how calculations of risk and gain yield faulty assessments of self-interest. While the ship appears undamaged, it seems risky to clamber into an open lifeboat and drift away into the freezing night, while the supposed gain (saving our life) is questionable: from the warm deck of the ship, it seems that clambering onto a lifeboat would place our life far more at risk than staying on board the mighty ship.

This assessment of self-interest was tragically flawed, and by the time the impossible (sinking) had become the inevitable, it was too late to change the fate we'd selected back when all seemed permanent and secure.

The point of this exercise is to reveal just how illusory our assessment of self-interest and security can be, and how prone we are to making decisions based on the present even when our rational minds are well aware that it is unsustainable.

The Central State offers us plentiful reasons—incentives, promises and threats —to believe it is in our self-interests to accept the Central

State and bank policies, even though it is obvious they will lead to moral, political and financial bankruptcy.

This dynamic can be illustrated by an examination of the Medicare system that promises us with lifetime medical care after we reach 65 years of age. This is unsurprisingly an extremely popular program, and thus politically untouchable except for minor policy adjustments.

Yet it is also visibly unsustainable: program costs rise by 6% or more annually, while the underlying economy that must fund it grows by 2% at best. Demographics render the program unsustainable, too; 60 million Baby Boomers are beginning to enter the system even as people live longer and the range of possible treatments expands every year. Anyone who looks into the costs and demographics concludes that Medicare alone will inevitably bankrupt the nation. The only way to paper over the reality is to assume rapid growth of the entire economy will suddenly outrace the costs of Medicare—in other words, the same old hope that's supposed to solve every problem: future growth that is so rapid it outraces debt, demographics and an ever-expanding Central State.

All of this should make us question our political devotion to the program, but that's not even the worst of it. Numerous studies have found that 40% or more of Medicare expenses are fraudulent, and another significant percentage is wasted on needless or even counterproductive tests, care, medications and procedures.

We know all this but we refuse to renounce our share of the illusory promise: if everyone else is going to get their share, then I deserve mine, too. The fact that no one can possibly receive what has been promised simply doesn't register in our calculation of self-interest.

In effect, the Central State has bribed us into complicity with a modern-day version of bread and circuses: don't dare question the system, because you'll be placing your share of the goodies at risk.

This is an interesting phenomenon, for our perception of self-interest is clearly delusional: there is no way that Medicare can fulfill what has been promised, yet we cling to the promise because it seems to serve our self-interest. Like the passengers in the warm interior of the *Titanic* gazing out at the cold sea, we cling to our belief in the mighty ship's invulnerability until it's too late and we're sliding down the tilting deck into the very sea we feared.

But this is only the leading edge of what's interesting about self-interest: even when told the program will bankrupt the nation, we still want our share. In other words, what's real and immediate to us is going to the hospital and paying almost nothing for treatment; the destruction of the nation's finances is abstract and apparently disconnected from our windfall of nearly-free visits to the hospital.

We will not believe the program is unsustainable until it fails.

This self-delusion has a great cost: rather than face reality when the situation could be salvaged, we refuse to believe our perception of self-interest is misplaced until it's too late.

This delusion has been institutionalized within the sprawling, expansionary Central State. The Central Intelligence Agency (CIA), for example, appears to be keenly aware of the risks to national security posed by America's dependence on unstable or unfriendly nations for its oil supply, by extremes of weather, geopolitical tensions, etc. Yet it appears, at least publicly, to be completely blind to the threat posed by the domestic death spiral of financialization.

As I write in March 2012, the Federal Reserve and the Federal government's policies of masking the inevitable outcome of exponentially expanding debt appear to be intact; but these policies have done nothing but buy time even as they hasten the eventual reckoning.

To many, it seems impossible that such a powerful nation could be brought to its knees by mere debt, in effect digital zeroes and ones. But debt is now the lifeblood of the nation and its global empire, and if that debt machine shakes to pieces then the nation will be unable to pay its mounting expenses by issuing more debt.

I liken the present to the final days of the mighty Ming dynasty in China. In 1640, the dynasty's power and stability were unquestioned; four short years later, the dynasty collapsed in a tangled heap of shattered stability and illusory strength.

The Chinese have an apt saying: when you're thirsty, it's too late to dig a well. We're not yet thirsty in America, so we have no interest in digging a well. When we do suddenly feel thirst, it will be too late.

This delusional faith in the Status Quo is not entirely self-directed; the Status Quo actively markets the illusion that it serves our self-interest as a way of promoting its self-preservation and masking the great divergence of our real interests from those of the Elites atop the Status Quo.

But it is merely another iteration of self-delusion to think that our delusion is only political and financial; its roots extend deep into human nature and our basic insecurities that are exploited so effectively by the Status Quo's marketing machine.

Stripped of illusion, we can now understand the Status Quo is unsustainable, that the interests of its Elites and the citizenry have radically diverged, and that the dominance of these parasitical, financialized Elites is ruinous to the nation.

The renunciation of the Elite's heavily promoted version of our self-interest is the first step in liberation. The second step is to recognize that the citizenry do not need the approval or permission of the Elite or the Central State they rule to pursue their own positive transformation.

Why do we accept a Status Quo that will inevitably fail to fulfill its promises? Why do we continue to believe that the Status Quo serves our self-interests? Why do we submit to a framework of beliefs that render us powerless to change our circumstances?

Our faulty assessment of self-interest has several deep causes that range across the social, political and economic spectrum. Balancing risk and gain is the foundation of our self-interest, and only by exploring risk can we understand how our calculations of risk and gain can be so spectacularly self-destructive.

Control of beliefs, myths, worldviews, contexts and agendas is also political control, and so we must understand how the media-marketing complex shapes our perception of the world and our own definition of self-interest. Control of the financial system ultimately translates into political power, too, and so we must understand these mechanisms as well.

To fully understand all these interconnected forces, we must examine human nature, marketing and the nature of groups, societies and economies. Though this may appear to have little to do with resistance, revolution and liberation in either a political or spiritual sense, this integrated understanding is essential to our synthesis of these two modes of positive change.

Revolutions, peaceful and non-peaceful alike, occur when two conditions are met:

1. The Status Quo is no longer able to serve the interests of its non-Elites as promised.

2. The non-Elites finally recognize that the Status Quo is designed to serve the interests of Elites and thus it has lost the capacity to serve their interests.

These may seem to be restatements of the same condition but they are quite different. The first condition has already been met, though it is not yet apparent because the financial *Titanic* still appears mighty. The second condition will only occur when the ship is finally sinking beneath the waves.

Chapter Two: **Understanding Systemic Instability**

People respond to their social order and government in three basic ways: they actively support it, they comply or they resist/opt out. Those who believe the Status Quo serves their self-interests will actively support it; those who feel the benefits of complicity outweigh the risks of resistance will comply, and those who realize the Status Quo is doomed and cannot possibly serve their best interests will resist or opt out.

As the Status Quo is unsustainable, then the belief that the system serves the interests of the non-Elites will become increasingly disconnected from reality. Why is this so? The core dynamic of the Status Quo is that the system's gains flow to the Elites while the risks and losses are transferred to the citizenry. Once the Status Quo can no longer mask this reality with vast sums of borrowed or printed money, then the reasons to support the system disappear.

As long as the vast majority of the people feel it is in their best interests to support the regime, then the Status Quo can marginalize resistance with minimal effort. But once a critical number of the populace realize the system cannot possibly serve their interests, then the Status Quo must devote an increasing share of its surplus to suppress resistance and persuade everyone else that the system serves their interests. Since the Status Quo is designed to benefit Elites by concentrating the gains into their hands and transferring risk to the system itself, this reality must be masked by claims that the system nobly serves the interests of non-Elites.

This diversion of surplus to suppression and propaganda opens divisions within the various Elites, and their grip on power is eroded by this disunity.

But the Status Quo is unsustainable for reasons far beyond extreme concentrations of wealth and power. Focusing exclusively on the Elites distracts us from even deeper systemic sources of instability. From this perspective, parasitical Elites are simply one source of instability among many.

In summary, the claims on any system cannot exceed the surplus of actual goods and services generated by the system. As input costs rise and the surplus declines, then attempts to satisfy the claims will capsize the system. That is the U.S. economy in a nutshell.

Measuring risk and gain is fundamental to our assessment of self-interest. Once it becomes clear that the risks of complicity outweigh the possible gain, resistance and self-reliance become the lower risk, higher gain options. Once the reality of domination by extreme concentrations of wealth and power has been exposed, then public anger will render active support of the regime an increasingly risky option.

Governments and Elites do not arise by magic. People enable the Central State and private Elites with their support. Once their support is withdrawn, apparently stable regimes crumble like sand castles hit by the rising tide of history. The same can be said of financial systems.

We have seen how financialization is unsustainable, and the Status Quo is papering over this reality with the temporarily successful expedients of financial artifice and propaganda. But financialization is not the only reason the Status Quo is increasingly unstable; there are a number of other sources of rising instability, and they arise from the very nature of systems. We have been trained to believe that policies shape our world, but these are ultimately surface phenomena of much deeper dynamics.

Once we understand these systemic sources of instability, we will better understand how our perception of self-interest can be so misaligned from reality.

The Ecosystem Model

We intuitively understand the symbiotic nature of ecosystems: that the various plant and animal species and micro-organisms that make up an ecosystem interact in symbiotic ways, and that various feedbacks from the environment affect every organism in the ecosystem. Ecosystems provide endless examples of the dynamics that affect humanity as well as all other organisms: competition, cooperation, feedback, mutation, adaptation, selection and diversity.

Human societies and economies can be understood as ecosystems driven by these same dynamics.

We can observe that sustainable, resilient ecosystems are populated by a wide diversity of species and individuals within the species. This diversity fuels the dynamics which enable individuals, groups, species and ecosystems to adapt and thrive.

Conversely, we can observe that ecosystems which are depleted of diversity become monocultures that are prone to collapse.

Modeling human societies and economies as ecosystems offers practical insight into why some human systems stagnate and collapse and why others are robust and adaptable. In general, systems in which diversity and variation—what we call dissent, innovation and experimentation—have been eliminated in favor of monocultures that offer greater efficiency are increasingly vulnerable to disruption and collapse.

The monoculture appears stable on the surface, but this stability is illusory; ultimately the surface calm is a result of stripping out volatility and diversity, the very dynamics that create systemic stability, and of a massive investment in brute-force suppression of variation, volatility and dissent.

We can understand this dynamic by considering another natural system, the immune system. Our immune system is enormously complex and requires a significant amount of energy to maintain. Our efficiency and the surplus we generate would be much higher if the immune system were shut down; all that energy could then be harvested as "work" or gain. This mirrors the efficiency of monocultures.

But we all know what happens when the immune system is suppressed or shut down: the organism soon dies as it has lost the ability to dynamically adapt to threats and disruptions caused by infections or accidents. In a sense, monocultures eliminate the small failures of low-intensity instability and in doing so they also eliminate the key dynamic of success, which is the constant feedback of low-intensity variation and experimentation, much of which we register as failure.

The forces of low-intensity instability—risk, threat, failure, feedback, fluctuation, variation, volatility, mutation, innovation, experimentation, competition, transparency, natural selection (meritocracy), accountability, consequence, accurate communication of facts and the free exchange of information —inevitably pose a threat to those benefitting from the monoculture of the Status Quo, as any change in the system might weaken their power and increase their exposure to risk.

(Note: to avoid listing all the features of low-intensity instability repeatedly, I will use the acronym LII to represent the essential elements of success: risk, threat, feedback, fluctuation, variation, volatility, mutation, innovation, experimentation, competition, transparency, selective pressure (meritocracy), accountability, consequence, accurate communication of facts and the free exchange of information. These forces lend dynamic stability to any system.)

Those inside the system perceive low-intensity instability (LII) as risk. But in suppressing LII, they are in effect suppressing the system's immune system and thus dooming the entire system to instability and eventual collapse. The one essential element of success is unimpeded low-level instability, and that is precisely what is eliminated in monocultures and tyrannies.

What appears to be in the self-interest of those inside the Status Quo actually leads to the destruction of the system they depend on for their power; thus their sense of self-interest is completely and utterly self-destructive.

Another way to understand monocultures is to see them as brute force attempts to make natural systems yield only what we desire, that is, steadily rising gains, by suppressing the very elements that give the system its stability and adaptability. In mismanaging natural systems, we eliminate the features that offer stability and conserve the very features that guarantee the system's self-destruction.

Monocultures are not limited to agriculture; financialization is also a form of monoculture, as is globalization. Corporate-backed electioneering is a form of monoculture, as is a mass media owned by six corporations. "Just in time" global supply chains are strings of monocultures. In effect, the entire Status Quo is an interlocking series of monocultures, all attempting to make natural systems yield only gain by eliminating risk and the "inefficient" foundations of stability with brute force: the Federal Reserve's monetary policy, the Federal government's massive deficit spending, and in agriculture, vast quantities of pesticides.

The entire modern global economy and the modern Central State are economic monocultures that have suppressed the social "immune system" and stripped the economic ecosystem of diversity in pursuit of efficiency, concentrated capital and political control.

In Chapter One, we saw how financialization and its handmaiden, the expansive Central State, are intrinsically unsustainable. If we understand our economy and society as ecosystems, we can see that they are unsustainable for an even more basic reason: the very dynamics essential to systemic stability have been stripped out in service of efficiencies (also called profits) and concentrations of capital and political power. What is left is a series of increasingly unstable monocultures that dominate an ecology strip-mined of every force that could threaten the dominance of Status Quo Elites. Since those forces are essential to systemic stability, the Status Quo's suppression of risk is akin to suppressing the nation's immune system. Without the dynamic protection of an immune system, the system, unable to adapt, inevitably expires.

We have been trained to believe that minor policy modifications can fix whatever ails the nation's economy. Once we understand that systemic instability is far beyond the reach of mere policy tweaks, we see that policy modifications are like applying a new pesticide to a monoculture. In the short-term, they successfully suppress variation, competition and dissent (low-intensity instability) with brute force, but eventually these temporary suppressions create systemic instability that no longer responds to policy tweaks or another dose of poison.

At that point the entire system implodes in an unpredictable cascade of destabilization. That is the U.S. economy and Savior State in a nutshell.

S-Curves and Fractals

If we observe ecosystems and organisms, we find that the trajectory of their histories often traces out patterns that are found across Nature.

For example, if we chart the emergence and advance of organisms and trends, we find they follow an S-curve, a pattern of emergent growth followed by a period of rapid expansion that plateaus and then declines. This pattern can be found in everything from epidemics of plague to the adoption of software.

Remarkably, all the things that seemed to "matter" in the growth phase of the S curve have little effect in the stagnation or decline phases. For example, the plague moving to another city seemed to drive the infection rate in its most virulent phase, but once the epidemic plateaus, its spread to another city does not restore the previous rate of expansion.

The same can be seen in oil production, which is following the famous "Hubbert's Peak" S-curve; each new discovery of a large recoverable oil field does not restore the global production of oil to rapid growth; it merely maintains the current level of production.

Thus we can anticipate further discoveries will do little to change the decline phase of oil production.

We can see an S-curve in virtually all the major components of the global economy. For example, the expansion of housing and mortgage lending began slowly in the late 1990s and then exploded in a high-growth phase from 2002-2006, after which it plateaued and then declined. Attempts to reinflate the bubble with low-cost mortgages and massive Federal subsidies have completely failed, at the cost of trillions of dollars in costs transferred to savers and taxpayers.

Just as we saw in ecosystems and monocultures, systems in the decline phase of S-curves do not respond to policy tweaks or brute-force fixes.

China offers many examples of S-curves: the explosion of industry, foreign direct investment, construction of housing units, exports—all are tracing S-curves in which the explosive growth stage has plateaued. Despite claims to the contrary, all of these will inevitably enter a decline or collapse stage.

The plateau stage can be followed by stagnation, decline or collapse. As a generalization, we can conclude that the greater the application of brute force to suppress instability, the greater the systemic instability. Those systems with masked instability are the ones that implode once the instability is unleashed. Systems in which the forces of low-intensity instability (LII) have not been ruthlessly suppressed are more likely to experience stagnation or decline.

This model can be observed in non-renewable resource extraction: the plateau phase is abbreviated, and the decline phase is sudden and sharp, i.e. collapse. These systems are characterized by increasing systemic friction or costs of production. While production is rising, the concurrent rise in friction or production costs are masked. Once these costs exceed the value of the production—the result of costs continuing to rise while production declines—production is prone to sudden collapse.

These transitions can be viewed as "phase transitions" of the sort popularized as "tipping points": in a common example, a sand pile rises as grains of sand are added, but at some point, the sand pile collapses. Up until the moment of collapse, the pile appeared stable. This illusory stability is also a feature of many political and economic systems.

As Nassim Taleb of "black swan" fame has explained, it is misleading to say the last few grains of sand on the pile are responsible for the entire sand pile collapsing: the masking of risk was systemic, and thus the sand pile was doomed to collapse regardless of the nature of the final few grains of sand.

In this model, natural feedback results in fluctuations that we experience as volatility. As Taleb has explained, feedback is information, and limiting feedback also limits information that is vital to adaptation. Suppressing feedback and communication to tame the system in a manner favorable to those controlling the system—market manipulators like the Federal Reserve, for example—suppresses volatility. Suppressing volatility (feedback) saps the resiliency and adaptability of systems and makes them vulnerable to large-scale disruptions that are viewed as low-probability events, the infamous "black swans." In Taleb's words, "Complex systems that have artificially suppressed volatility tend to become extremely fragile, while at the same time exhibiting no visible risks."

Misguided attempts to engineer a false stability by suppressing "undesirable" volatility create intrinsically fragile systems that are doomed to crises of ever greater dimension even as the periods of calm between crises shrink.

Risk is like water in a closed system: it can never be squeezed into nothingness. The more pressure that builds up, the more inevitable it is that the risk will burst out in some part of the system that was viewed as "safe" and "stable," for example, home mortgages.

This is how financial events that are widely viewed by conventional economists and government officials as "impossible" can occur with increasing frequency.

One model for apparent stability that is disrupted by unpredictable spikes of volatility is stick/slip destabilization. In "sticky" systems—for example, those with major forces creating credit to maintain the financial Status Quo—pressure builds up within the system that is invisible to those looking at an apparently stable surface. But at some unpredictable moment, the built-up pressure within disrupts the system, and it "slips" or destabilizes into a new configuration.

A similar dynamic is what I call the supernova model in which a system (in the case of a supernova, a star) rapidly consumes the fuel that supports it. Throughout this "hollowing out" the system appears stable until the critical moment when the internal structure can no longer maintain the system and it implodes in a catastrophic collapse.

Another common pattern in Nature is fractal geometry, in which irregular or fragmented shapes are scale-invariant, meaning that they remain self-similar regardless of scale. A common example is a coastline, which appears similarly irregular when viewed during a seaside walk and on a larger scale, for example, from an altitude of 1,000 feet.

Fractal geometries don't just model physical structures; they also model financial systems such as the stock market. One feature of such fractals is that they are intrinsically prone to unpredictable periods of disorder. As a result, statistical models that predict the probabilities of severe disruption to be extremely low are repeatedly shown by history to dramatically underestimate the probabilities, as "low-probability" disruptions occur with remarkable regularity.

Later, we will examine social fractals, but for now the point of fractals is once again that systems operate on a scale that impervious to policy tweaks or State intervention. Indeed, as we have seen, Central State and bank intervention acts to suppress the very elements (low-intensity instability and dissent) that keep systems healthy and stable. The State and central banks thus doom the very systems they claim to be "saving."

In Chapter One, we saw how financialization and its handmaiden, the Savior State, are intrinsically unsustainable, and as a result the Status Quo will inevitably be replaced by a new social and financial arrangement.

By analyzing the Status Quo as a system, we now understand that its fundamental unsustainability cannot be repaired by modifying policies; its instability is profoundly systemic. We also recognize that financialization, including the expansive Savior State that enabled financialization, has run its course. It has plateaued and is now in the decline phase. This cannot be changed by money-printing, zero interest rates or any other policy tweaks. Due to their suppression of risk, dissent and low-intensity instability, the financial system and its partner in predation, the Central State, have doomed themselves to collapse. A new social and financial order will take their place, and the nature of that replacement is in our hands.

Pareto Distributions

Vilfredo Pareto, an early-20th century Italian economist, found that 80% of the land in Italy was owned by 20% of the populace. This and similar observations are the basis of the principle that 20% constitute a "vital few" that exercise outsized influence on the remaining "trivial many" 80%.

This "80/20 rule" appears in a wide range of distributions. For example, Microsoft noted that by fixing the top 20% of the most reported bugs, 80% of the errors and crashes would be eliminated. Global studies have found that 20% of the world's populace owns 80% of its wealth.

This distribution rule (not a physical law, such as gravity, but an observable pattern) is, like fractals, scale-invariant, meaning that about 20% of a town's populace will own 80% of the population's aggregate wealth, just as 20% of the planet's seven billion people own 80% of the world's wealth.

This distribution can be further reduced to 64/4, as the top 20% of the top 20% (4%) garner most of the distribution. Thus the 4% "vital few" exert outsized influence on the "trivial many" 64%.

This was the basis of my February 2007 prediction that 4% of U.S. homeowners defaulting on their mortgages (roughly 2 million of 50 million mortgages) would bring down the entire housing/credit bubble. That the credit bubble did pop once this threshold was reached is yet more evidence that the Pareto distribution is a powerful pattern of Nature that extends to human constructs.

This distribution does not imply causation; why this pattern holds across such a wide spectrum is not explained by the distribution itself. We can surmise, however, that Nature asymmetrically rewards significant advantages, such that 20% of the pea pods in Pareto's garden held 80% of the peas, and the most efficient 20% generate 80% of the production or profit.

The Pareto distribution also suggests that phase transitions/tipping points and the inherent instabilities of fractals are additional evidence that natural systems have stick/slip points of resistance and cascading positive feedback, and that these cascading effects can be triggered by a relatively modest small number of interactions or participants.

The Pareto distribution may well have much broader applications than generally surmised. For example, perhaps practicing the top 20% of preventative health measures (eating a diverse diet, maintaining a moderate weight and exercising daily) might garner 80% of the gain in health and longevity.

Referring back to risk and gain and human nature, we might further surmise that the top 20% of any hierarchy controls 80% of the hierarchy's resources. This would explain the attraction of political power.

We could extend this even further by suggesting that devoting 20% of an investment to a hedge might protect 80% of the entire investment. For a natural-selection example, perhaps the 20% of children resulting from illicit mating provide a genetic hedge for the parents' children born in wedlock.

These concepts suggest that the Pareto Principle has practical applications in hedging risk and concentrating competitive advantages in political power. This further suggests that limiting increasing concentrations of wealth beyond the 80/20 rule, while accepting asymmetric advantages as inevitable, would be practical features of sustainable political and economic systems.

For example, enabling the most productive members of a group to generate 80%of the gain might well serve the entire group's interests as long as power and wealth were not allowed to concentrate into politically protected Elites, and the producers' asymmetric productivity benefited the entire group in a tangible fashion.

From the point of view of the most productive, sharing gains with the group is a hedge in favor of the security and trust offered by the group. From the point of view of the trivial many, enabling the most productive to fulfill their efficiency while limiting their concentration of power and wealth increases the resources available to the entire group, and thus enhances the security and competitive standing of the entire group. In this fashion, the asymmetric distribution, if properly limited by transparency and feedback, can be seen as a low-risk, practical hedge for both the trivial many and the vital few.

We can also speculate that when 20% of a protected Elites' wealth is devoted to maintaining their asymmetric hold on power via suppression of feedback (LII), then the instability inherent in systems which have suppressed feedback as a method of concentrating power beyond the natural distribution will suddenly be unleashed.

In a similar fashion, we can anticipate that when 20% of a neighborhood's homeowners are delinquent on their mortgages, then the market price of the neighborhood's homes will decline, and when 20% of a household's disposable income is being spent on interest payments above and beyond mortgage payments, then the finances of the household enter a death-spiral.

Pareto distributions help us understand how systems that appear placid and stable on the surface suddenly tip into instability when an invisible threshold is reached. They also help us understand how systems can become increasingly imbalanced as power accumulates in the top levels.

The Pareto distribution offers us a key understanding: asymmetry is as natural as low-intensity instability, and attempting to suppress either one is ultimately counterproductive, as this suppression leads to uncontrollable systemic instability. Attempting to concentrate 80% of the wealth into the top 1% is as unstable as attempting an even distribution of all wealth. Both will fail as Nature rewards successful adaptations asymmetrically and distributes the advantages through the entire population to enable survival of the species.

In terms of the gene pool, very successful adaptations enable individuals' offspring to survive and reproduce at much higher rates than those without the adaptation. Over time, the adaptation is distributed throughout the entire species, giving every individual the benefits of what was once an asymmetric advantage held by only a few.

In terms of technology, the development and marketing of specific technological advantages reaped vast fortunes for the innovators (for example, Steve Jobs), but the advantages of the innovation were quickly distributed throughout the populace, sparking a vast number of creativity-enhancing advances that benefitted the entire economy and everyone in it.

Though they appear to be fundamental features of natural systems, Pareto distributions do not imply stability or sustainability. For example, those who control 80% of the wealth now may not control it in the next decade. The great fortunes built upon railroad cartels in the late 19th century traced out an S-curve and went into decline, and new financial Elites arose to claim 80% of the nation's wealth. Though 80% of the wealth continued to be controlled by 20% of the populace, a new class replaced the previous owners.

If we consider a grassy island without predators inhabited by a small population of rabbits, we may find that 20% of the rabbits consumed much of the grass and produced 80% of the offspring. But when the last tufts of grass have been consumed by the expanding horde of rabbits, then the Pareto distribution will not save the population from mass starvation.

Ultimately, the Pareto distribution helps us understand two principles: that major shifts tend to be triggered by thresholds that are not apparent on the surface, and that Nature rewards successful adaptations asymmetrically in order to distribute the advantages to the entire population.

Once again, we see that apparent stability only masks systemic instability until a phase shift occurs. At that point, of course, it's too late: too late to escape the apparently-unsinkable *Titanic*, and too late for the thirsty to dig a well.

Systemic Friction

Friction is a concept that helps us understand how apparently stable systems can tip suddenly into instability and also how low-intensity instability acts as an "investment" in what we might call the virtues of innovation and competition.

There are two types of friction: productive and unproductive. We might assume all friction is unproductive, but this overlooks the value of investing some surplus in redundancy and experimentation. Some may argue that this is an investment, and an investment is not friction. But if the duplicate systems are never used and the experiments fail to yield useful innovation, on a gain-loss basis the expenses look much like friction.

The efficient monopoly enterprise doesn't "waste" any profit on the risky and possibly fruitless attempt to innovate via experimentation, and from this perspective innovation is a form of friction. Maintaining a second supplier that costs more than the primary supplier is also "useless" friction, for what yield do we receive from the added cost? Buying a hedge against commodity prices can also be viewed as friction, as it reduces profit by increasing costs.

Competition is also a form of friction, as there is a cost to innovations and enterprises that fail. A monopoly is highly efficient, as it has no need to spend profit on competitive advantages. This is why monopoly or cartel-capitalism is the lowest-risk and highest profit apogee of State-controlled capitalism.

Democracy is also friction, as monarchy is much more "efficient" in transferring power and reaching policy decisions. Democracy requires an inordinate amount of "wasted motion" in debating, tallying votes, drafting laws, contesting those laws in the judiciary, and so on.

As we have learned, all these sources of friction are the "cost" of system stability: innovation, competition, dissent and democracy are all manifestations of the forces of low-intensity instability. The second supplier adds cost but provides resiliency should the primary supplier suffer a reduction in output. A hedge adds cost as well, but provides a form of insurance against volatile commodity prices.

"Efficiency" in simplistic terms is best served by monopoly and cartels, as monopolies sacrifice innovation and competition to lower risk and increase profits. But as with monocultures, this sacrifice of low-intensity instability and risk greatly increases systemic brittleness and vulnerability.

Classic (non-productive) friction reduces surplus by siphoning off energy as wasted heat. In political and financial systems, corruption, the transfer of risk to others and parasitic Elites who skim the cream while producing nothing are all friction.

Corruption and parasitic Elites skim the surplus from an economy and concentrate it in the hands of a few. Unlike an investment of surplus in innovation, there is no potential gain to be distributed; there is only a net loss. Like parasites, these forms of friction undermine systemic stability by raising costs while yielding no gain.

We can visualize this destabilizing dynamic in a number of ways. This rise in unproductive friction (fraud, graft, corruption, transaction fees, and so on) can be quantified as the cost basis of a system. As costs rise, the net surplus dwindles correspondingly, as total output remains flat-lined: friction doesn't increase efficiency or production, it saps the net surplus left after the costs are subtracted from the output. The increase in friction offers no competitive advantage; rather, it lessens the system's competitive standing by diverting surplus that could have been invested in innovation into the parasitic Central State and its protected cartels.

If we visualize the system as an engine, the input (fuel) remains constant but the work (net output) keeps decreasing as systemic friction rises. At some point the engine will seize up, just as a high-overhead company will slide into bankruptcy when the firm's diminishing net income cascades into losses.

We can also understand rising unproductive friction as marginal return: as parasitic Elites divert more and more of the system's dwindling surplus, the system is starved for investment in innovation and productive capacity, and so the surplus declines. The parasitic Elites have no incentive or desire to reduce their share, so progressively smaller surpluses are available for productive investment.

Referring back to the Pareto distribution, we can posit that when parasitic Elites, fiefdoms and cartels divert 20% or more of the system's surplus to their own consumption, the system destabilizes and enters a death-spiral of falling surpluses and investment.

Put another way: unproductive, parasitic friction increase the vulnerability of the system, just as parasites weaken an organism. The organism doesn't die as a direct result of the parasites draining its vitality; it becomes prone to opportunistic threats that its weakened immune system cannot counter.

Understood in this light, we see how complex Central State regulations (often designed to protect cartels from competition) act as a form of unproductive friction on the economy. While simple regulations can act as productive friction to limit monopoly and exploitation, overly complex regulations are manifestations of crony-capitalist cartels buying State protection.

Complexity itself is a form of unproductive friction, and this helps explain why complex systems follow an S-curve trajectory: in the beginning, the complexity provided some powerful competitive advantages that fuels growth. But as the expansion of complexity outpaces the improvements in productivity, then the complexity becomes a source of unproductive friction that leads to increasingly marginal return. As those who depend on complexity for their share of the dwindling surplus defend their fiefdoms, the system reaches a breaking point and collapses.

Bottlenecks Create Systemic Brittleness

Bottlenecks create another type of systemic brittleness. The classic example of a systemic bottleneck is a critical shipping lane in a narrow strait, for example the Strait of Malacca. In stable eras, the supply of oil passes unhindered through the strait, and the price of oil doesn't reflect any risk of the bottleneck being blocked. If the bottleneck is suddenly restricted, then the price of oil leaps as the now-visible risk is priced in.

Systems with numerous low-visibility bottlenecks are much more fragile than those without bottlenecks. Much of the global supply chain is littered with bottlenecks such as single-source factories for critical components. (The tsunami and earthquake that struck Japan on March 11, 2011 illustrated how many critical components were single-sourced.)

These bottlenecks arose because of the selective pressure to increase efficiency and specialization. In this way, bottlenecks are the equivalent of specialized bird beaks: they offer narrow competitive advantages that dramatically increase the potential for collapse.

In ecosystems, this declining surplus can be seen in species that have to work harder and harder to find enough food to maintain their population. It may appear that the population is stable, but once the work of gathering food exceeds the calories gained, then the population crashes.

Bottlenecks can also be found in social, legal and financial systems.

The dynamic of hidden bottlenecks triggering collapse is similar in some ways to the stick/slip phenomenon described earlier, where pressure builds invisibly within a system until a critical threshold is breached and the system slips suddenly into instability.

Marginal Return: Maladaptation and Malinvestment

Marginal return or diminishing returns describes a dynamic in which the return on an investment steadily decreases over time. Either the system yields less, or it requires an increasing input/investment to obtain the same yield.

Debt saturation is a telling example. In the 1960s, adding $1 dollar of debt to the U.S. Economy added about 70 cents to the gross domestic product (GDP). By the early 2000s, this yield had diminished to 7 cents. Now as I write in March 2012, adding $1 of debt actually reduces the GDP: it no longer has any yield whatsoever, as the costs of servicing the debt exceed the value of the economic activity generated by the debt.

This is a classic example of marginal return, but there are many others. In financial matters, diminishing returns characterize systems that have weak feedback, for example, government which is not exposed to the discipline of the marketplace.

In systemic terms, we can identify a number of causes for diminishing returns. One is the friction of unproductive costs. If a State employee's healthcare insurance costs double every few years, the cost of that employee increases annually but his work output remains constant: costs rise incrementally but output stays constant.

Another cause is what we might term maladaptation—systems which are maladapted to the task at hand and therefore intrinsically inefficient. Maladaptation characterizes any enterprise or institution that is a monopoly and lacks the selective pressure created by competitors. Thus tyrannies and economies dominated by monopolies and cartels are prone to maladaptation and malinvestment.

In advanced economies, a series of false choices presents the illusion of choice and feedback, but in fact the feedback has no effect on output or efficiency. If there are two stores in a "company town," both owned by the ruling corporation, then the "competition" is illusory, created for public relations purposes. Our two-party system is in effect a false choice, as little changes regardless of which party is nominally in power.

Lastly, the diminishing returns dynamic can be created by chronic malinvestment, a feature of systems that divert scarce surplus to unproductive speculation or outsized compensation to parasitic Elites. Since there is only a limited surplus available for investment, diverting a significant percentage to unproductive bets and consumption necessarily means that productive investments are starved for capital.

In the mid-2000s housing bubble, Central State incentives and lax financial regulation led to vast sums being invested in isolated luxury subdivisions. Since the homes only made sense in a speculative fever, once the fever had passed the homes were revealed as negative yield investments.

Since that capital was squandered on speculation, there was less capital available for productive uses. Over time, capital diverted to low-yielding investments will lower the system's overall output to the point of destabilization.

Marginal return quickly encounters negative feedback in natural systems, but in human organizations, members of protected castes will devote scarce resources to protect their positions, lowering output to do so.

As we have seen with debt saturation, human systems lacking feedback and accountability will continue to zero yield and beyond, as those benefiting from the Status Quo resist any reduction in their personal security.

When surplus rises as a result of a windfall such as cheap oil or conquered assets, then diminishing returns are masked by the flood of new funding. Once the windfall has been consumed, then the underlying diminishing return is exposed.

Natural Selection and Meritocracy

Natural selection is the non-linear process of sorting through the information and feedback provided by mutation, experimentation, variation and volatility to conserve those traits that are advantageous and deleting those which are not. In the context I am presenting here, natural selection is the process of accepting risk for greater gain by conserving those traits that lower risk and enable potentially higher gains while paring away traits that increase risk for little payoff.

One of the distractions of ideology is the notion that there is a moral code implicit in natural selection, that eliminating traits that increase risk while lowering surplus is "wrong" when applied to human culture.

As I have endeavored to explain, suppressing risk (LII) causes a rise in system instability. Thus suppressing natural selection—a supreme expression of risk in Nature— is an ideal way to guarantee self-destruction.

In the human sphere, natural selection can be understood as meritocracy: the participants and ideas that manifest advantages while lowering risk benefit the group, while those that increase costs and impose disadvantages will sap the group and potentially send it into a positive-feedback loop of systemic collapse.

Financial systems that attempt to mask or suppress risk inevitably implode, and societies that attempt to suppress in their people and ideas end up withering or collapsing via the same dynamics.

Risk is uncomfortable but necessary, as there can be no gain without risk and no stability without free-flowing low-intensity instability. Suppress risk, volatility, transparency, experimentation and meritocracy and the system loses resiliency and stability.

Brittleness and Dependency

We intuitively understand the selective advantages of flexibility over brittleness. Systemic flexibility arises from free-flowing communication and feedback, experimentation and wide channels of movement. Brittleness results from rigidity and ossified systems that do don't allow experimentation and which demand strict compliance to rules.

Thus transparent systems tend to be flexible systems, and flexible systems tend to be resilient systems. In political systems, democracies tend to be flexible and thus robust, while tyrannies tend to be inflexible and thus brittle. In systems with little flexibility, any instability breaks the entire system. When information, fluctuation and volatility are repressed, then the brittle system becomes vulnerable to cascading disruption.

This causal connection between flexibility and resilience and brittleness and vulnerability is scale-invariant, meaning that it is observable in households, groups, enterprises and nations.

Though it may seem unrelated, dependency is correlated to diversity and flexibility. When an organism or society becomes dependent on one source of food, it becomes extremely inflexible and vulnerable to collapse. For example, for a variety of reasons, the Irish became increasingly dependent on the potato as their primary source of calories. When blight destroyed most of the potato crop, a terrible famine ensued. (One branch of my family can be traced to County Down, Ireland; they left for America in the mid-1840s, the era of the famine.)

In the present era, many people have become solely dependent on the Central State, what I term the Savior State. The destabilization of the State will reveal the brittleness and vulnerability of this dependency.

An ecosystem that is dependent on one food source is highly vulnerable to collapse, while one that draws sustenance from a symbiotic network of food sources is much more resilient. These traits go together, just as inflexibility, repression, brittleness, dependency and vulnerability go together.

Political and economic systems that breed inflexibility, repression, brittleness and dependency are thus highly vulnerable to instability and collapse.

Institutional and Individual Risk

Individuals naturally seek to offload risk onto an institution, which stores the risk until it become large enough to capsize the institution. Individuals who seek to suppress information within an institution to maintain their own security are acting rationally in terms of self-interest. But when all these individuals acting in their own self-interest are aggregated, their attempt to lower the risk that information could threaten their position leads to institutional stagnation and eventual instability/collapse.

This is one of the risks of consciousness, which enables organisms to modify their behavior. An organism which is directed entirely by genetic encoding cannot choose to evade natural selection, which responds to reproductive and survival pressures. A human, in contrast, will resist being treated as disadvantageous friction. Once a certain threshold of people within an institution have evaded selective pressures—what we might call the organization's "immune system"—then the institution enters a downward spiral as an increasing share of the budget is siphoned off by unproductive friction.

It is a matter of faith in some ideologies that the pursuit of self-interest alone is sufficient to construct a resilient system. But this faith overlooks the core divergence of individual and institution. The individual conserves his position by suppressing information, transparency and feedback that inevitably threaten his security and which the institution needs to sustain itself.

The group is only sustainable as an ecosystem if the risk implicit in meritocracy is freely manifested. Once individuals have the power to suppress information and feedback to protect their own private gain, then they doom the institution and the very security they sought to protect.

Thus we see that unconstrained self-interest is ontologically prone to undermining the group as a byproduct of the effort to preserve individual gain. This capacity for secondary self-destruction—that is, the destruction of private security via "accidental" destruction of the institution which enables the individual's security—is the risk implicit in consciousness.

Put another way: the ontological drive to suppress risk as a means of securing individual gain deprives the institution of the mechanisms that enable its adaptation and stability.

In a biological analogy, the individual's personal gain is necessarily threatened by the institutional "immune system" which selects for meritocracy, experimentation, feedback and transparency, and pares away sources of friction, stagnation and brittleness within the ecosystem, what we might term either "deadwood" in a forest ecosystem or "cancer" in an individual organism.

The individual or subgroup which contrives to protect private gain by bypassing the immune system's weeding out of unproductive friction is akin to cancer. If left to pursue their self-interest, these cancer cell-like individuals end up consuming so much of the ecosystem's resources that the system's surplus completely disappears. Once the difference between overhead costs and output drop below zero—that is, costs exceed output—then the ecosystem crashes.

This is why symbiosis is the key feature of ecosystems, and perhaps why conscious self-interest is so intrinsically dangerous. Once it gains enough power to suppress risk and information to conserve its own advantageous position, it destroys the entire ecosystem.

In our current economy, the financial system's Elite is the cancer which has crippled the nation's economic ecosystem.

Ideologies blind us to this ontological divergence between the self-interest of individuals and the survival of the group/ecosystem.

Anything which suppresses low-level instability in effect destroys the immune system which protects the institution from collapse. The only way individuals or subgroups can secure their position is to undermine the very immune system which protects the entire ecosystem. This self-serving strategy necessarily destroys the entire organization and the gain the individual tried so mightily to protect. Self-interest is ironically self-destructive.

Eliminating meritocracy, transparency and feedback leads to self-reinforcing instability and criticality, i.e. collapse.

Individual cancer cells are not aware that their desire to live forever will destroy their host; they are only aware that they want to live forever and to do so they must evade the immune system's cleansing of systemically dangerous threats. The individual cells that seek to expand their control at the expense of the immune system will, if they succeed in fulfilling their self-interest, destroy the system and themselves.

The great irony of human institutions is that those benefiting from maintaining the Status Quo rightly perceive transparency and consequence as risks to their share of the system's surplus, but their suppression of these "immune responses" leads directly to the very collapse they sought to avoid.

The risk created by feedback is also the system's source of adaptability, resilience and stability. Suppress the risk and you also suppress the system's ability to innovate, experiment, adapt and endure. Suppressing risk to maintain stability actually insures the rise of instability.

The individual desire to secure one's slice of the pie regardless of the cost to the organization infects groups which then infect departments which then infect the entire institution which then infects the entire economy.

This is an example of what I call social fractals: the individual and departmental desire to secure personal gain and avoid risk create self-same structures within institutions. As we shall see in later chapters, social fractals also work from large to small: corrupt institutions create corrupt departments which foster corrupt individuals.

Here is the primary point: the pursuit of self-interest is rational on the individual level, but it eventually causes institutions to ossify and implode under their own weight as all the forces of low-intensity instability are neutered as "threats" to individuals' security. As institutions invest ever more heavily in self-protection, then they become ever more brittle. Once the demands on the institution exceed its share of the economy's surplus, the institution collapses.

The Grand Tradeoff between Conservation and Experimentation

We have briefly touched on the institutional bias for conserving the Status Quo. This is merely a reflection of life's grand tradeoff between conserving existing traits that have worked well enough to aid survival, and risking precious surplus on wagers that some variation (innovation) will yield an advantage.

We can understand the tradeoff by thinking of the organism's limited bank of surplus energy. If it wagers that surplus constantly on innovation/mutation, then it might find itself without the reserves needed to survive a crisis. Making wagers in the hopes of gaining selective advantages has a cost that could potentially threaten the life of the organism.

Thus every species has to strike a shifting balance between "investing" limited resources on innovations that may come to naught and conserving existing traits which may prove inadequate in the next crisis.

This is the ontological uncertainty described earlier: there is no way to predict how much surplus should be wagered on adaptations, or whether conservation of the Status Quo will be a successful strategy or a doomed one.

What is certain is that organisms that invest little to nothing in adaptation, mutation and experimentation (LII) will eventually find their Status Quo is no longer suited to the environment and they will destabilize into extinction.

The fossil record is littered with species that were unable to adapt quickly enough to rapidly evolving environments. Thus the ability to evolve quickly and produce robust adaptive responses is a great selective advantage.

If we had to describe the selective advantages of culture over genetic mutation, it would be culture's innate capacity for extremely rapid adaptation via experimentation, feedback and communication.

Life has a default setting that guarantees constant instability: random genetic mutations occur constantly over time, and those individuals who have been weakened by mutation die without reproducing, while those with advantageous mutations bear more and stronger offspring, and so the improvement is slowly distributed throughout the species' gene pool.

Though genetic mutation and selective pressure may appear constant, we have observed that some species are able to adapt relatively quickly to rapidly changing environments. They accomplish this with an explosion of experimentation that results in what is termed punctuated equilibrium.

In periods of relatively unchanging conditions, species' Status Quo is more than adequate for survival, and so mutations are generally passed over: they simply weren't that much better than the Status Quo.

But when the environment changes rapidly, some species are able to unleash a cascade of highly beneficial adaptations which spread fast enough through the species to save it from extinction. Thus the process of experimentation and selection is not a steady-state; it too is adaptable depending on the pressures created by crisis or rapid environmental change.

We have seen that individuals within institutions have tremendous incentives to suppress any threats to their own security, and that the selective pressures of meritocracy and feedback pose threats to the security of individuals within organizations.

But human organizations are also capable of rapid evolution when selective pressures mount and conditions change.

This feature of culture is scale-invariant, meaning that we can see human groups from households to communities to corporations to nation-states that clung to their Status Quo (conserving existing strategies) suddenly abandon the Status Quo and move to new strategies.

Thus we can conclude that punctuated equilibrium is a model that illuminates human behavior as well as genetic mutation.
Transformative change is possible; so is choosing to conserve the Status Quo by suppressing dissent, fact, feedback and transparency, and sliding to extinction.

Separating Risk and Gain Creates Systemic Instability

In Nature, it is difficult to detach risk from gain: actions have consequences that cannot be avoided. Experimentation and adaptation have costs, and not every mutation leads to stellar results. Suppressing experimentation /mutation creates the great risk that the organism/species will be increasingly ill-equipped to survive the next round of environmental change.

Thus risk and gain are ontologically bound together in Nature. It is impossible for organisms to detach gain from risk, that is, transfer the risks of adaptation to some other organisms while retaining the gains of successful adaptation. The best that Nature can manage is to isolate the genetic mutations in individuals who bear the full brunt of maladaptation—that is, they perish without taking down the entire species with them. Any positive adaptation will benefit the species over future generations.

Humans, being conscious organisms, can bypass natural selection via deception, collusion, lies and persuasion. Humans are quite adept at detaching risk from gain, as our specialty as a species, as it were, is transferring risk to others while retaining the gains for ourselves.

Even in relatively small groups, leaders can accrue the power to wage war, for example, while staying safely out of harm's way. The losses—death in combat, for example—are shunted onto others, while the spoils of victory will flow mostly to the leader. If the war is lost, the leader may escape with his life and plot a return to power.

In large institutions, members of the select caste at the top of the institution can use the power of the institution to divert risk to those outside the power circle while using the institution to increase their own gains.

In a modern example, State institutions can pass costs and risks onto the taxpayers while retaining the institution's power and perquisites for the upper caste.

In a private-sector example, a healthcare insurance cartel can raise prices of insurance unilaterally, in effect shifting the risks of higher expenses to its members, while retaining the profits for the insiders who control the cartel.

From this understanding of the immense gains to be had by separating risk from gain—put another way, removing accountability from the system—we can discern that modern Capitalism is not about conserving competition, which places risk, accountability and gain on the same square: profits are maximized by subverting competition and passing the risk to others while retaining the gain.

Institutions are the means for separating risk from gain. Without the power concentrated in institutions, eliminating accountability would not be possible for long, as those burdened with the risk would rebel. The institution is necessary to enforce compliance and repress any rebellion.

In financial systems, the eradication of accountability via the shifting of risk to others leads to two destructive dynamics: what has been summarized as "gains are private but losses are socialized," that is, spread over a populace which never had any hope of sharing in the gain, and the immense incentives for malinvestment when risk can be transferred to others.

Malinvestment occurs when risks have been off-loaded onto others while all gains are conserved. In this happy circumstance, there is no rational reason to wager conservatively; the incentive is to wager as aggressively and with as much leverage as can be managed. It is the equivalent of being given cash and a line of credit in a casino where your losses will always be paid by others. Betting on long shots with huge potential payouts makes sense, as does betting spectacular sums on low-risk, low-return wagers, as the monumental size of the bets insures that any gain, however modest in terms of percentage, will be outsized simply as a result of the bet size.

Thus separating risk from gain creates intrinsically unstable systems, as the negative feedback of responsibility and accountability has been decisively broken and replaced by a positive feedback loops that reinforces the most destabilizing elements in the system: the more expansive the credit and leverage, the bigger the wagers can be, and thus the richer the gains from bets whose risks have been shunted onto others.

This feedback rewards speculation and malinvestment, which diverts the system's scarce resources to bets which benefit the few at the expense of the many. This is an inherently unstable disequilibrium, as scarce resources are not being invested in innovation but in predation.

This positive feedback suppresses any information that might restabilize the system and creates additional positive feedback loops within institutions. As the bets increase in size, the institution's wealth and power grow, extending its ability to suppress feedback and push risk onto others.

With individuals, this ability to shunt risk onto others creates delusions of grandeur and reinforces self-aggrandizement, the very traits which feed detachment from reality.

This separation of risk from gain generates another kind of positive feedback loop, what we might term the tyranny of financial power. As financial institutions such as banks and corporate cartels gain the power to offload risk onto the State (ultimately, the taxpayers), then their increasing wealth enables them to buy political influence, which strengthens their ability to transfer risk onto the State.

In this way, any shift of risk away from those who will garner the gain leads to the suppression of capitalism and the corruption of the Central State.

Distributing risk to those who have no share in the gain creates a dynamic that inevitably leads to financial tyranny and speculative malinvestment.

Financial tyranny becomes political tyranny, and vice versa. Once risk is offloaded and gain can be concentrated, the power of private wealth and the State become one.

Our Understanding Thus Far:

We have seen how the financialized expansive Central State model is unsustainable and will be replaced by some other social/financial order, regardless of our wishes or desires.

In this chapter, we have reviewed some of the system dynamics that characterize the Status Quo.

In general, the Status Quo seeks to limit risk by transferring it to the system and seeks to concentrate gains by eliminating the forces of low-intensity instability that act as the system's stabilizing immune system. Once these have been eliminated as "inefficiencies" or "threats," the system will inevitably self-destruct.

Though the Status Quo presents itself as permanent and stable, we have seen that it has traced out a classic S-curve of rapid growth and stagnation and is now poised to begin the decline/collapse phase. Its stability is illusory, as its brittleness and vulnerability are building beneath an apparently stable surface. We have seen how the social fractal of individuals protecting their security by neutering the "threats" posed by low-intensity instability eventually destabilizes institutions.

We can now see why the Status Quo no longer serves the interests of its citizenry. This will become increasingly clear in the years ahead as these systemic dynamics overwhelm vain attempts at "reform" via trivial policy tweaks and leadership changes in political Elites.

Since the separation of risk from gain is the critical step in systemic collapse, the next chapter delves more deeply into systemic risk.

Chapter Three: **Understanding Systemic Risk**

The relationship between risk and gain is the ontological foundation of life. Life is ontologically at risk and the gain from any action or mutation is, like the future, unknowable. All organisms must balance risk and gain, and there is no way to know which action to favor or avoid at any moment in time.

This uncertainty that can never be resolved is somewhat akin to the Heisenberg Uncertainty Principle in quantum mechanics that states that the more precisely a particle's position is known then the particle's momentum is inversely less precisely known, and vice versa.

This is not an exact analogy to risk and gain, but it offers a taste of the pairing's innate uncertainty: the larger the potential gain, the larger the risk and the lower the risk, the lower the gain. But always choosing the low-risk option could eventually lead to a loss of security if those who pursued high-risk strategies corner scarce resources. In other words, the lower-risk choice is unlikely to yield outsized results, and so a preference for low risk could over time lead to a systemic underperformance that threatens the organism's survival.

The more information we have about risk, the more accurate our assessment will be. But avoiding risk also lowers our odds of reaping windfalls, which remain unpredictable. Any precision we claim in assessing risk is incomplete when it comes to assessing the future consequences of our strategy.

To take a hunter-gatherer example: if we take shelter in a shallow cave frequented by other passing groups, risk is certainly lower than if we wander into unknown territory, but so are the possibilities of finding a windfall. On rare occasions we might find a low-risk windfall in a sheltering cave frequented by others, but the probabilities rise considerably if we pursue higher-risk strategies that have led to windfalls in the past.

As a result of being alive, each organism is faced with balancing the risk that loss or even death will result from pursuing an advantage with the risk of taking no action.

This concept of movement is both physical and metaphorical. Organisms that are capable of motion choose a direction or choose to remain motionless; each is fraught with risk. All organisms have the potential for genetic drift, that is, the addition or deletion of genetic instructions via mutation and natural selection. These too are fraught with risk.

Humans have the additional opportunity to add or delete cultural knowledge that is passed on not by genes but by communication and social order. Like genetic change, this body of cultural knowledge also confers an advantage or disadvantage to groups and individuals within groups.

Risk and gain can be illustrated by a simple scenario from humanity's early hunting and gathering history. Suppose rainfall began declining in a particular valley, reducing the harvest of wild foods for gathering and the feedstock available to game animals. Does the group take the risk of leaving the known (and dwindling) resources of the valley for unexplored, inherently risky regions beyond, or does it accept the risk of remaining in the valley? If the drought worsens, staying could lead to starvation and death, but striking out into the unknown might well yield the same results. There is no way for the group or its leaders to know which choice will lead to gain or hardship and loss—and perhaps even extinction.

Suppose some intrepid members want to risk the unknown beyond; their leaving the main group could weaken the remaining member's resources to the point that those left behind would become vulnerable to other groups (invaders or competitors) or roaming predators.

The same calculations and unknowns occur throughout life's great choices: will choosing this mate yield healthy offspring? Will an investment of scarce capital, time and energy yield a windfall, or will it result in a catastrophic loss of irreplaceable capital and time?

All organisms are keenly attuned to the scent of windfall: a tree loaded with fruit, an available mate with much greater resources than our own, an investment which yields ten times the initial investment, and so on. If we need to cooperate to reap a windfall, we will do so; if we can secure it by low-cost, low-risk persuasion, we will do so; if we can secure it by deception, thievery or coercion, we will also be tempted to do so, as our eventual survival may depend on that windfall.

Alternatively, if deceit could cause us to be ejected from the group that sustains us, then that is essentially risking a life of solitary hardship in a harsh and unforgiving environment. Few windfalls would be worth risking life itself.

As organisms with multiple pathways for communication, cooperation, deception, alliances, coercion and hedging, humans have an extraordinarily powerful set of tools to assess risk and gain, make nuanced decisions, and modify the plan of action if the results are counterproductive. With a rich array of communication tools, humans have multiple ways to deceive or persuade others to lower risk and increase the probability of gain. As social, cooperative beings, humans have multiple opportunities to increase their individual or family gain via mutual projects, alliances and open exchange. As aggressive creatures jostling for scarce resources in a dynamic hierarchy that asymmetrically distributes risk and security, humans have the potential to undermine or harm others to avoid risk or secure a gain that is otherwise unattainable.

Understood in this way, we see that humans are intrinsically, even necessarily, political, as the ontological uncertainty of risk and gain force every individual, mating pair, family and group to assess risk and the potential for gain/loss in aggression, exchange, cooperation, deceit, theft, persuasion, alliance and punishment of transgressors—all the elements of political order.

We can also say that humans are intrinsically, even necessarily, investors who accept or decline the opportunity to invest scarce resources, time, energy and political influence for future gains.

Chance may bring us a windfall, but the accretion of a powerful mind is proof that the ability to improve our odds via prudent political and investment choices is highly advantageous. In this sense, we can even say that increasing our political and investing skills is the driving force behind the development of the human mind and its greatest innovations, language and the wealth of knowledge incorporated in a culture that is readily modified and passed on to the next generation.

The constant balancing of risk and gain has this ontological core: there is no gain without some level of risk, and so all of life seeks out low-risk, high-gain "bets" and avoid high-risk, low-gain ones.

Risk Cannot Be Eliminated, It Can Only Be Transferred

Risk is an ontological state of being and cannot be eliminated; it can only be transferred to others or masked. Transferring or masking risk separates it from the causal feedback of consequence, i.e. success or failure. Breaking the ontological link between risk and gain leads to catastrophe as the feedback loop of action and consequence is the key dynamic of successful innovation and adaptation. If the consequences of actions are lost, then mal-adaption and misallocation of scarce resources is the inevitable result. Once the negative feedback of consequence has been lost, only positive feedback (a self- reinforcing runaway reaction) remains. Positive feedback inevitably leads to systemic collapse.

This series of ontological truths manifests on many levels.

Ontologically, the causal feedback between risk and consequence is the one key feature of sustainable success for all of life. Risk, threat, failure, consequence—these are four descriptions of the same feedback loop from the real world. Transferring risk to others increases the security of those who keep the gain—after all, now they can't lose their jobs, pensions, bonuses, contracts or whatever has been guaranteed—but this security is only temporary.

Once risk and consequence have been disconnected, risk enters a self-reinforcing, explosive expansion far beyond the scale of the initial transfer of risk. Two dynamics mask this dangerous rise in risk. Once risk has been transferred to a system, for example, the Federal government, then that risk is distributed among all the participants. As long as the risk and loss remain small, the risk and loss distributed to each participant remains almost invisible.

But since the feedback of consequence and reality has been lost, the system has lost the ability to recognize or assess the risk that is being transferred to it.

Another way of expressing this dynamic is to say that once the feedback loop of risk and consequence has been broken, then capital and risk are inevitably mispriced. Once capital and risk are mispriced, then capital is misallocated and adding risk is rewarded: those placing the high-risk bets get to keep any gains if the bets pay off and transfer losses to others if they lose.

Sever the feedback of failure and the system loses touches with reality. Lacking the information of feedback and failure the system is unable to adapt and eventually collapses.

This is the grand irony of risk: by transferring risk to the system, the participants feel more secure as they perceive their own risk has vanished. Since risk cannot be eliminated, it can only be transferred, this perception of security is illusory; by transferring risk to the system, the risk of systemic failure rises to 100%. The elimination of risk via transfer to others is dangerously illusory.

Eliminating consequence generates perversely unintended consequences. Remove the risk of flunking out and students tends to slack off; why bother studying if you're going to pass anyway? Remove the risk of loss and participants feel free to make high-risk wagers.

The same mechanism spawned the credit/housing bubble and the mortgage documentation mess: lax regulations and zero enforcement created an illusory risk-free environment for speculation, fraud and embezzlement.

The results of this disconnect between risk and consequence are always and necessarily catastrophic, a truth that can be illustrated with a casino gambling example.

The Casino Example: How Disconnected Risk Brings Down the Entire System

The entire global economy's fundamental financial instability can be traced back to one simple rule of Nature: risk cannot be eliminated, it can only be transferred to others or masked. When it is transferred to others, then the causal feedback between risk and consequence is severed.

As noted above, once risk has been disconnected from consequence, then it is impossible to discover the price of capital and risk. Once capital and risk have been mispriced, then the inevitable result is misallocation of capital and a positive feedback loop of self-reinforcing risk.

Imagine yourself in a casino where a consortium will guarantee your losses up to $1 million. We call the disconnect of risk from the resulting gain/loss "moral hazard," and to understand the ramifications of moral hazard, we need only compare the actions of two gamblers in the casino: one is using his own money, the other has none of his own capital at risk, and his losses will be covered up to $1 million.

How much risk will you accept if you can lose $1 million without any loss to yourself? Obviously, we will accept enormous risks because if we win a high-risk bet, the gain will be ours to keep while any loss will be transferred to the consortium. Since low-risk bets yield low returns while high-risk bets yield high returns, why bother with low-risk bets?

Once risk has been freed from consequence, then the incentives are all to maximize and increase risk at every opportunity.

If we actually reap a few high-risk wins, this success further feeds our risk appetite. This is a positive feedback loop: our wins reinforce our risk appetite, while negative feedback (the losses from losing bets) no longer registers as losses have been eliminated from our calculations of risk and gain.

This positive feedback eventually leads us to make stupendously large bets. Eventually, we bet $1 million on a high-risk play and lose. We are wiped out, but oh, well, it was fun while it lasted. If we were especially disciplined and clever, we squirreled away some of our winnings in our own account, that is, we kept the gain and the consortium took all the losses.

The risk didn't disappear, of course; it was simply transferred to others who now bear the cost of the unfettered risk being played with abandon. The consortium that financed the no-risk gambling spree now has to absorb the $1 million in loss. If the consortium masked its own risk by presenting a phantom financial security to the casino, then the casino will have to absorb the loss.

In effect, the risk was transferred to the entire system. Since the consortium is made up of many investors, and the casino has many investors, then the risk and loss was effectively spread over many participants. The $1 million loss, catastrophic to any one player, was distributed to everyone in the system.

If the risk was masked by misrepresentation or purposefully misleading information, then the risk will end up being distributed asymmetrically, that is, some participants will end up bearing the majority of the risk while those who misrepresented the risk will have a much smaller share of the losses. In this way, withholding or manipulating information becomes a method to mask risk and transfer it to everyone with less accurate or complete information.

When losses are trivial compared to the size of the system, then this distribution of transferred risk results in a modest loss to all participants.

But let's suppose the player with the $1 million backstop was extraordinarily successful with high-risk bets, and he built the $1 million stake into $100 million, which he then rolled into several stupendous bets.

He loses, because the risk of gambling hasn't been eliminated, it has only been transferred to others. Now the consortium faces a loss 100 times its guaranteed backstop, and since its capital is only $10 million, it is wiped out and leaves the casino with $90 million in uncollectible debt.

If the casino needs that $90 million to pay its own debts, then it too will be wiped out.

This is how one player who manages to transfer risk to others can bring down entire systems. The risk only appears trivial and manageable at the start, but since the negative feedback of consequence has been eliminated from the players' perspective and the positive feedback of spectacular gains is all that he experiences, then risk piles up in a self-reinforcing geometric expansion.

Since the system itself has disconnected risk from consequence with backstops and illusory claims of financial security, then it is has lost the essential feedback required to adapt to changing circumstances. As the risk being transferred to the system rises geometrically, it is incapable of recognizing or assessing the risk being transferred until it is so large it overwhelms the system's meager reserves set aside for what was perceived as modest amounts of risk.

The banking system offers another example of this systemic inability to recognize and assess risk. If a bank has $100 million in deposits, the guarantor of depositors' accounts assumes the total potential loss is limited to $100 million. That is, if the bank were to lose all its capital, then the guarantor would be responsible only for replacing the $100 million entrusted to the bank by depositors.

But suppose the bank leveraged this $100 million in depositors' cash into $100 billion in high-risk bets on mortgage-backed securities, credit default swaps (CDS) and other derivatives supposedly guaranteed by another financial institution (the counterparty to the bet).

Now the guarantor is facing losses in the $50 billion range, and if the system fails to make good the entire $50 billion, then the failure of the bank to back its derivative bets will trigger a domino-like chain of failures in the entire global financial system as counterparties owed by the failed bank can no longer make good on their own obligations.

This is precisely what occurred in the 2008 global financial meltdown.

Returning to our casino example: the consortium has only two ways to create the illusion of solvency when the punter's $100 million bet goes bad: borrow $100 million from credulous owners of capital or counterfeit $100 million on a printing press. These are precisely the strategies being pursued by central banks and states around the globe.

But since risk remains disconnected from loss, then capital and risk both remain mispriced. Risk is being transferred to the entire global financial system at a fantastic rate, as counterfeiting money or borrowing it on this scale to cover losses creates new self-reinforcing feedback loops.

As long as risk is being transferred to others who don't reap the gain, the system is doomed to self-reinforcing instability and eventual collapse.

The only solution is to enforce the causal connection between risk and consequence: those who took the risk have to absorb all the loss. Since risk cannot be eliminated, it can only be masked or transferred, all the financial trickery of the central banks and states in Europe, Asia and the U.S. are only enabling risk to pile ever higher in the system itself.

At some unpredictable point, the accumulated risk will implode the system like a supernova star.

Once we understand this, we realize that the "security" created by the Savior State's welfare system (corporate and "transfers to individuals" alike) is illusory: all that has occurred is the risk has been transferred to the system, which is starved of the information it needs to adapt.

Real security flows only from the dynamic of adaptation fueled by risk, threat, consequence and failure, the very feedbacks we ruthlessly

eliminate with paper-money guarantees and empty promises of
entitlements to come.

Risk is masked by deception but also by complexity, which is itself a
form of tyranny when imposed by the State or financial institutions.
When risk has been transferred to the system as a whole, consequence
is easily lost in thousands of pages of obtuse legislation and
impenetrable shadow systems of banking.

Risk and failure are necessary for adaptation, innovation and thus
for success. Mask or transfer risk and you've eliminated the possibility
of sustainable success.

The Role of Ethics in Controlling Systemic Risk

The temptations to use deceit and coercion to transfer risk and loss
to others and these techniques' potential for undermining the social
order is the ontological foundation of ethics and religious morals. In the
modern world, we study this risk-gain matrix with game theory; in less
analytic times, ethical and religious constructs were devised to maintain
consequences for deceit (deception, lying, withholding critical
information, embezzlement, fraud, misrepresentation of risk, etc.), theft
and coercion via the mechanism of religious edits (internally
experienced as guilt) and socially administered punishment.

When the punishment or disincentive is asymmetrically puny
compared to the potential gain, ethics and indeed the rule of law pose
little restraint to human behavior. If I can embezzle $10 million and
escape punishment with a $100,000 bribe (called a "campaign
contribution" in the U.S.), then from the point of view of risk-gain
analysis, financial embezzlement is simply too grandiose a windfall to
pass up.

The Threat-Exploitation-Repression Matrix

Elite-dominated societies have an additional layer of risk-gain
calculation that I call the threat-exploitation-repression matrix. When
power and wealth are concentrated in the hands of a relatively few

members of a society, for example, a tyranny, monarchy, aristocracy, oligarchy, theocracy, kleptocracy, etc., then that Elite possesses a compelling risk-gain opportunity: when its power is not threatened by the citizenry below, then the Elite can increase its share of the economy's income (i.e. increase its level of exploitation, parasitism and predation) with impunity.

Conversely, when the Elite feels its position at the apex of power is threatened by a restive populace, then it increases its repression to suppress the risk to its power posed by rebellion.

These forces interact dynamically rather than linearly, and thus we have witnessed eras in which an external power threatens the local Elite by offering its oppressed citizenry a "better deal," for example, more freedoms and a greater share of the national income.

In this scenario, the Elite may voluntarily lower its share of the national income to enable a larger distribution to the citizens below—in effect, buying their compliance and cooperation with a larger share of the national income.

At the same time, the Elites actively increase repression of any elements it sees as supporting the external threat. Thus income disparity can decline even as repression increases.

The key point is that the Elites of any society respond to the unique opportunities that come with concentrated power and wealth, i.e. systemic, centrally controlled exploitation and oppression. While conspiracy and evil certainly exist in human experience, they are not necessary to understand the behaviors and motivations of Elites.

We can also detect the pendulum of history in the threat-exploitation-repression matrix. Elites can exploit their populaces to near-starvation, sparking mass migration or revolt, and they can also repress the strata that create their society's wealth to the point that rebellion is seen as the low-risk, high-gain option. The pendulum of history then swings toward egalitarianism and a wider distribution of wealth until new Elites arise to supplant the ones who over-reached their power and privilege.

This context enables us to understand why those in academia, government and State-dependent private sectors avoid threatening the Status Quo in their writings and public actions: membership in the Elite offers uniquely low-risk, high-gain positions while threatening the Status Quo creates the potential for dismissal from the favored class.

It is thus highly irrational for anyone benefitting from the Status Quo to pose a threat to its intellectual foundations, or even be perceived as posing such a threat, and highly beneficial to parrot the ritualistic appeals, social control myths and pseudo-realities that the marketing /media complex uses to shape the non-Elites' perception of their self-interest in the Status Quo.

The Grand Tradeoff between Increasing Gain and Vulnerability

As a general characterization, systems that specialize to increase their gain also correspondingly increase their risk and vulnerability.

We might call this the specialization/diversity spectrum. Consider a bird species that has been selected to feed on tall, narrow blossoms by developing an exquisitely thin, curved beak. This specialized beak enables the species to occupy a limited but calorie-rich niche of the ecosystem. The specialization has been driven by the advantage gained, but it has also greatly increased the species' vulnerability, as any decline in these specific flowers would doom the species to starvation, as its specialized beak is poorly adapted to feeding on blossoms in other already-crowded niches.

Birds which can feed on a diversity of flowering plants are constantly competing with a variety of other species, so their lower risk is traded for lower yield: their food supply is unlikely to vanish, but sharing ecological niches with other species reduces the potential bounty. Compared to the bird which dominates a single niche, they must work harder and longer for calories.

We can summarize this tradeoff as one between high/low risk and high/low gain: the higher the risk, the higher the potential gain, and also the greater the vulnerability.

Species which favor diversity over specialization can be said to have hedged their food sources, and that hedge lowers their vulnerability but also lowers the potential gain. By sacrificing the advantage of specialization, they've sacrificed higher gains for the increased security offered by diversification.

This same tradeoff plays out in financial markets. If an investor wants to reap the maximum gain on an investment, he makes an "all-in" unhedged wager on a single trade. This high risk is accepted in exchange for the potential of a windfall: high risk yields either potential high gain or catastrophic loss.

Investors who choose low-risk hedged wagers or diversified portfolios also accept lower gains for the relative safety of limited losses.

If an investor has a distinct advantage in the marketplace, then taking hedged wagers reduces the value of that advantage, in effect sacrificing it for no gain. In this sense, a meaningful advantage significantly lowers risk while maintaining the potential of outsized gains.

We can discern the outlines of the Pareto distribution in this tradeoff: those with a real advantage have the potential to reap outsized gains without necessarily taking on more risk, as their advantage acts as a kind of hedge. This may help explain how the top 20% garner 80% of the gains: they possess substantial competitive advantages that offer outsized gains and lowering risk without dissipating the gains via diversification.

We can visualize this in another way, as concentrating risk and gain, or diffusing them via diversification. Agriculture concentrates risk and gain by planting a single crop at a time: monoculture. This enables increases in yield—gain—while increasing the risks that an insect or micro-organism infestation could devastate the monoculture crop.

These concepts—specialization/diversity, concentrating risk/gain, hedging/vulnerability—all describe the same tradeoff of taking on heightened risk to increase gain or accepting lower yields to reduce risk.

The ideal investment is of course low-risk and high-gain. Such opportunities are rare and fleeting in Nature, and in the financial world, such investments have been revealed as illusory: despite claims to the contrary, risk was not lowered to zero, it was simply transferred or masked.

Recognizing Systemic Risk

Widespread recognition of risk is dangerous to the Status Quo, as public fear that promises of stability will not be kept feed doubts about the ruling Elites' ability to suppress systemic risk. Once risk reaches the surface of public awareness, the Status Quo devotes itself to pretense, propaganda and shadow intervention to maintain an increasingly fragile Status Quo. Political Elites offer soothing reassurances that all is well, but behind the facade, the rule of law is sacrificed in favor of political expediency; protecting the system from unraveling is the sole goal of the political and financial Elites.

Ironically, these heavy-handed attempts to stem a loss of faith actively undermine what's left of public trust by shredding the rule of law to protect Elites.

The Status Quo's basic claim is that the financial system and the Central State are self-regulating systems that will auto-correct without public sacrifice, given enough time. As we have seen, transferring risk to the system and masking this transfer can at best delay the inevitable collapse.

Risk cannot be stored for long. When the system breaks down despite all the official attempts to maintain the Status Quo, then the public will see that the risk was not permanently buried in the system— it was only stored there temporarily until it fell to them.

Revolution occurs when the level of systemic risk perceived by the public (low) suddenly re-aligns with the real risk (high). The public suddenly realizes the system's gains have been concentrated in the hands of a few at the top and the risk has been distributed to everyone below who shared little of the gain but are now left to shoulder the dire consequences of systemic instability.

Once the public recognizes runaway systemic risk has exploded beyond the Status Quo's control, the threat to their security is severe enough to warrant dramatic change, that is, the wholesale dismantling or replacement of the ruling Elites.

We only risk systemic change when our personal stake in the Status Quo falls below a critical threshold. At that point the risk of revolution "becomes worth it" because the alternative strategy, hoping the Status Quo Elites will set things right again, has demonstrably failed.

The same mechanism of systemic risk being recognized can be seen when people are trapped deep underground in a mine; their recognition that risk is systemic, that is, it weighs equally on all participants, illuminates advantages of mutual aid and support. The trapped people bond in ways they would never have experienced in their previous life, and "all for one and one for all" ceases to be an empty slogan. But once they are freed and return to normal life on the surface, they quickly revert to the standard self-centered strategy of focusing on lowering risk and increasing gain in their own individual lives.

We think and behave differently once we recognize systemic risk: the self-centered conception of self-interest that served us well in secure times is suddenly revealed as counterproductive as our interests become one with the community's, and we need the cooperation of others to survive.

Risk Is the Ontological Foundation of the Political Economy

By now we can see that risk is the ontological foundation of the political economy, for it underpins humanity's incentives to spread risk and gain across a group via cooperation and concentrate wealth in the hands of a few by transferring the risk to others. Social groups are necessarily political groups of investors, as the driving motivation of social order is to increase gain and lower risk for participants.

We can also see how transferring and masking risk is the foundation of Elite domination and control.

In totalitarian police states, the Elites can physically steal from non-Elites with impunity. In nominally democratic, nominally capitalist societies such as the U.S., then the theft and control are exercised more subtly via transferring the consequences of risk to the citizenry while retaining all the gains. Maintaining this transfer is accomplished by buying control of the machinery of governance within the Central State. Nominally democratic states enable this purchase via election campaign contributions, lobbying, shadow systems of influence, revolving doors between concentrations of wealth and the State regulatory agencies, and so on.

This wholesale transfer of risk to non-Elites is masked by a carefully maintained facade of democracy and quasi-capitalism that lends a veneer of legitimacy to what is in essence a kleptocratic partnership of concentrated capital and political power.

This transfer of risk must be masked lest the citizenry awaken to the institutionalization of Elite dominance. The ideal method of masking this is to transfer risk to the Central State, whose very size and complexity mask the inevitable buildup of systemic risk until it's too late to stop the implosion.

Understanding the essential role of risk in establishing Elite dominance gives us a clear vision of what a truly democratic, just and free system must guarantee along with the freedoms of speech, assembly, religion, etc. stated in the Bill of Rights: that risk cannot be separated from consequences and transparency in all financial and Central State arrangements so the transfer of risk cannot be masked.

It is not just Elites that benefit from transferring risk to the system. All of us who expect a guaranteed pension or entitlement from the government are in effect transferring the risk that the nation's economy can't generate enough surpluses to pay our entitlement to the system.

No nation, no matter how mighty, cannot generate infinite surplus to be spent on "pay as you go" pensions and entitlements. At the most basic level, all government is a luxury paid out of surplus. In a truly subsistence economy, the only surplus is the seed reserved for next year's crop or the food left over from the day's hunting and gathering; there is no government because there is no surplus to spend on government or any other institutionalized overhead.

Ultimately, an economy can only afford to spend what it generates in surplus. Even if the government harvests the entire surplus, it cannot spend more than the economy generates in surplus. (And if the Central State does harvest the entire surplus, then there is no capital left to be invested in the private economy, which then slides into the positive feedback death-spiral described earlier.)

Thus "guaranteed" pensions and entitlements cannot exceed the surplus being generated by the economy. The only way to mask this reality is to borrow or print money, and this strategy carries the multiple risks outlined above. Everyone who expects to get paid regardless of the health of the economy has transferred risk to the system. When the claims on the Central State exceed the surplus generated by the economy, then the system is unsustainable: the only ways to sustain the illusion of solvency is to borrow or print money in increasing quantities, and both pathways lead to the same end-point, collapse.

Since this systemic risk is carefully masked by the Status Quo, each individual reckons it is in his self-interest to demand his "guaranteed" entitlement, a guarantee that neatly separates risk from consequence and substitutes lofty promises for what the real economy actually generates in surplus.

Once the transfer and masking of risk is institutionalized, then financial and political Elites have the means to maintain their domination. If risk can be transferred to the system with impunity, then justice is impossible, security is impossible and reforms are nothing but window dressing. Once risk has been separated from consequence, the system is doomed to collapse. We ignore this ontological truth at our own peril.

The *Titanic* Analogy

We now understand why the Status Quo is unsustainable: the only way for the Elites to concentrate gains and maintain political power is to distribute risk to the system itself and then mask that transfer with illusory promises of security supported by vast sums of borrowed or printed money.

Since risk cannot be eliminated, it can only be transferred and stored temporarily, the system itself becomes increasingly risk-laden. At a critical threshold that is impossible to identify, the steadily increasing hidden risk explodes "out of nowhere," destabilizing the system.

Since this buildup of risk in the system was masked by the Status Quo's marketing machine, participants do not recognize it. Since transparency has been eliminated to obscure the risk transfer, information about the dangers of systemic risk is marginalized. Lacking this information, the non-Elites believe that supporting the Status Quo serves their self-interest.

As in the first moments after the *Titanic* struck the iceberg, non-Elites naturally believe the false reassurances of their leaders that all is safe and secure, as there is yet no visible evidence that the ship is already doomed. Since the ship is so visibly massive and its safety has been guaranteed (the ship is routinely declared unsinkable), the typical reaction to declarations that the ship will sink is disbelief.

Since the vast majority of passengers and crew cannot yet see the water pouring through the damaged hull, their conception of self-interest is fatally flawed: they believe their self-interest is best served by accepting official reassurances and staying on board. Ironically, the very strategy that would save their lives once the ship sank—leaving the ship by whatever means are at hand and depending on self-reliance rather than official pronouncements—appears exceedingly risky early on. But as the Chinese saying has it, when you're thirsty, it's too late to dig a well; by the time systemic risk has become undeniable, it's too late to pursue a long-term strategy.

Just as with the *Titanic's* woefully inadequate lifeboats, the Status Quo's claim that there is adequate financial surplus to "save" us all from systemic collapse is illusory. The claims on the economy far exceed its actual surpluses, and only those who recognize systemic risk early on will have the time and insight needed to survive the inevitable foundering of the Status Quo.

Resisting a reassuring authority appears risky when systemic risk is masked, as does a strategy of self-reliance. But by the time systemic risk is undeniable and self-interest shifts from delusion to realism, it's too late to save the system or the mass of people who believed it was in their self-interest to accept the Status Quo's false assurances.

We can now see that the techniques of marketing and propaganda used to mask systemic risk are critical to the Status Quo's maintenance of power and control. To understand how and why these techniques work so effectively even as the ship is visibly sinking, we must first understand the key dynamics of human nature which can be manipulated by the Elites' marketing machine.

Their basic strategy is two-fold: one, mask the fact that behind the façade of pseudo-democracy and crony capitalism, the system is institutionalized to serve their interests, and two, promote the illusion that the system serves your self-interests to win your support and compliance.

Chapter Four: Human Nature and Social Control

We cannot understand how our assessments of self-interest can be so misguided without understanding human nature and social systems. This is a tall order, and though a complete answer is impossible and a partial answer would fill a small library, I will endeavor to do so in a few pages.

Humans are complex beings, and there are limitless variations of human society. Since complex systems are generated by a small set of dynamic elements, we must first extract the essential characteristics of human nature. These interact non-linearly, giving rise to the endless variation of human experience.

Our World is Both Social and Internal

The human species combines three distinct dynamics, each nurtured and conserved over thousands of generations because they offer distinct selective advantages to individuals, groups and our species.

In the social realm, humanity organizes itself along the two axes of hierarchy and cooperation. In some sense we can fruitfully view these as two elements of one social dynamic, as each serves the self-interests of individuals and groups.

Social hierarchy is an organizational trait we share with our primate cousins the chimpanzees as well as many other mammalian species. Hierarchy provides irresistible incentives (better access to mates and resources) to struggle for status and an identity within the group. If we view a social order as a group of competing groups, the benefits of hierarchy fuel our social drive to establish and maintain dominance via aggression.

The second social dynamic is cooperation, which provides equally powerful incentives to establish and maintain trustworthy groups, extended families and alliances with other groups via the process of establishing and renewing trust with communication, trade, negotiation, compromise, gift-giving, festivities, communal rituals, forgiveness and expressions of empathy.

The third dynamic is the internal world of the individual. This includes the experiences of romantic love, spiritual insight, creative expression, solitary study and self-knowledge. While many of these have social components—for example, religious faith may be expressed in communal worship, and marriage may express a social/financial alliance of families—the essential characteristics of this dynamic are nonetheless private in nature.

Our Identity Is Constructed Internally

Counter-intuitively, at least at first glance, our sense of identity is ultimately a product of our internal world. I say counter-intuitively, as identity includes our membership in various super-groupings where anonymity is the norm: global religions, nation-states, ideologies, political parties, sports teams and "brand identity," i.e. loyalty to various corporate brands. Our identity is a dynamic assemblage of our place in social hierarchies, our membership in various anonymous super-groupings and our self-selected identity with various behaviors, strategies and values. Our internal model of the world is a complex taxonomy of class, status, education and cultural associations, and our identity is established by where we place ourselves in each of those overlapping taxonomies.

The inner private world is also home to the cue-activity-reward loops of personal habits: our level of self-discipline, for example, and our place in the spectrum of "consumer identity and behavior": whether we are an "early adopter," "aspirational shopper," and so on. Our behaviors and habits naturally flow from our identity and character: if we value the status of being first on the block with a new gadget, we will become an early adopter. If we value the status of owning a luxury brand, then we become an aspirational shopper, and so on.

Our Three Methods of Getting What We Want From Others

Within this basic framework of social dynamics and internally constructed identity, we are equipped with three basic methods to acquire what we want/need from others:

1. Free exchange of mutually agreed value: this exchange is transparent, cooperative, and based on mutual trust. It can occur as a private transaction or in an open marketplace.

2. Persuasion: one party seeks the acquiescence or agreement of another to an exchange or commitment. When the exchange is asymmetric, that is, it benefits one party more than the other, we call it sales, seduction or propaganda. In this type of persuasion, trust is carefully established to mask the asymmetry, and the purported benefits of the exchange are heavily promoted by the side with the most to gain while the risks are downplayed or obscured. The techniques of persuasion and the asymmetry are purposefully opaque to the losing party.

3. Coercion: one party compels acquiescence to an asymmetric arrangement with threats or force.

Our Tools of Assessment and Decision-Making

The human mind, though non-linear and enormously complex, has three basic levels of assessment, analysis and response—what Colonel John Boyd encapsulated as the OODA loop—observe, orient, decide, act:

1. Limbic: instinctive emotions and reactions such as "fight or flight," what we might call the genetically hardwired, automatic reactions to threats or surprises.

2. Intuitive: subconscious assessment and decision-making based on available information and past experience.

3. Deliberative: conscious analysis and decision-making based on experience, acquired knowledge, pattern-matching, inquiry, data collection, testing and modeling of reality and feedback.

Our Three Existential States of Being

Stripped to their essence, we experience and express three primary existential states:

1. Security: choosing what is known as it offers relative safety; this is the realm of habit and of conserving everything that appears to be keeping us out of high-risk, low-gain situations.

2. Fate: passively awaiting events and others' actions before responding, i.e. being "resigned to our fate."

3. Opportunity: risk-taking for the possibility of a windfall in wealth, status or security; this is the realm of actively seeking low-risk, high-gain windfalls and managing high-risk, high-gain situations.

Our Ontological Insecurity

In philosophy, we use the word *ontology* to describe the study of being. Conversationally, ontological means fundamental, something that has been boiled down to its essential nature and cannot be further reduced to a more fundamental state.

Humans are ontologically insecure on two distinct levels: one is shared with all life, the unknowability and permanence of risk; the other is unique to humanity.

Humans exist in a perpetual state of active insecurity. We are not ruled by instinct alone, but neither are we born with an innate sense of self. We are born with various personality traits and tropisms, but not with an identity; that must be forged and renewed within a group, and by an internally coherent model of the world that renders our place in it intelligible and meaningful.

Being both solitary and social, we have two intertwined insecurities. As social beings, we have a profound emotional need to establish and actively renew our standing within the social matrix of marriage, family, group, workplace and culture. As individual beings with inner states and dialogs, we hunger for an internally coherent framework that bestows meaning on a chaotic world and establishes our identity within that framework. If we fail to establish a rewarding social identity and a framework for making sense of our experience of the world, then our default state is a gnawing, debilitating insecurity that expresses itself as angst, anxiety, depression and alienation.

This ontological need to establish and renew an interior world of meaning and an external identity within a group is the primary force that powers our thoughts, emotions and actions, and it interacts dynamically with our basic life-force instincts to secure the essentials of food, water, shelter, safety and reproductive/mating opportunities—the basic level of Maslow's Hierarchy of Needs.

This need to overcome our innate insecurity is the key to understanding the entire spectrum of human experience: our inner states, our culture, our society, our political structures and our economy. It is not a psychological state or a cultural trait; it is the ontological state of being human.

Our Innate Vulnerabilities to Social Control

The advantages these traits and tools give us as a species is evident in our domination of our home planet; clearly, these traits and tools have leveraged extraordinary evolutionary success. While we could while away time indulging in the many pleasures of debating which traits bestow the critical advantages (12 menstrual cycles a year, grandparents and opposable thumbs all earn high rankings), our focus here is on the critical vulnerabilities created by our matrix of traits and tools.

Why focus on these vulnerabilities? In less complex species, Elites generally gain power through raw physical dominance or by reaching leadership via seniority. While humanity shares these two dynamics, human nature opens up vulnerabilities that Elites can exploit to maintain a predatory system that diverts the gain to them and transfers the costs and risks to the non-Elites.

These vulnerabilities can be leveraged by often-subtle tools of social control which we will now explore. These methods of social control are not cost-free; indeed, their basic mechanism is to transfer risk from the Elites to the system as a whole, which then becomes vulnerable to stagnation, brittleness and collapse.

Extremes of Dominance

We might start with the costs of being able to establish extremes of dominance. In the Animal Kingdom, only viruses and bacteria rival humanity's ability to establish extremes of dominance. Unfortunately for microbial empires, their dominance—for example, killing most of their hosts in short order—leads to their own fall as the annihilation of their hosts causes their own demise.

Other animals use dominance as a selective tool: the dominant male gains access to the most mates, and so on. The relative advantage of the dominant few (the Elite) is rather modest, and the ritualized battles to establish dominance rarely result in death. Even then, death is the result of accident rather than intent. Furthermore, dominance is often rather fleeting in the animal kingdom; the stresses of maintaining dominance against the constant challenges of younger rivals generally take a severe toll on the leadership, and as a result their reign is often brief.

Humans, on the other hand—or at least the males of the species— have enthusiastically embraced eradication and wholesale slaughter as irresistible benefits of extreme dominance. Such dominance has often been established with a technological or tactical innovation coupled with leadership that understands how to exploit the advantage on the battlefield. But extremes of dominance can also be established by material wealth drawn from superior resources or religious institutional power.

For example, a political entity that discovers how to grow three crops of grain per year will establish an overwhelming material advantage in kilocalories available to feed an army over those still laboring to get two harvests a year.

In the Middle Ages, fear of eternal damnation gave the Holy Roman Empire tremendous leverage and dominance, as it wielded the sole power of granting absolution.

In our era, extreme concentrations of wealth and political power have established extremes of dominance that are largely hidden from non-Elite eyes. The average American does not understand that the difference between owning $5 million in assets and owning $500 million is not the luxuries one can buy; the meaningful difference is in the political power one can buy.

Evenly matched rivals and a relatively level playing field limit potential extremes of dominance. In this setting, no one can gain an advantage for long, and the advantages will necessarily be modest.

In contrast, asymmetric situations where an initial toehold of dominance enables quick ascension to extremes of dominance lead to ossification, brittleness and Elites that cannot be dislodged except in times of extraordinary crisis or by the concerted efforts of the entire non-Elite populace.

Just as with overly successful bacteria, regimes of overwhelming dominance lead to excessive exploitation and eventual collapse.

There is another dark side to extremes of dominance: such sociopathological systems excel at distributing and enforcing social defeat, the bitter fruit of being dominated with little hope of liberty or escape. This has a number of negative consequences across the entire spectrum of social order and eventually triggers systemic instability and collapse.

Social defeat is the state of powerless isolation and low status where opportunities to renew a positive identity within the social and financial order are few; in this state, self-worth turns negative and the person feels as if they are becoming invisible. Stripped of positive opportunities to establish and renew an identity, the person suffering social defeat is prone to depression, anxiety, self-destruction, alienation, frustration, addiction and other expressions of chronic trauma.

Social Fractals

We typically think of fractals—structures that are scale-invariant—as features of Nature or finance. Scale-invariance means the feature retains certain characteristics regardless of the scale being viewed. For example, a coastline has the same characteristically ragged appearance from 100 feet, 1,000 feet and 10,000 feet in altitude, and the hourly, weekly and monthly charts of a stock share the same basic characteristics of alternating periods of high and low volatility.

The concept of social fractals can be illustrated with a simple example. If the individuals in a family unit are all healthy, thrifty, honest, caring and responsible, then how could that family be dysfunctional, spendthrift, venal and dishonest? If we aggregate individuals into a family unit then the family will manifest the self-same characteristics of the individuals, and if we aggregate those families into a community, then the community will reflect those self-same characteristics. This is the essence of fractals.

If the individuals in a department focus their energies on dodging consequence and feedback to increase their private security, then the department will devote itself to self-protection. If this proves successful, then the other departments will also devote their resources to self-protection, and the entire institution will also follow the same strategy.

But social fractals also work in the other direction, from the largest feature down to its smallest aggregates. For example, in a social order controlled by Elites that do not allow upward mobility via open markets and merit, then the characteristics of those Elites will manifest in the lower layers of the social order. If the Elites dominate with strong martial spirit and discipline, then the communities, families and individuals will manifest those self-same values. If the Elites maintain power via corruption, then every institution of the State and every department of those institutions will also manifest and reward corruption.

An entire volume could easily be written describing the complexities of social fractals, but we will make do here with a few key points.

Extremes of dominance (arising from extreme concentrations of wealth and power) also exhibit a self-same concentration of whatever social characteristics fuel their dominance. If financial dominance results largely from mastery of a certain form of cleverly disguised pathological dishonesty, then that trait has a great selective advantage in the Elite castes. In societies governed by extreme dominance, this type of clever dishonesty may have relatively little advantage in the lower reaches where honesty is still the norm. In this scenario, sociopathological dishonesty is soon concentrated in the upper reaches where the payoff for that mastery is the greatest.

A strong case can be made that this precise dynamic is at work in the U.S., where the financial Elites maintain their extreme dominance not by creating honest value via transparent enterprise but by institutionalizing corruption and dishonesty on an industrial scale via deliberate misrepresentation of material facts, legerdemain accounting, financial instruments designed to defraud and embezzle, the formalized debauchery of credit and the corruption of democracy via the purchase of political favors to thwart any organized attempts to limit their profits and power.

Social Control Myths

Another key dynamic of social fractals is their roots in belief structures: value systems, religious faiths, national identities and what is known as social control myths. A simple example illustrates the power of cultural norms: some cultures are incapable of forming queues, except perhaps at gunpoint (and even then a few line jumpers might have to be dispatched to impose order), while others "self-organize" into queues without coercion.

The ideal arrangement for Elites is a society that essentially submits itself to domination by internalizing (i.e. believing) a set of values and social norms that enable the Elites to dominate with very little expenditure of wealth or energy.

One example of this is the caste system, in which the lowest caste's belief in the dominant social control myth (that karma from previous lives has doomed them to this fate) enables domination by the Upper Castes with little effort. A few judicious killings of troublemakers is usually more than enough to enforce a wildly extreme form of domination.

Social control myths can extend the Elites' domination in a variety of ways. In the U.S., a dominant social control myth is upward mobility, the belief that anyone can, with hard work and perseverance, rise to the top ranks of status and wealth. Famous examples of this opportunity are raised to demi-god status and worshipped via massive media coverage.

But actual measures of social mobility have found that upward mobility has not just stalled but reversed for the majority of Americans. And what upward mobility does exist seems to be a function of gaming the system to gain entrance to the technocratic, managerial Upper Caste that serves the Elites.

The myth of upward mobility works not by banning certain behaviors but by offering false hope and a false explanation for one's low status: if we believe the system is a meritocracy, then we must conclude that our low status and insecurity result from our own deficiencies rather than from asymmetries built into the system. We also must conclude that we could succeed if only we worked harder.

This belief gives us hope in a better future for ourselves, even as it distracts us from looking at the system with less starry eyes.

The ideal setup for low-cost dominance by Elites is a populace who believes a set of social control myths and further believes they operate at every level of the society, i.e. as a fractal. If the social control myth is that honesty and hard work will loft you into the relative security and comfort of the Upper Caste, then the Elites are free to use dishonesty to expand their wealth and power as long as their corruption is hidden from those below.

This leads to a society in which the vast majority of people are working hard to create wealth that the Elites then siphon off via lying, cheating, fraud, embezzlement and political corruption. The key feature of this social-mythology mechanism is the Elites' use of shadow systems that are hidden from the view of non-Elites and informally operated so it is impossible to even prove their existence.

Here is a typical example of how Elites use shadow systems to maintain their dominance. The offspring of an Elite couple gains entrance to an Elite university via "legacy admission," an opaque shadow system that lets children of alumni or even major donors into the university regardless of their work ethic or intelligence.

The top Wall Street firms make a show of accepting applications from a range of jobseekers, but the shadow system only recruits new partners from two or perhaps three Elite universities. Informally, a member of the financial Elite places a phone call to a senior partner and asks him to place his son/daughter at the firm as an intern. If the son/daughter has sufficient social skills to schmooze with clients and willingness to engage in sociopathological looting, their graduation with poor marks from an Elite university and their parents' social/financial connections grant them immediate access to the heart of extreme dominance.

Later, when the firm needs an investigation quashed or sidetracked, calls will go out to other alumni or former associates of the firm who have secured top positions in government. These fellow members of the Upper Caste will dutifully find "insufficient evidence to pursue the investigation further" or similar rationalization to derail a potentially troublesome inquiry.

Non-Elite parents must hope their child has enough innate brilliance and a sufficiently relentless work ethic to gain entrance to the private elementary school which places most of its graduate in the Elite prep school which then places most of its graduates in Elite universities. The brilliance and hard work of the few aspirants who actually gain admission to the Upper Caste will be put to work solidifying and extending the already extreme dominance of the Elites.

The irony of their success is that the upward mobility myth they so fervently believed is at bottom a selective tool for recruiting the best and the brightest to dutifully serve the Elites. In this way, the self-interest of the most productive non-Elites is channeled to serve the self-interests of the Elites.

Exploiting Our Ontological Insecurity

As noted before, the ideal social control myth generates a social order that submits to the rule of Elites without coercion, as if their dominance was as natural and irresistible as the seasons. Once the populace internalizes the myth, they willingly sublimate their own interests to those of the Elites and rationalize this subjugation serving their self-interest.

Since social control myths reside in the minds of the ruled, they must satisfy our inner need for a coherent worldview and slake our ontological insecurity by providing us a meaningful identity in that internalized world.

Totalitarian police states can impose their will on their people by force, but this is a costly and risky way to gain compliance. Not only does this heavy security bureaucracy absorb much of the national surplus, the constant repression lowers the will of the people to be productive. The combination of low surpluses and high overhead costs eventually collapses the system.

The only sustainable, low-cost way to transfer risk to the populace is to persuade them to internalize social control myths that enable Elite political and financial domination. This requires constant repetition in the mass media and a psychologically appealing model of the world.

Lastly, the system must offer incentives for compliance and negative consequences for resistance.

Compare police states which reward spying on one's neighbors with those that nurture a social control myth that it is one's patriotic duty to spy on one's neighbors. In the first case, the State eventually collapses for the reasons noted above and the snitches are executed or punished. Nazi-ruled France provides a 20th century example: Nazi collaborators were widely loathed and suffered the consequence of their betrayal after the Nazis lost the war.

In the second case, the belief system causes some people to perform the dirty work of spying with relish, and without compensation other than recognition for their fine service to the State. This lowers the cost of repression and also lowers the internal thresholds to an activity (spying on neighbors) that is normally viewed with distaste.

If the social control myth gained widespread acceptance, the aftermath of the inevitable collapse is quite different. In the first case, the snitches were seen as individual traitors and punished appropriately. In the second, the populace is forced into a cultural reckoning as they must accept, often with great pain and regret, their own role in the national self-destruction: their belief in the myth led directly to their support of a system that could not have endured without their complicity.

Regardless of the flavor of the repressive state (theocratic, fascist, totalitarian, etc.), the key to implanting an effective social myth is strict control of the media and the textual sources of authority. For example, the translation of the Bible into the language of the people was deemed a capital crime in medieval Europe, as the Bible was the ultimate source of the Church-State's authority.

While repressive regimes are generally quite adept at controlling the media and "news" (victories are trumpeted, defeats are ignored), they often fail to distinguish between brainwashing, i.e. the repetition of what are clearly falsehoods or half-truths that only erode the credibility of the State, and the nurturing of a social control myth which is internalized as "making sense" and "serving my best interests."

If authority is ultimately granted by appeasing the gods with human sacrifice, for example, then the ideal social control myth elevates the role of being sacrificed to the noblest religious honor. (A steady supply of unwilling but eminently sacrificial prisoners of war helps limit the risk to the average citizen of being so honored.)

If the only way left for the State's military to sink enemy ships is by instructing pilots to crash their aircraft into the ships in a suicidal sacrifice, then raising suicide to a noble duty that cannot be shirked is an effective social control myth. (Dishonoring the family is the disincentive in this case.)

All control myths prey upon our ontological insecurity, i.e. our need to establish a coherent internal view of the world and develop an identity in that world. Social control myths function to the degree they offer up a compelling worldview and offer us a positive place in it. Once this structure has been internalized, then we feel it serves our best interests and are loath to replace it or even question it. In terms of natural selection, this can be understood as conserving what works because doing so is a low-risk strategy: since the worldview and our identity "works," then why risk modifying or replacing it? That process is fraught with risk and uncertainty, so better to avoid it if possible.

This explains why we cling to a conception of self-interest long after it no longer actually serves our best interests.

One key dynamic of our ontological insecurity is the need to constantly renew our identity; identity is not a project that can be finished and set aside, it is a process that must constantly be renewed by displays, interactions, signifiers, rituals and so on.

Uniforms offer a ready example. When we wear a uniform, we are renewing our identity as a solider, sailor, police officer, nurse, etc. While it may be possible to maintain unit coherence, esprit de corps and discipline without uniforms, it is certainly easier to do so when members put on a uniform every day to reaffirm their identity. The experience of those wearing uniforms is certainly different from those who do not. (I have long wished writers had a recognizable uniform.)

Attending worship services is a way of reaffirming our faith but it also serves to renew our membership in a specific congregation. If our internal world assigns the color black to artists and non-conformists, then wearing black reconfirms our identity as an artist/non-conformist. If our vehicle is our primary signifier of status and identity, then we will experience a positive sense of renewing our identity every time we sit in the driver's seat.

This process can also reinforce social defeat. If the auto is our primary signifier of status (and thus to some degree of self-worth), then driving a battered old car reinforces our sense of deprivation and low status.

We can distinguish two general categories of ways we establish and renew our identity: material goods of the sort I call *market-economy signifiers* that are purchased in the market economy and *non-market social signifiers* that arise from transactions, gatherings and rituals in the family, group, neighborhood, community, church, etc. This is the realm of social capital and the experience of belonging to a real-world group of people with some commonality, as opposed to an amorphous corporate brand in which identity is staked by wearing an item emblazoned with a logo.

Coercive States engender a politically useful identity by forcing the populace to wear uniforms or standardized clothing, attend large public rallies in support of the regime, join the ruling political party, and so on. Everything from paper money to billboards reaffirms the solidity and beneficence of the ruling Elites.

Nominally democratic and capitalist societies with a free press and open economy cannot force-feed a mass identity or worldview on their citizenry; they must use market-based persuasion and shadow systems to nurture social control myths.

They accomplish this critical task in several ways:

1. Economic data is presented in ways that reinforce the perception that the ruling Elites are competently managing the system to serve everyone's interests.

Journalists are bribed, influenced or browbeaten into disseminating "news" and data that reaffirms this perception management.

2. The Central State actively seeks to make the majority of the populace dependent on the State for rights, employment, retirement, food coupons, etc. In this way, identity is soon defined in terms of our relation to the State—employee, entitlement recipient, taxpayer, voter, supplicant, etc.

3. The State and private-sector Elites emphasize the market economy as the sole source of identity: once the market economy becomes the dominant paradigm of identity, then the populace defines themselves almost exclusively in terms of their roles in the market

economy: employee, business owner, investor, consumer and displayer of consumerist market signifiers.

Non-market identifiers and social capital are replaced by market and State definitions of self-interest and identity. In other words, there is an ontological connection between the dominance of a consumerist market economy and an expansive Central State: they are essentially two aspects of one system, the consumerist State economy.

Dependence on the State and the market-economy discredits and dismantles the non-market sources of identity: faith, communities, voluntary associations, enterprise and individually assembled identity, in sum, the sources of authentic identity, are replaced with intrinsically inauthentic but financially and political useful identities provided by the State and consumerism.

A human being stripped of authentic sources of identity becomes depressed, anxious and alienated, and no amount of market signifiers or State dependency can fill the void within. Dependence on the State and consumerism further deepen the void even as they claim to fill it. Ironically, with few other sources of comfort and identity available, people pursue consumerist digital distractions with even greater intensity as the failure of atomized consumerism to calm their insecurities eats away their sense of self.

Indeed, let us ask this key question: what is the ideal social control worldview for an expansive Central State ruled by financial Elites that hold extreme dominance over the State and economy? The answer is a society of atomized, socially isolated individuals who are largely dependent on the State, individuals who define their identity, status and self-worth in terms of the State and consumerist signifiers that must be purchased in the market-economy.

The ultimate expression of this worldview is when the act of purchasing become the primary renewal of identity, and the possession of the purchased object is secondary; thus the "perfect consumer" is one who must buy more shoes (for example) to renew her identity, even as the shoes previously purchased pile up in her closet, untouched and unworn; the value was imparted in the purchase transaction, not in the ownership.

Since market-economy signifiers are intrinsically inauthentic, they cannot fill the ontological need for identity for long. Rather, the insecurity quickly returns as the market-economy is like a wheel mounted in a cage: whatever you buy today will be surpassed and lose its status value tomorrow. The transactional "high" experienced in the moment of purchase quickly dissipates, and renewed ennui rushes in to fill the void.

It doesn't really matter if the person is inside the market-economy wheel, busily running to buy enough signifiers to avoid social defeat or if they have been pushed off the wheel into social defeat and total dependence on the State: in either case their primary emotions are anxiety, insecurity, depression and alienation. Both are firmly trapped in the cage of the consumerist market-State economy.

This exploitation of our ontological insecurity for profit and power has profound consequences. It is not just the economy that is hollowed out by this financialization of human nature; the entire society is also hollowed out and replaced by a monoculture consumerist, expansive-State financialization.

We will explore the subtle and pernicious nature of this hollowing out in the next chapter.

Chapter Five: **The Derealization of the Non-Market Social Order**

It is difficult to understand the pathology of the consumerist-State worldview because it's like the air around us—it is a given that we accept without questioning. This acceptance is not a matter of chance, as the non-market, non-State social order has been *derealized* and replaced by a consumerist market and State whose ontological imperative is expansion and control.

Derealization and depersonalization are clinical psychiatric terms, but I use the word here in a philosophic manner to describe the ontological disconnection between our lived experience and what the marketing/State complex reports we should be experiencing. This creates an emotional and cognitive dissonance that renders both our internal experience and the marketing/State's interpretation of the real world into dream states that we never fully inhabit. This derealization creates a society and economy that is ontologically sociopathological.

All that is presented by the marketing/State complex as real is actually abstract and illusory, as the sources of authenticity have been derealized and replaced by a monoculture of inauthenticity, consumerism and State control.

This derealization manifests in many ways: eating disorders and obesity; difficulty sleeping; trance-like apathy; lack of engagement with real life; inability to maintain meaningful relationships; a life devoid of intimacy, passion and purpose; reliance on medication and drugs; addictive behaviors and attachments; inability to concentrate; fragmented sense of self; avoidance of responsibility; proclamations of victimhood; inability to discern right from wrong; the substitution of soaring rhetoric for logic; escapism; serial lying; chronic rage, frustration, depression and anxiety and a generalized sense of emotional hunger, incoherence, imbalance, disquiet and loss.

These are neither isolated psychiatric phenomena found only in a few mentally-ill individuals, nor are they unique to modern consumerist-State societies. But we dodge the self-evident is we refuse to recognize that these manifestation are normalized in our current social order.

Our ontological need for intimacy, purpose, identity and social connection is not recognized by the consumerist market State; the social order's key dynamics have been reduced to profitable, mass-marketable consumables or experiences that are centrally produced, marketed and managed.

For example, meals have been derealized into facsimile-food gobbled on the go, and the experiences of growing food, cooking and eating have been replaced with profitable simulacra of those once-authentic experiences. As a result, we are malnourished, physically, emotionally and spiritually, even as we are constantly told we live in the ultimate state of abundance.

Recent history has been derealized into a state of *induced amnesia*, decontextualized into an account that serves the interests of the Status Quo. Authentic non-market sources of identity have been eroded or delegitimized as the marketing/State complex tirelessly seeks to legitimate illegitimate concentrations of wealth and power in finance, governance and the social order.

Derealization is such an alienating process that we cannot even identify the sources of our isolation, anxiety and depression. It is little wonder so many people feel powerless and resigned to life in a sociopathological order they do not consciously recognize as pathological.

Since the consumerist market economy and the Central State are ontologically one, it is impossible to separate a political revolution from an economic and social one, and impossible to understand this without a revolution in our understanding of marketing, authenticity and the replacement of the non-market social order by the consumerist State economy.

A typical response to this is to deny derealization, and to claim that since governments and markets have existed for thousands of years, the present consumerist State economy is simply an extension of these pre-modern examples of shopping and central control.

This response only proves the completeness of the derealization, for the social order of traditional, pre-financialization, pre-Central State capitalism is qualitatively different from the financialized, centralized consumerist State capitalism of today.

We cannot possibly understand liberation without understanding how the non-market, non-centralized social order has been largely lost, and with it our sources of authentic identity.

The Qualitative Differences between the Traditional Bazaar and Consumerism

In what we might call the "folk economics" view of "shopping," the modern consumerist State economy is simply an extension of the ancient bazaar: the only difference is now we have more bazaars to browse.

This naïve summary of consumerism not coincidentally fits the Wall Street/State conception of consumer self-interest perfectly: becoming a politically pliant "consumer" of debt to "live large" via consumption empowers the banks and their partner in domination, the Central State.

Unfortunately for the citizen reduced to a passive "consumer" and the nation, consumerism is a sociopathological construct whose sole purpose is to undermine authentic identity and drive the populace into a debt-serfdom ruled by centralized concentrations of capital and political power.

The only way to understand this distortion of citizen self-interest is to parse the qualitative differences between pre-financialization markets and the consumerist State economy.

We can start by noting the key differences in what many would assume is the common feature of all markets, shopping.

The universal appeal of shopping arises from humanity's attractions to novelty, routine, acquisition, windfall and social activities. Browsing bazaars fulfills all these desires: routine visits to markets provide the comfort of routine, while the variety of goods offers the stimulation of novelty and finding a "good deal" satisfies our innate search for windfall and a new "addition" to our prosperity. A crowded traditional market offers the stimulation of being with "novel" strangers and opportunities to meet friends to socialize over tea or coffee or a snack.

In other words, shopping fulfills our innate need to renew social connections, engage in the practical calculation of maximizing the value of our trade (get a bargain, turn our labor into cash, etc.) and enjoy the stimulation of novelty while also experiencing the comfort of "familiar and safe" routines.

On the surface, shopping at the mall appears no different from shopping at the traditional bazaar. The superficial similarities are deceptive, for the financial and social fractals of each are entirely different.

In traditional markets, the pleasures of browsing and socializing are the primary experiences; purchases are either essential (basic foods to take home to prepare) or modest (a tea or snack). In the mall, essentials are secondary and offer little pleasure; buying basic groceries is a chore. The primary goal of shopping is to ward off social defeat by purchasing something that can be displayed—finger nail polish, jewelry, clothing, etc.—and that display is the primary source of self-identity.

In the traditional market, the renewal of identity is based on the social connections made, not the process of acquisition. In the mall, it is the transaction itself and the acquisition of some item to display or consume in public which renews a sense of self.

In the bazaar, each transaction is settled: cash or goods are exchanged and the transaction is complete. In the mall, acquisitions are paid with credit, and the debt accrues interest long after the transaction is completed.

In traditional markets, credit is informal and scarce; in consumerist-State markets, credit is not just commonplace, it is the essential lifeblood of commerce and thus of establishing identity and our place in the world.

In the traditional market, there are no guarantees in life, and so surplus income must be assiduously saved to safeguard the household in emergencies and to build capital to be invested in enterprise or some other income stream.

In consumerist-State markets, the Central State guarantees loans and promises to pay everyone's pension and healthcare costs as they age. Saving is thus not just unnecessary but counterproductive, as it diminishes the amount of income that can be devoted to buying a larger self and life, i.e. becoming a different person by consuming differently. Enterprise, like consumption, is funded by debt.

In traditional market capitalism, a distinction is drawn between consumption of essentials, consumption of non-essentials, and investments that create income streams. Income left after buying essentials and saving capital is scarce for most people, and so consumption of non-essentials is rare and thus recognized as a signifier of status.

In consumerist-State markets, the line between essentials and non-essentials is blurred. Since identity is dependent on consumption of "status identifiers," then what is considered "essential" is widened to include a spectrum of non-essentials that are perceived as essential to identity.

We can define essential as what is necessary to sustain life: basic foodstuffs, shelter, utilities, etc. Everything beyond this strict utility-value is non-essential consumption.

Thus all housing above minimal utilitarian shelter is a form of non-essential consumption. Recognition that housing is consumption is anathema to the Status Quo, which must insist that debt-based consumption of housing (mortgages) is a form of "investment" to mask the unproductive nature of most housing expenditures.

The definition of investment is quite simple: an investment generates an income stream. Everything that does not generate an income stream is dead money or unproductive consumption.

Thus most of what is spent on higher education must also be recognized as a form of non-essential consumption. In terms of productive skills and knowledge acquired, an entirely free online education or a low-cost state university education satisfies the requirement for an "essential" education needed to navigate the modern global economy. The "non-essential" segments of higher education—the status value of "going away to college," the status of prestigious diplomas and multiple degrees, etc.—account for most of the cost, which is of course paid for with debt.

Defenders of the Status Quo vociferously defend this non-essential consumption of education as "an investment," claiming that the status and social connections imparted by the prestigious diploma pay enormous dividends for the rest of the student's life. While examples "proving" these contentions are easily found, so are counter-examples.

Setting aside the fact that the costs of non-essential education have skyrocketed solely as a result of student loans being made universally available, such claims of "investment value" may be true in in a thin slice of the total sum spent on education. But since the number of plum positions in the Upper Caste serving the financial and State Elites is actually quite restricted, then it is impossible to claim that the vast sums spent on tens of millions of college diplomas are "investments" that will yield plum positions and salaries.

As with everything else in the consumerist-State economy, what was once high-status in cash-based traditional markets—expansive private residences, university educations, foreign travel, multiple vehicles, superfluous decoration and consumption, etc.—is now available to everyone with credit via the magic of expanding debt.

As a result of this widespread availability, the status value of these non-essential forms of consumption has plummeted merely as a result of supply and demand. Once one-third of the workforce has a college degree, the value of that degree is considerably lower than when only 15% of the populace had a university education.

In traditional social orders, the rarity of credit and surplus income to spend on non-essentials meant that identity and one's place in the world were based on social connections and behavioral attributes such as enterprise, devotion, generosity and integrity.

In the consumerist-State social order, non-essential consumption is the primary source of identity, as credit and State guarantees have eroded the need for savings and income-producing investments. Ironically, the ubiquity of credit means that almost everyone can buy the same mass-produced signifiers, and so the "competitive advantage" flows to those with some "hustle", i.e. fraud, that leverages an asymmetric advantage into higher consumption, or those who can leverage modest incomes into vast mountains of credit.

Expanding debt and an intrinsically unstable identity based primarily on consumption are the key attributes of consumerist-State social orders. These economies are qualitatively different from traditional pre-financialized market economies, and their dependence on ever-expanding debt and consumption of non-essentials is both sociopathological and unsustainable.

An example will help clarify the essential characteristics of consumerism.

If I need a new suit because the ones I own are worn or no longer fit, then it is in my self-interest to buy a well-made and designed suit that enhances my appearance for the lowest possible price. This is pragmatic replacement. If I go into debt to buy a new suit that I don't really need, this is debt-based consumerism.

If I enjoy browsing a variety of suits before deciding on the one I will buy, this is shopping. If I browse store after store as my primary source of socializing and entertainment, this is consumerism.

If I enjoy wearing the suit because it fits properly and I like the cut but otherwise give it no mind, this is pleasure in ownership. If my identity is dependent on the brand of the suit and those around me knowing the brand, this is consumerism.

If I sacrifice capital accumulation (savings) that can be invested in acquiring skills and income-producing investments to buy items I can easily do without, then that is consumerism.

The key features of consumerism are that purchases are non-essential, they are purchased with credit and the motivation for the purchase is to enhance identity via the act of purchasing and displaying a high-status brand label.

It is natural to enjoy the novelty and social aspects of browsing the bazaar. What is not natural is to buy goods you don't need with debt that outlasts the brief boost to self-worth offered by the status identifier. Basing one's identity on consumption creates an inauthentic, fragile sense of self that is vulnerable to social defeat, and sacrificing capital accumulation (savings) to fund debt-based consumption leads to lifelong servitude. That is the essence of consumerism.

The Financialized Consumerist Social Order

Most Americans have little direct experience of a pre-financialization (i.e. traditional) decentralized market economy and social order, and so imagining such a world is a challenge.

One way to highlight the difference between our consumerist-market economy and the traditional model is to simply describe the everyday life and built environment of each social order.

In the typical American urban or suburban zone where the vast majority of people reside (85%), most people do not know their neighbors beyond the most superficial acquaintance, and few have even that with neighbors a few doors down the street or hallway. A visit to the police department, café or other traditional gathering place will yield little to no information about the individuals in the neighborhood; everyone is equally unknown and anonymous.

The primary expressions of status are the home and vehicle, both of which explicitly exclude informal, uncontrolled social contacts ("the outside world") and privatize consumption and experience. Indeed, the entire purpose of the home and private vehicle is to carve off private space that is controlled by the individual owner.

While we can say this is an overt manifestation of the value our social order places on privacy, that characterization misses the wider significance of this privatization of experience. While such private spaces offer opportunities for privacy, they also offer equally capacious opportunities for social isolation and extreme emotional poverty. While it suits the ideology of consumerist individualism to trumpet the opportunity for privacy, what is ignored is the withering of opportunities for social connections and a social identity that isn't entirely dependent on consumerist signifiers.

This elevation of the individual's extreme isolation to the peak of social status—that is, a walled-off mansion and a private fleet of luxury vehicles are the very pinnacle of consumerist status in our social order—are pathologically counter to human nature. Stripped of authentic sources of positive identity, humans seek to blot out of the inner void with drugs and distraction (entertainment) or with a monomaniacal pursuit of additional consumerist signifiers, as if the next trophy purchase, diploma or experience (for example, exotic travel) will magically fill the void that only deepens with the failure of each purchase to renew a meaningful identity.

It is not accidental that such solitude comes at a steep price. Maintaining ontological insecurity is the primary purpose of marketing, and the high costs of the home and vehicles push the vast majority of households into debt serfdom as the initial purchase requires staggering loads of debt.

Stripped of authentic sources of establishing and renewing social identity, people turn to external consumerist signifiers: we don't establish identity by actually belonging to a real social group, we claim an entirely meaningless "membership" in a corporate brand or consumerist "tribe" by displaying tattoos, clothing brands, various mass-media musical tastes, and so on.

If we understand individual identity as an ecosystem of nodes and connections, then we will recognize that the isolated individual constructed of mass-produced brands and mass-marketed "tribes" is a chimera, a pretense, an illusory identity fashioned in an environment that has been strip-mined of authentic sources of identity. Though we give lip-service to devotion, service, accomplishment and a number of other behavioral signifiers, who among us would trade a walled mansion and fleet of luxury vehicles for devotion and feel we got the better end of the deal?

An ecosystem with numerous nodes and connections will be resilient, adaptable and robust; once that has been stripped of diversity will be brittle, vulnerable and unable to adapt to change. In terms of identity and self-worth, the consumerist market economy is a monoculture: the only meaningful way to establish and renew identity is to buy a signifier of status and worth.

The promise of the consumerist monoculture is that we can each construct a larger life and self by consuming differently. We can distill this down to a simple question: does this make me feel larger or smaller as a person? Owning a spacious mansion, luxury name-plate vehicle, high-status diploma, etc. makes us feel larger, and being too poor to own a private vehicle makes us feel much smaller. This sense of reduced selfhood and value is what I term social defeat, and our social order excels at generating and distributing social defeat.

At the extremes of social defeat, the individual feels as if they have ceased to exist. In terms of the consumerist social order, they have indeed vanished into invisibility.

This secular worship of social isolation serves two other consumerist purposes: it leaves the individual aching for distraction from isolation and boredom, and it reinforces "the outside world" as a threatening place to avoid.

The "solution" to ennui and isolation is of course digital distraction, i.e. entertainment, social networking, assembling lists of mass-marketed music on mass-marketed digital devices, etc., and the purpose of marketing is to elevate these abstractions of actual connections to high-status activities. The ideal scenario in the consumerist market is individuals whose primary claim to high status is the interconnectedness of their digital distractions and the size of their personal archive of mass-produced entertainment, all consumed in splendid isolation.

That the outside world is threatening is not accidental. Once the rising cost of private space exceeds the ability of the lower 20% of the populace to pay the price, then this population is forced out into the public spaces for distraction and solace. In societies with relatively low inequality in income and status, public spaces tend to be safe and lively as a variety of social classes intermix in the normal course of daily life.

In highly unequal societies, a perverse dynamic develops: those on the bottom rungs turn to begging in public spaces, attaching themselves to any high-status, high-income person who come by, and those in the top rungs avoid this unpleasantness by abandoning all public spaces except those small quadrants that can be policed, for example, around the opera house and tony shopping districts.

The mass-media long ago established that sensationalized crime and fear both command attention that they can sell, so crime and threats are relentlessly broadcast to the point that they dominate the inner perception of those who consume multiple channels of media.

What are lost in this dynamic is non-market public spaces and the sense that being social is actually safer than isolation. The isolated, fearful consumer can be sold much more than the individual who values non-market social activities and finds isolation heightens emotional impoverishment.

We can observe the manifestations of these dynamics in everyday life.

Most people remain inside their homes except for yard work or other tasks that cannot be accomplished indoors. A walk down the street in the evening typically reveals a line of windows dimly illuminated by the computer and television screens within.

When people are outside, they are ensconced in the cocoons of their private vehicles or in the sensory cocoons of their private musical playlist. The majority of conversations occur via phones.

There are few if any public spaces for informal non-market gatherings and those that do exist are either uninviting paved expanses or parks occupied by the marginalized populations who have no permanent private space. The only safe places to meet in public are for-profit zones—malls, fast-food restaurants and formal venues such as theaters.

There are few safe, inviting promenades for pedestrians and bicyclists, and few public spaces that are not designed primarily for autos and trucks. Those pathways and bikeways that do exist are on the margins of the urban zone, either in "scenic" areas with no access to public urban life or on leftover land that has lost its commercial value such as abandoned rail lines.

There is little informal gathering or mingling of diverse members of the community; events are formalized and commercialized, such as concerts, or strictly limited to formal commercial zones such as farmers markets. There is no public space available for informal commerce, and any non-formalized gathering for non-market activity is viewed with alarm and suspicion.

People tend to eat out frequently, but rarely meet up with friends; many people have no real friends, only circles of acquaintances, few of which overlap. Each social circle revolves around a formalized, often abstract purpose: work, spectator sports, etc. If someone meets one person in one context, they are unlikely to see them in another context: atomized individuals have limited connections to other atomized individuals, and since people live, work and pursue recreation in widely scattered locales, individuals only make fleeting connections with other people in the real world. In other words, few people would recognize the butcher in their local supermarket, and even fewer would ever meet that individual outside the supermarket.

Security is measured by firearms and other weapons, high-technology security alarms and multiple lights, locks, etc. The ideal home is a locked-down isolated fortress bristling with firearms.

Few people practice real-world skills; yards are "beautified" for show, and vegetable gardens are frowned upon unless safely hidden from view. Cooking may be viewed on television more than it is than pursued in the real world. Music is seldom played live non-commercially; it is generated by recordings and devices. The social gatherings that do occur are formalized; many people eat alone, hurriedly, or while they absorb four to six hours daily of television, films, music, spectator sports, web-surfing or other individually consumed digital entertainment.

Shopping is the primary pastime of many people; it is their entertainment, relaxation and fun. Much of the shopping occurs in "big box" discount stores, malls or urban districts dominated by national retailers. A significant share of shopping is done online in the privacy of the home or office.

Most people's homes, be they one-room studios or multi-room mansions, are crammed with mas-produced belongings. This is true regardless of the wealth of the household; low-income homes are just as crowded with consumer goods as middle-class homes.

A large percentage of the typical suburban home is rarely inhabited, being devoted to abstract uses such as formal dining rooms and living rooms intended for social gatherings. These supposedly public spaces are rarely inviting and many are cold, overly formalized displays of consumerist signifiers, i.e. "tasteful art," etc.

Political gatherings are typically formalized meetings of professional politicians and lobbyists and a smattering of special-interest citizenry who have come to specifically influence particular policies that affect their interest. The average citizen has never attended a political meeting of any kind, and those few that did found that the meeting often ran late and they were unable to speak or were limited to 30 seconds of testimony.

Many people spend most of their time alone with digital devices, in their office, home or vehicle. Most of the social "scripts" and explanatory narratives they are familiar with are drawn from commercial programming and films, i.e. entertainment.

These are of course generalizations, and there are many exceptions. But on the whole, can anyone honestly claim these attributes are not the common experiences of the 85% of the American populace that lives in urban and suburban zones? Indeed, these are also the common experiences of many rural and small-town residents, as these attributes are social fractals that are found everywhere in the culture.

The common denominators are: life revolves around earning or collecting money to consume centrally manufactured, distributed and marketed goods and services in formalized settings; much of one's time is spent alone, at home, the office or in a vehicle, consuming digital media and entertainment; public life is limited to formalized, for-profit single-use environments and most of life is, beneath the day-to-day routines, centrally controlled, manufactured and marketed.

The point here is not to issue a value judgment—after all, I spend a great deal of my time alone staring at a digital screen, I shop at Costco, and so on—but to ask two questions of this social order:

1. Is this social order in any way causally related to the negative characteristics listed previously?

2. Does this social order limit opportunities to renew identity and status in non-market, informal settings?

The honest answer to both questions is yes. It is self-evident that the normalized manifestations listed above are causally connected to the Status Quo's generosity in distributing social defeat and its erosion of all non-consumerist sources of identity and self-worth.

It is self-evident that the consumerist-State social order has pruned away informal, decentralized non-market opportunities for social connections so that participants must pay money and be controlled by State directives.

Alternatives to this consumerist-State order are few and far between; many of the traditional non-market institutions have been infected with market-type extremes of competition (parents demanding "winning seasons" of child athletes and assaulting other parents who are seen as impediments to that goal) or the subtle substitution of market concepts of well-being (for example, churches that promote consumerist measures of prosperity).

We can best understand the sociopathological nature of the current social order by looking at it as an ecosystem. In effect, the modern consumerist-Central State social order has been stripped of diversity and non-market opportunities to establish a positive identity via social interactions so all that remains is highly profitable, centrally controlled market-economy transactions.

Market-economy signifiers have high value, and non-market social signifiers have low value. This social order enables concentrated private profits and expanding State control.

A simple analytic tool for understanding the social order as an ecosystem is to mark each participant with a dot and draw lines between them to signify a transaction or relationship.

If we break down the average household income, we find that the vast majority of the income flows to a very small number of institutions: the Central State and local government (income, sales and property taxes), a handful of global banks (mortgage, credit cards, student loans, auto loans), a handful of global retailers, a handful of global fast-food/restaurant chains and a handful of global media/entertainment corporations.

If we break down the time spent by the household, we would find once again that the majority of time was spent working (to consume and service debt, not to save), commuting, usually in a private vehicle, consuming some centrally distributed, marketed and produced good or service or consuming digital entertainment produced and distributed by a handful of corporations on devices produced by a handful of global corporations.

In other words, were we to draw a chart of what controls and consumes the vast majority of everyday life in America we would have a chart with the Central State at its center surrounded by local governments, and lines drawn to a handful of global banks, global retail chains, global media companies, global fast-food chains, supermarket corporations and a global digital device manufacturers.

Once a large ecosystem has been reduced to a series of monocultures and cartels, it loses resiliency and adaptability. In essence, the opportunities for low-intensity instability—the spontaneity and creativity of informal, non-market, non-State controlled activity--have been stripped away. What's left is centrally controlled and highly profitable, so profits and power can be concentrated in financial Elites and Central State fiefdoms.

Is it any wonder that people who have limited opportunities to establish an authentic individual and social identity are emotionally and spiritually impoverished?

In non-market, less centralized social orders, vendors set up shop informally along a street; this is the norm in many areas of so-called "developing world" cities such as Bangkok. In our social order, this is banned as a "public hazard" as the food might be unsafe (never mind food poisoning epidemics trace back to highly centralized agribusiness) and cities demand high fees for any commercial activity.

Where kids once gathered for informal games in empty lots, that kind of activity is viewed as a "public danger" (they might be a gang) and the only allowed games require organizational fees, coaches, centralized management and so on. There is a place for organized youth sports, of course, but is informal, non-centralized sports really such a threat? If so, why?

If we draw connections between each individual and the handful of cartels and institutions that dominate their lives as transactions that offer minimal or plentiful opportunities to make meaningful social connections and renew identity with non-market interactions in the real world, we find that the American social order offers very few such opportunities. The point is that informal, non-market gathering places are proscribed and marginalized so all activity is driven into the market-economy where fees can be collected and concentrated into distant hands.

Between working in a private office or cubicle, commuting for hours alone in a vehicle, dining alone, shopping alone and consuming media alone, then the only "convenient" opportunities for renewing identity and establishing social status is as consumers of marketed goods and services, or as abstract connections on social media.

This explains the obsession with surface identifiers such as tattoos, hairdos, clothing, jewelry, vehicles, etc., as interactions and deeds have no "place" in the social order nor do they have value in an ecosystem where everyone is reduced to an anonymous consumer.

The other ontological point about this social order is its extreme level of abstraction. Consumers pay for purchases with an abstraction, credit, and an abstract identifier, a plastic credit card. Though whatever they buy has some utility value (a meal, an item of clothing, etc.), the social value—that is, the value in terms of identity and status—is also an abstraction.

An abstraction is traded for an abstraction, and the real world is either a display case for the consumable or a workplace that generates the abstract money to pay the abstract debt.

Not only is the worker alienated from the product of his labor, as Marx noted, in this social order the worker is alienated from most of the real world, which has largely been reduced to financialized abstractions and consumer signifiers. There are few ways to establish and renew a positive identity, and escaping social defeat is difficult without an income ample enough to consume market-economy goods and services in quantity.

Even the Central State, the ultimate guarantor of abstract money and debt, is an abstraction; it is only rendered real when it conjures up coercion.

Contrast this impoverished, brittle and unhealthy ecosystem with a traditional market social order. Though it is all too easy to sentimentalize or romanticize a traditional social order, we will avoid that, for sentimentality is itself a form of derealization. The goal is simply to note the fundamental attributes of life in a pre-financialized, decentralized market social order. Examples of this social order can be found throughout the world (including America) and throughout history.

Once again we can best understand such a social order as an ecosystem that can be traced by drawing lines of social connections and interactions between people and institutions, and listing opportunities to establish and renew identity and status in market and non-market settings.

In non-financialized social orders, people interact with others across a variety of social circles; you may or may not like the lady who sells homemade cheese in the square, but you will see her in the post office, in the corner café and in the building next door. In America, this is usually experienced in small, close-knit towns where "everybody knows everybody."

In the pre-financialized social order, much if not most income is derived from informal activity; the bakery bakes homemade loaves, cookies, trays of nuts, etc. for a small fee, a motorbike acts as a taxi and so on. Other than the money spent on a few liters of petrol or other fuel, cheap appliances and electronics, spare motorbike parts, etc. very little of the community's money flows to the Central State or global cartels; most remains circulating in the community. There is little formal bank debt and little contact with the Central State.

Though decentralized, localized enterprises typify small towns in America, in non-financialized societies these traits also typify urban neighborhoods: everyone knows everyone else via family, clan, church or neighborhood connections, and security is derived not from gated, armed fortresses but from the security of being known in a number of overlapping circles, i.e. the opposite of anonymity.

Identity and status are of course imparted by "high status" globally marketed corporate "brand" items, but there are still abundant sources of non-market social capital and identity in these communities: gatherings at the churchyard or temple, informally created music, acts of generosity, unpaid mentoring, etc. The closest analogy in America is once again small towns where much of the social activity results from unpaid volunteer work.

Once again we can derive an understanding of the resilience and robustness of an individual's identity by mapping out each source of identity, each opportunity to renew that identity positively and each socially rewarding transaction or connection. The individual who draws sustenance from worship, devotion, study, pursuit of a skill, the public free performance of music and dance, the creation of non-market art, the communal growing, preparation and partaking of real food, participation in the community on some level, be it religious, security, politics, sports, food, education or commerce, and spends informal time with friends, extended family and associates has a wealth of wellsprings of identity and self-worth.

In contrast, the "ideal citizen" to the expansive Central State/consumerist market economy (which is to say easily manipulated and debt-indentured) devotes most of their time to earning money to service their overwhelming debts, has few if any other sources of identity other than corporate brands and mass-marketed "tribes," and consumes vast quantities of mass-media "news" and "entertainment" in isolation that increase their ontological insecurity with marketing and propaganda. This citizen is dependent on mass-marketed status identifiers, medications and the Central State in equal measure, and has no non-abstract (i.e. real-world) social sources of identity or self-worth. The loss of income needed to buy consumerist identifiers is equivalent to a loss of self.

The reader may wonder what social order and identity has to do with political revolution; my answer is twofold.

Changing the leadership of the State changes nothing of substance; is it impossible to transform the Central State and its financial Elite partnership without also transforming the entire debt-based, financialized consumerist economy that supports the State and financial Elites. It is not just the financial Elite or the expansive State that is unsustainable; the entire social order of financialized mass consumption is equally unsustainable.

The point of this book is to demonstrate that the State, concentrations of wealth and power and the debt-based consumerist social order are all facets of a single social order. It is not possible to transform one aspect without also changing the others.

The second answer is entirely practical. As I write this in March 2012, there are 313 million Americans, of which only 115 million have full-time employment of the sort that enables survival in a high-cost consumerist economy. Another 21 million eke out a modest income from part-time work while 7 million others have two or more part-time jobs.

The Central State and central bank (the Federal Reserve) have borrowed or printed at least $9 trillion and pumped this unprecedented sum into the economy over the past four years to prop up the Status Quo. In we add corporate debt ($7 trillion) and private debt ($13 trillion), we find that the past four years of "extend and pretend" were purchased at the cost of trillions of dollars in additional debt on every level of the economy. As noted in Chapter One, this is not sustainable; the national debt already exceeds the nation's gross domestic product ($15 trillion), a threshold which research has found inevitably leads to destabilization.

As a result of this folly, the economy will eventually be unable to borrow enough to support the Status Quo and service the debt piled up in previous years. The Status Quo will then destabilize and be replaced with another more sustainable arrangement.

Regardless of the political or financial nature of this arrangement, it will operate without borrowing trillions of dollars annually. That means it will be smaller and "poorer" in terms of spending, debt and leverage. The debt-based consumerist economy will no longer exist in its current form, and formal employment will be increasingly scarce. Though no one can predict the future with any accuracy, the above facts suggest that formal full-time employment will fall well below 100 million jobs, meaning that less than one-third of the populace will have formal full-time employment. Everyone else will either be dependent on these workers or they will have to generate income in the informal economy, as the vast majority of people in the developing world currently do.

A society in which only a third of the population can escape crushing social defeat will be an exceedingly unhappy and unstable one. Many observers claim that technology will increase wealth to the benefit of all, but if history is any guide, technological innovations destroy jobs by replacing costly human labor with increasingly cheaper machine labor and intelligence. As noted previously, scalable technology requires vast investment of capital, which is precisely what will be wiped out as the Status Quo system of leverage debt implodes under its own weight.

Counting on technology to extend the life of debt-based consumerism is a form of fantasy science fiction. Recent history suggests the Internet destroys established industries and job bases at a far faster rate than it creates stable employment. Even worse, much of the Web's revenues are marketing and advertising. Once debt-based consumerism implodes, there will be far fewer consumers with the means to respond to adverts and marketing.

It seems self-evident that the only possible positive solution to the self-destruction of the debt-based consumerist market economy is to dispense with consumerism as the basis of identity and widen the foundation of identity to include the traditional non-market sources that the consumerist economy and Central State have eroded or marginalized.

Financialization has not just rendered our financial and governance systems brittle, unstable and self-destructive; it has also rendered our identity and internal worldview brittle, unstable and self-destructive. The sociopathology of the Status Quo is fractal, and manifests in individual's manic pursuit of a store-bought identity and impoverished sense of self and in the highly centralized concentrations of wealth and political power that have fatally weakened the healthy forces of low-intensity instability (LII).

The ecology of consumerist-based identity and the financialized economy are both fractals of systemically vulnerable monoculture.

Once these self-destructive systems destabilize, we will have a choice as to the replacement. A decentralized ecology of authentic identity and definancialized political systems which protect and encourage the "immune" forces of low-intensity instability is the only stable, sustainable model. We ignore this at our peril.

Consumerism as the Centralized, Profitable Source of Identity

Why is consumerism so appealing? Why do people cling to a visibly pathological model that generates insecurity, debt-serfdom and social defeat as its core function? Certainly the immense power of marketing plays a key role, for the modern marketing-propaganda complex has mastered the manipulation of our limbic and cognitive levels of response. Advertisements play on our insecurities and fears, emphasize alluring sexuality, activate our innate desire for social status, trigger our intuitive decision-making with impulse buying and appeal to our risk-return calculations with assorted "bargains."

But mass-marketing manipulation of our innate capabilities is not the only dynamic behind consumerism; there is another equally powerful ontological appeal: buying something tangible with an abstraction feels like windfall. What could be more wonderful than getting possession of something valuable without having to sacrifice anything in the here and now?

A consumerist purchase made with abstract money (cash or credit) is experienced in the moment as all gain and no risk. Though we know intellectually that we're making a trade-off of some sort in the purchase, i.e. there is some eventual cost or risk, the exchange of abstract credit for a tangible good or service feels like the optimum situation that we have been selected to favor: low risk, high gain.

In a consumerist economy, the act of purchasing is imbued with multiple layers of meaning and reward. Most importantly, it triggers a cascade of self-worth and renewal of identity that feels like a windfall: through this purchase I have value. The immediacy of this reward is akin to the "high" of a mind-altering drug, and as with a drug high the cost or risk is not experienced. The abstract nature of the exchange feeds this illusion of zero cost and risk; the fact that the debt incurred must be paid by future labor or sacrificing other consumption or accumulation of capital is buried under the avalanche of positive rewards.

Each purchase offers multiple levels of gain and reward, each on different spatial and time lines.

The initial rush soon fades but the good or service is displayed to gain social status and expand the sense of self (recall the question: does this make my life feel smaller or larger?): people see me eating at this restaurant; the brand logo of the clothing is seen by others, and so on. This reward may last from a few minutes to hours to weeks, but the product cycle of a consumerist economy spins so fast that few purchases have value for long.

The most costly purchases continue to renew identity with every use: the expensive watch, the luxury vehicle and the mansion continue to provide a dose of renewed identity with each use.

But the consumerist economy has a contradictory ontology: to expand the base of consumers, high-status goods and services have to be made available to a constantly expanding audience. But this expansion dilutes the value of the brand's status, so a new, limited-issue iteration of the brand must be marketed to keep the hound chasing the mechanical rabbit of higher status.

Thus we have the absurdist ratcheting up of credit cards from standard to silver to gold to platinum to black (the marketing claims it is reserved for only the top 1% of high-worth individuals), and the many levels of airline frequent-flyer status. Each new level of status degrades the value of the previous "high status" and thus triggers a new round of social defeat and yearning.

This is a dynamic of dependence of addiction: the windfall is transitory and decays quickly, and a new injection of identity must be obtained soon to stave off the many discomforts of insecurity and social defeat. The pervasive, low-level trauma of social defeat feeds a cult-like acceptance of the consumerist mindset; everyone else is benefiting from obeying the directives, and those who rebel or resist suffer marginalization or ridicule.

The dynamics of dependence, addiction and centrally managed cult-like reinforcement explain the power of consumerism. Once again the models of monoculture and risk transference illuminate these interactions: consumerism is a monoculture that requires ever greater expenditures of capital and debt to keep the "yield" of status high. The greater the "yield" of gain, the more risk is transferred to the system.

As a result, the system becomes increasingly brittle and maladapted and thus increasingly prone to collapse.

Both risk and cost are masked by the limbic reward mechanisms of consumerism; like a drug addiction, the focus is on the immediate gain, which feels god-like in its power, while the costs have been shunted into the future. Just as the addict gives no weight to the future costs of addiction, the consumer gives little consideration to the lifetime burdens of consumerism: an atrophied sense of self, the sacrifice of potentially valuable capital and an insatiable yearning for identity and security that can never be fulfilled by the "fun" of shopping.

Debt is the key financial abstraction that enables the consumerist economy. Debt is the ultimate expression of a low-risk, high gain windfall: for a modest monthly payment, anyone can expand their life and self. The gain is immediate and compelling—the answer to the question "does this make my life feel smaller or larger?" is always "larger"—while the risk (debt penury and loss of authentic self) is invisible.

Debt also enables the expansion and dominance of the Central State, and so debt binds the consumerist market economy and the Central State into one centralized, financialized system which depends on debt and the illusion of risk transference.

There is a terrible irony in the consumerist market economy: our primary motivation is to avoid social defeat and isolation by expanding our sense of self via the windfalls of consumption. Yet making our sense of self dependent on debt-based consumption actively increases the risk of the very things we sought to avoid, isolation and social defeat. Though the trade-off feels painless, we sacrifice our authentic self and our future security (capital) for the illusory gains of store-bought identity.

Consumerism makes a claim that seems in our self-interest: every purchase is a windfall gain with near-zero risk. But this conception of self-interest is illusory, as the costs and risks have simply been aggregated into the future. What we sacrificed—an authentic sense of self and the potential to accumulate productive capital (savings)—is not visible in the transaction, any more than the true cost of servicing the debt is visible. Consumerism only functions if these costs and sacrifices are invisible.

In a consumerist market economy, social defeat is risk; it can never be eliminated, it can only be staved off or masked for a limited time. We stave it off until our income can no longer support more debt, and then our consumption ceases and merciless social defeat shreds our store-bought identity.

The Ontological Oneness of Debt and Consumerism

Just as buying something tangible with something abstract (money) feels like a windfall—something for nothing, as it were—buying something with credit also feels like a windfall, for the future payment has none of the reality and immediacy of the good or service just purchased. Both payment and the accruing interest are known but diminished by time-distance to an abstraction. In the decision-making process, the gain reaped by the purchase far outweighs the distant burden of modest monthly payments; indeed, the modesty of the payments—"affordable"—creates another abstraction, for the cumulative size of the payments is only an intellectual concept, featherweight compared to the emotional/limbic sense of immediate windfall. Thus borrowing $500 to buy a desirable consumable "makes sense" even when the borrower is presented with information that the cumulative cost with interest is $1,000.

The reverse process of debt is savings. In savings, the point in time when enough capital has been saved to make the purchase seems distant, and imagination and discipline are required to conjure the future value of the present sacrifice. The emotional appeal of future possession is nowhere near as strong as the appeal of impulsive possession in the moment, and so credit and consumerism are ontological twins, going hand in hand to fulfill our innate preference for immediate windfall and our innate avoidance of sacrifice for some future goal.

Immediate gratification and the transfer of cost and risk to the future via credit are "convenient," and this debt-enabled convenience appears to be in our self-interest. Given the immense risk-gain appeal of buying on credit, it "makes no sense" to forestall the immediate benefits of credit-based consumption for the abstract future benefits of being debt-free. The gain of being debt-free is obscure and abstract; the freedom of movement and peace of mind this offers has little value compared to the gains in status and emotional pleasure offered by credit's immediate gratification.

A food analogy helps illuminate the distortion of self-interest wrought by debt-based consumerism. When we're hungry, the process of preparing a healthy meal has little appeal compared to a juicy burger and sugary soda that can be had immediately "for next to nothing" if bought with credit. The tangible will always be more appealing than the abstract, and the immediate more appealing than the distant. The cumulative cost of an unhealthy diet is akin to the cost of debt-serfdom: it's too abstract and distant to outweigh the immediate windfall of the burger and soda.

Once again we can understand this dynamic in terms of risk: sacrifice for a future goal is loaded with risk, for something could arise that waylays the plan and renders the sacrifice a loss. Immediate consumption, by contrast, is low-risk: once the item is safely in hand, then the risk has been transferred to the future payment and thus to the lender.

The powerful appeal of debt and consumerism is thus innate; marketing need only nudge the low-risk gain of immediate gratification forward and push the abstract future costs into the background. The banking sector can profitably extend credit to anyone with disposable income, and easily calculate the maximum amount of income that can be devoted to servicing debt.

This calculation is a fractal, that is, it applies to households, communities, companies and entire nations. Once the maximum amount of income that can be diverted to debt service has been calculated, it is only a matter of extending the credit to capture the income stream. The debtor is thus reduced to a debt-serf, as there is insufficient income to pay off the debt without accruing interest.

Since the banking sector funds political power and debt-serfs are typically too anxious and overworked to be politically restive, the Central State also benefits systemically from debt-serfdom. This dynamic binds the entire Status Quo of financialization, consumerism, marketing and the Central State: all the power Elites benefit from debt-serfdom, as debt generates the leverage, the profit and thus the power.

The Illusion of Individuality

Of the many paradoxes in the consumerist worldview, none is more obvious than the contradiction of individual identities based on mass-produced goods and services. How individual is an identity that is nothing but an overlay of mass-marketed goods and simulated-tribal brand affiliations?

The reason we fall for this illusion is once again risk-gain calculus: it is extremely convenient to construct an identity and worldview from pre-assembled pieces. The gain is immediate and tangible—presto, we "belong" to a brand and tribe—while the risk—social defeat and isolation—seems to be eliminated or vanquished by the immediate-gratification gain.

The ease of transaction masks a devil's pact: "buying into" consumerism only appears to stave off social defeat, ennui and isolation. Beneath this illusion, it actually guarantees social defeat, ennui and isolation. There are no other end-states possible when the authentic sources of identity—all the forces of social capital invested in a stable ecology of identity and purpose—have been set aside as too risky and low gain compared to the convenience and ease of a consumerist identity.

Social defeat is terribly painful and corrosive to our inner well-being; in psychological terms, it is a form of trauma that leads to stress disorders (obesity, inability to sleep, anxiety, depression, etc.) and cult-like obedience to group-think as a way of gaining social approval and avoiding the pain of social defeat. A consumerist identity is a "convenient" way of gaining social approval, and corporate brands offer cult-like comfort to their "members."

Every transaction in a consumerist economy is an exchange of value. In terms of individuality and identity, the "value" of the consumable is entirely illusory: the centralized global corporations hawking illusory identifiers of status get the gold (i.e. tangible purchasing power) and the consumer gets a handful of sand that quickly runs through his fingers. The corporations concentrate the gold into political power that extends and protects their wealth, and the consumer spends the rest of his life servicing the debt taken on to buy the abstract "value" offered by a "convenient" consumerist identity.

The promise of consumerism is convenience: you can get a "larger" self and life without sacrifice or troublesome (i.e. exposed to low-intensity instability) internal assembly and non-market social renewal. Convenience "sells" because it is simply another expression of debt-based consumption's primary appeal: the gain is immediate and significant while the risk of future payment is distant and insignificant.

This is a fractal of the ultimate promise of financialization: "something for nothing," a windfall gain at near-zero risk. This same fractal dynamic underpins the entire system of centralized control via concentrations of wealth and power. Debt-based consumerism and debt-based expansion of the Central State are simply two manifestations of financialization fractals.

The Derealization of the Non-Market Social Order

Financialization, consumerism and the Central State did not expand to dominance in a vacuum; they undermined, marginalized and dismantled the non-market social order that bestowed identity and sustainability as functions of decentralized low-intensity instability.

A political movement that simply swaps Elites to enable yet another extension of financialization is only a simulacrum of transformation. A true revolution must change the fractals that construct the entire system; it must dispense with the false promise of something for nothing via debt and leverage and the disconnection of risk and gain. It must enable the recovery of a non-market, decentralized social order with a radically lower cost-basis and secure its stability with the free forces of low-intensity instability.

For many people, this derealization is so complete that they find it impossible to imagine a future without a debt-based consumerist social order and ever-expanding Central State. But since these are systemically unsustainable, they will pass away regardless of our current conception of what is possible or impossible and a new arrangement will take their place.

Our Understanding Thus Far:

We can understand consumerism's brittle and self-destructive dynamics as a fractal of financialization's false promise of immediate gain and zero risk. We now understand that the consumerist economy and the dominance of financial Elites and the expansive Central State are all manifestations of a single interlocking system of increasingly unstable monocultures.

In the next chapter, we explore the specific dynamics of the expansionist Central State and its institutions.

Chapter Six: Institutional and State Dynamics

In Chapter Two, we surveyed systemic dynamics that are observable in the Status Quo. In this chapter, we will examine systemic dynamics which are unique—we might even say perversely unique—to human institutions of governance.

The Central State's Imperative: Expand Control

Though the popular imagination focuses on the Central State's current leadership as drivers of policy, to understand the State we must view it as an organism that is driven by an *ontological imperative* to expand its control as a means of lowering risk and increasing gain. In pursuing this goal, it is just like any other organism.

To believe the State is directed at a fundamental level by individuals is equivalent to believing individual ants control their species' evolution. In aggregate, mutations within individuals do spawn changes that spread throughout the species, just as ideas created by individuals spread throughout cultures. But the State cannot be understood merely an as aggregate of individuals; the State is powered by its own ontological imperative regardless of which individuals are serving the State at any one moment in history.

We can best understand this ontological imperative within the framework of the grand tradeoffs in life between risk and gain and conservation and experimentation. As an organism within the ecosystem of the nation, the State holds two unique powers that make it a super-organism: the power to print paper money and the power of coercion via imprisonment, repression, taxation and involuntary servitude in the Armed Forces.

Within the ecosystem of human society that encompasses organized religions, regional loyalties, cultures, communities and markets, the State alone holds the power to create money from thin air and coerce its citizens with force.

Merely holding these unique powers creates an ontological imperative to use them, and if we fail to understand this then we fail to understand the single most fundamental characteristic of the State.

But there is another driver to use these powers—the ontological imperative to lower risk and increase gain. The way the State lowers risk to extend control over the entire ecosystem that sustains it; once it controls all the other subsystems, then it can transfer risk from itself to the system as a whole while concentrating the gains reaped by its dominance.

In sum: the best way to lower risk is to control everything that can be controlled. Once the potential sources of risk are controlled, risk can be shifted to others.

The other grand tradeoff of life is between conserving the Status Quo and investing in experimentation. The State has a unique advantage on both ends of this spectrum: it can coerce its citizens into conserving the State and pass the costs of that coercion to the citizens via taxation, and it can expropriate the positive results of any private experimentation without having accepted the risk or cost of that experimentation.

It is critical that we grasp the ontological nature of the State as a super-organism whose imperative is to limit risk and increase gain by expanding its control of everything within reach.

This unique set of powers and imperatives gives the State the means and desire to impose control over the entire nation, either via outright tyranny or via the cloaked tyranny of limited choices, propagandistic persuasion and financial tyranny.

Our current system of governance assumes, incorrectly, that a "separation of powers" within the State will limit the State's appetite for control. Rather than limit the entire State's expansion, the State's subsystems—the institutions of Executive power, legislative power and judicial power—are only competing to gain as much control as possible over both the State itself and the nation's social and financial ecosystems.

This competition doesn't weaken or limit the State; rather, it lends the State a fearsome competitive advantage, as each institution gains power as the State expands. So even though the competition between the three may appear to limit the power of each, in aggregate this competition only increases the State's expansion as each seeks to outdo the others in reach, influence and power.

Regardless of which institution wins or loses each squabble, the State inexorably expands its control and power. And just as inexorably, those Elites within the State—systemically protected from the risk created by their policies—will experience a rising sense of omnipotence as their private power rises in tandem with the State's expansion.

These powers also offer Elites a unique way to radically lower their own risk and dramatically increase their private gain by leveraging the State's vast powers to their own benefit. Just as the State harvests the surplus of the entire ecosystem and redistributes the risk of its control to those laboring beneath it, so too does it redistribute these vast gains to its own Elites and their private-sector cronies.

As noted in previous chapters, separating risk from gain inevitably creates an uncontrollable systemic instability. From the point of view of the entire ecosystem the State dominates, this separation of risk from gain is the entire project of the State.

If we understand the ontological imperative of the State, then the State's uncontrollable expansion, its leveraging of State power for private gain and its eventual destabilization are all inevitable.

State Institutions as Fractals of the Central State

Institutions have the same self-interest as individuals, and if they gain the power to evade the system's immune system via suppression of information, feedback and experimentation (the forces of low-intensity instability), then just as individuals acting in self-interest will collapse an institution, a preponderance of self-serving institutions within the Central State will eventually collapse the entire State.

All systems have thresholds for systemic cost and surplus, and the State is no different. Once the Central State's institutions consume the system's surplus, the system collapses. From the point of view of those within each institution, the costs of their employment and security are more than offset by the service they provide to the institution. From a point of view outside the system watching it approach collapse, the protected Upper Caste working within the walls of the State are largely unproductive friction, sequestered by the State's power from market forces or selective pressure.

Each institution within the State acts as a fractal of the entire State, seeking to offload consequence and risk to others while expanding its share of the State's income, just as the State seeks to redistribute risk to the entire nation while expanding its own power.

Control as Suppression of Risk

In terms of system dynamics, low-intensity instability (LII)—risk, threat, innovation, competition, variation, experimentation, transparency, meritocracy, selective pressure, feedback, accountability, consequence, accurate communication of facts and the free exchange of information—is the one key feature of dynamic stability.

Suppress these forces of equilibrium and the system becomes increasingly unstable beneath a veneer of stability. At some point this rising instability triggers disorder and collapse.

The State expands its control to lessen its own risk and increase its own power. Given its power to print paper money and force compliance, the State is ontologically predisposed to extend control over the entire ecosystem, in effect transforming a vital and stable system into an unstable and brittle monoculture. Since the State's imperative is to lessen risk by separating it from its own gain, the stability provided by low-intensity instability are lost to the State.

That is to say, breaking the feedback between risk and gain also breaks the stabilizing feedback provided by low-intensity instability.

From the State's point of view—and recall that the State is a super-organism, not merely an assembly of individuals—low-intensity instability (dissent, transparency, variation, etc.) provides no benefits (it cannot, since the feedback between risk and gain has been severed) while posing a threat to the State's control.

Thus the State's ontological imperative is to suppress low-intensity instability both within the State's institutions and within the ecosystem it dominates. This is the grand irony of the State: in suppressing the low-intensity instability it views as a threat to its dominance, the State is sowing the seeds of its own destabilization and self-destruction.

If we follow these initial conditions and dynamics to their logical *telos* (end-state), we realize that the State is ontologically incapable of limiting its own expansion and tyranny. The only forces that can exert some limiting influence are those of the larger ecosystem that the State dominates: the subsystems of community and the marketplace.

To the degree that community and the marketplace offer potential counterbalances to State expansion, the State naturally views them as threats that must be limited or controlled. We will explore this process of co-option and control in a later section.

Suppressing Creative Instability Leads to Systemic Instability

Suppressing the creative instability of dissent, accountability, accurate reporting of facts, competition and experimentation to protect the State and its crony capitalism leads to a systemic instability. This is the grand irony of suppressing transparency, feedback, variation and competition: these are the system's immune system, the elements that dynamically lead to a systemically stable, "noisy" equilibrium. Suppress the "noisy" stabilizers of dissent and variation and the system tilts into imbalances that eventually trigger complete destabilization.

We can understand this suppression of transparency as another example of risk being disconnected from gain. If accurate data were widely available, then the State Elites protecting private Elites from scrutiny would be exposed to the threat of losing their cozy monopoly on power. To avoid that risk, the Status Quo suppresses transparency while keeping the gains skimmed from their monopoly on power.

In suppressing low-intensity instability, the Elites transfer the risk from themselves to the entire system. This breaks the key feedback and renders the system deaf to fact. Since risk cannot be eradicated, it can only be shifted, then the risk transferred from the State is shunted into the system itself, where it piles up to the point that the system destabilizes.

It is as if an organism so feared the immune response of low-intensity fever—the manifestation of restabilizing the organism by fighting off the infection—that the organism cripples its immune system so it cannot raise a "potentially disruptive" fever. As a result, the next infection will be the last, as the organism, lacking an immune response, spirals into a final fatal instability.

This is the Status Quo: to avoid the potential threat of a "fever" of transparent inquiry into fraud-based crony capitalism, collusion, monopolies, cartels, "shadow" banking systems and all the other mechanisms of a financial tyranny disguised as a democracy, then the Status Quo suppresses the "immune system" of transparency, dissent, competition and feedback. With these stabilizing dynamics suppressed, the Status Quo has doomed itself to self-destruction.

It is an irony lost on the Status Quo: in attempting to protect their hold on power by suppressing the risks created by the low-intensity instability of transparency, competition and dissent they fatally destabilize the very system they are attempting to preserve. Eliminating low-intensity instability to eliminate the risks of regime change only guarantees massive systemic instability later.

Imposing Control by Reducing Choices

The separation of risk from gain to benefit the few must be enforced by the Central State, which alone has the power to do so systemically. There are two basic methods of imposing this control: one is a legal system that punishes anyone who resists the State's diversion of risk, and the second is to limit the number of choices available to those who must bear the risk forced onto them by financial tyranny.

Limiting choice works in two ways: one, it suppresses dissent and secondly, it funnels non-Elite participants into pathways that benefit the Status Quo, a method of control that is masked by a series of false choices. In other words, the choices approved by the State all lead to the same destination—acceptance of financial and political tyranny.

For example, voters are given a choice of equally corrupt political parties, equally predatory healthcare insurers, equally parasitic banks, and so on, all under the guise of "free enterprise" and "free choice." The "choice" is illusory.

The political leadership of institutions from households to nation-states seeks to suppress threats to their control posed by the forces of low-intensity instability we have catalogued. The methods of imposing control include: repressing negative feedback, limiting experimentation by raising the cost of competition and reducing choices throughout the system.

Reducing choice and competition to protect the Status Quo leads to poverty as innovation and feedback are suppressed along with other types of instability. The net result of suppressing LII is that scarce resources are diverted to malinvestment and non-productive speculation by those who have transferred risk to the system.

Just as limited choice is a feature of all tyrannies, so too is a campaign of persuasion that claims this limitation is necessary and beneficial. This campaign is rightly labeled propaganda, as it benefits the Elites by "selling" a delusional notion of self-interest to the non-Elites.

Reducing choice is an excellent control mechanism, as it cloaks the control from the view of credulous citizens. But when it is coupled with the harsh repression of dissent, loss of purchasing power due to excessive money-creation, the petty harassment of fines and junk fees, the oppression of higher taxes and the expanding divide between those protected by the State and those exploited by the State, then an explosive, non-linear model of resistance manifests as profound political disunity.

Limiting Transparency Limits Stabilizing Feedback

Another key technique of State control is limiting transparency and feedback—two of the essential elements in creative instability (the others being mutation/experimentation and competition).

The State limits transparency and promotes opacity in a number of ways: it declares a variety of politically damaging material "top secret," it manipulates supposedly accurate official data such as the unemployment rate and inflation to suit the needs of political expediency (if the data counters what is politically expedient, then the basis for calculating the data is modified behind the veil), it reaches sweetheart legal settlements with high-profile Elite embezzlers with closed-door settlements based on "unknown facts," that is, facts which are zealously guarded from the public, and it requires citizens undergo arduous procedures to obtain records which should be freely available, such as precisely how many billions of dollars were transferred to private banks in bailouts funded by taxpayers.

For example, the State required a news service to file a Freedom of Information Act (FOIA) and pore through 30,000 pages of "secret" documentation to discover that two of the largest private bank-benefactors of the bailout had skimmed $13 billion from "secret" low-interest loans and other blatant giveaways.

The loss of transparency in the people's business leads to atrophied feedback. False information or information manipulated to serve as political cover is disruptive poison in the system; decisions made on falsehoods will necessarily be destructive because they cannot possibly align with reality.

The State as Protector of Private Gain/Self-Interest

The Central State is granted the sole power of coercion by its membership (citizenry) to protect the membership from the predation of individuals, concentrations of wealth and other subgroups seeking monopoly. They grant the State this extraordinary power to insure that no subgroup or individual can gain enough power to dominate the entire membership for their private gain and to protect freedom of faith, movement, expression, enterprise and association.

Granting this power to the State creates a risk that the State itself may become predatory, supplanting the parasitic elements it was designed to limit. To counter this potential, the State has self-limiting mechanisms such as an independent judiciary, armed forces under civilian control, etc., a separation of powers such that no one institution or agency can dominate the State and thus the nation. The goal is to create a stable but flexible equilibrium between comparably powerful institutions, all of which are tasked with enabling and defending the members' freedom of movement, expression, enterprise and association against the encroachment of powerful subgroups.

In this sense, the State is ultimately an immune system for the nation, a system designed not to dominate but to recognize and limit potentially destructive forces within the ecosystem (nation). To monitor and limit the influence of individuals and subgroups within the State itself, an internal immune system of regulation, auditing and enforcement is built into each institution.

The State is thus designed to be a self-regulating immune system, protected from abuse of power by its own internal immune system.

We can understand the tradeoff of the citizenry in establishing a State as a risk-gain hedge: the risk of granting extraordinary powers to the State is offset by the gain of being freed from local or foreign tyrannies and the predation of criminals and exploitative Elites. This establishment of liberty is worth the risk of a self-regulating State becoming predatory.

The self-regulation mechanisms are supposed to act as a hedge against a runaway parasitic State.

We can properly understand the State as a concentration of risk and gain: its extraordinary powers of coercion render it a great risk to the membership, even as its protective shield of liberty offers the freedom to pursue individual happiness and self-fulfillment.

Since the State is a concentrator of both wealth and power, it also concentrates the risk that ontologically accompanies concentrated power and wealth: with such great power, the abuse, repression, exploitation and predation which the State could unleash on its citizenry are fearsome.

This concentration of wealth and power makes the State the primary attractor in the ecosystem for those seeking to increase their private gain. What better way to enforce a monopoly than to persuade the State to limit your competition? What better way to lower the risk of enterprise than to persuade the State to grant its own contracts to your company? What better way to amass a fortune than to harness the coercive powers of the State to your own self-interest?

The State is thus the ultimate lever within the ecosystem. While $1 million buys little influence within the market, if spent to influence State policy then it will buy more power than $10 million spent in the marketplace.

There is a great irony in this concentration of power in the State: the power is concentrated to protect the citizenry from predation and exploitation, but that concentration becomes an irresistible attractor for all those seeking to increase their private gain via monopoly, cartels, collusion, fraud and other forms of predation.

The wealth that can be concentrated in private hands is not limited or self-regulated, and so private concentrations of wealth inevitably exceed the threat-gain threshold of individuals within the State. This structural imbalance leaves the State ontologically vulnerable to the influence of private wealth. Once this wealth has a foothold of influence within the State, it can then bypass the State's internal immune system and become the financial equivalent of cancer: a blindly self-interested organism bent solely on growth at the expense of the ecosystem as a whole.

This financial/political cancer of single-minded self-interest creates a self-reinforcing feedback loop within the State: the more power and influence it gathers, the more it can weaken the State's own immune response to its rising dominance. This erosion of restraint further frees it to increase its influence, which then gives it more power to weaken the State's immune system, and so on, until private concentrations of wealth, in partnership with self-serving State Elites, bypass the State's immune response.

At that point, the collusion of private wealth and State Elites comes to dominate the entire ecosystem. The State's function as the system's immune system has been subverted by private wealth and the State's own extraordinary powers have been directed to serve the self-interests of private Elites and their cronies within the State.

The Immune System Metaphor

I have used the biological term "immune system" to describe the limiting feedback loops within human institutions. This analogy is obviously imperfect, as the many cellular systems that make up our immune system operate without the benefit of conscious intent; they operate according to instructions coded in their genes.

As a result, when the immune system targets a cancerous cell for destruction (i.e. a "runaway" immortal cell that has evaded its self-destruct coding) and an immune cell arrives to destroy it, the immune cell cannot stop itself from performing its appointed task because the cancer cell offers it a bribe. In human systems, this is in essence how individuals and institutions avoid the regulatory systems which act as the immune system in human society.

In biological systems, cancer cells or invading organisms often develop via mutation (random experimentation and the feedback of selective pressure) ways to deceive the immune system into ignoring them. Human systems are equally prone to destructive agents developing ways to deceive the immune system into bypassing them as harmless.

For example, banks create deceptive accounts of their assets and liabilities via off-balance sheet activity, spoofing regulators into passing them as legitimate and solvent rather than what they really are, fraudulent and insolvent.

As noted earlier, humans are hardwired to seek windfalls of food, energy, power or reproductive opportunity. Since windfalls in Nature are scarce, this alertness to windfalls offers an obvious selective advantage; those who spot a windfall and exploit it fully may gain an edge that in a future crisis might spell the difference between life and death.

We have also seen that self-interest and windfall exploitation are served equally well by deceit, theft, fraud, collusion, falsification and persuasion as by merit, honesty and trustworthiness. The only factor that gives merit, honesty and trustworthiness any advantage is the "immune system" of the marketplace and the social group that extends and withdraws membership. In pre-State eras, those who chose the advantages offered by thievery and deception were, if caught, punished by social and economic ostracism—that is, ejection from the group. Once outside the social/economic network, the thief would no longer have access to people to deceive.

Since outsiders were viewed with a well-deserved suspicion, then the "stranger" would have little opportunity to practice fraud, as the new group would be actively examining his every transaction and behavior. In our metaphor of an immune system, any stranger is a potential threat and thus the group's immune system is on high alert until the new member is proven trustworthy via a lengthy process of tests and feedback.

The advantages offered by fraud and deception will also drive some percentage of the populace to seek chinks in the armor of any institutional immune system. Where the hunter-gatherer thief would wait for everyone to fall asleep before pilfering, the modern thief finds a way to bypass financial auditing and regulatory systems.

The ideal scenario for those seeking to bypass an organization's immune system is to control the immune system itself. Thus the primary suspect in accounting fraud is the auditing staff itself, as they know best how to spoof the system. Institutions have what might be called counter-intelligence methods to weed out internal fraud; for example, banks insist key auditing staff take a full two-week vacation from work every year, as they have found that any fraud is difficult to maintain in absentia.

In this way, the institutional immune system acts very much like the biological equivalents. There are always low-intensity attempts by individuals or organisms to spoof or evade detection, and the immune system must constantly evolve to counter these probes, as a low-intensity threat can quickly evolve into a system-destroying one if left undetected.

For example, one rogue trader can, if he evades detection, bring down an entire global bank when his gigantic wagers with bank funds go bad.

In Nature, evolution of the immune system is one strategy to counter constantly evolving threats, but another is the overall health and vitality of the organism. Thus plants which are stressed by lack of water or poor soil are more likely to be overwhelmed by infestations of pests. The insects, fungi, bacteria and other micro-organisms are ever-present, but it is only when the organism weakens that their proliferation exceeds the immune system's ability to detect and defend.

In a human example, we are constantly exposed to bacteria and viruses, but we most often come down with a cold after travel that disrupts our sleep and weakens us via stress and exhaustion.

The immune system is a perfect example of a system that benefits from low-intensity instability, experimentation, feedback and fluctuation, that is, the "information" offered by constantly evolving threats. If this low-level instability is weakened, then the organism becomes increasingly vulnerable to non-linear systemic instability:, a previously benign threat that expands rapidly once inside the organism (institution) and thus threatens to bring down the entire organism or institution.

We can see natural system dynamics repeating in immune response: threats arise in fractal, non-linear patterns, which randomly generate severe threats amidst a "noise" of low-intensity interactions of information and feedback. Threats can fester beneath the surface and then suddenly explode in a stick/slip phase-transition.

A State that is weakened by internal conflict, financial exhaustion or the accretion of unproductive friction will be increasingly prone to failure or hijacking of its regulatory immune systems.

The immune system is ultimately an expression of the same feature of all healthy, stable systems: the ability to enable the low-intensity instability caused by the free exchange of information, experimentation, feedback and dissent. If this low-level instability is limited or repressed, the system veers into self-destruction.

The Systemic Failure of the State's Self-Limiting Mechanisms

At the risk of repeating concepts that are already familiar to readers, I want to further explore how and why the State's internal self-limiting mechanisms have failed to limit the State's expansion.

As noted previously, the primary purpose of the State is to defend the membership from external threats and from the internal predation of private individuals or groups.

In this sense, the Central State is the immune system for society, actively seeking out and limiting parasitic and predatory individuals and subgroups. Examples include criminal gangs, corporate monopolies and companies that increase their private profits by dumping their waste into a river that serves as a "commons" used by everyone.

To function as the immune system which protects the stability of the entire ecosystem, the State has been granted unique powers of coercion by its membership: the power to collect taxes and raise armies by force, and to impose its will on every member and subgroup that threatens to exploit the membership for their own private gain.

This coercive power creates an ontological contradiction, as it also gives the State the power to become a super-predator, suppressing dissent and competition, rewarding its controlling castes and gathering more of the system's surplus for itself.

If the State alone holds coercive power to limit private predation, then what inhibits the State from becoming a super-predator? What limits are there on a State with coercive power?

Put another way: how does the immune system restrain itself? In Nature, there are mechanisms such as cell apoptosis, i.e. cells are programmed to self-destruct, that provide internal limits. But even these mechanisms of internal control can be bypassed if a virus gains the ability via mutation to enter and reprogram immune cells. Once the immune system itself is compromised, the organism is doomed to degradation and death.

In the Central State, these self-limiting mechanisms cannot be mechanical, as humans can consciously over-ride their institutional instructions: they can offer a bribe to avoid the State's control, and the State employee can accept the bribe and use the State's power for his personal gain.

Once the State's Elites gain the power to evade the State's own immune system, they are free to crowd out community and the marketplace as counterweights within the overall ecosystem.

This is a positive feedback loop: the more influence that individuals and Elites gain over the State's power, the more they use the State to repress dissent and competition. This increases their wealth, which is then used to increase their control over the State, which under their influence then further suppresses competition.

Eventually, the Central State dominates the entire ecosystem and becomes in effect a monoculture that serves the private interests of the Elites that control the State's enfeebled immune response, i.e. its regulatory agencies.

Once the State's regulatory systems have been neutralized, then the cancer of financial fraud is free to expand into every level of the State and the economy it controls.

One of the key mechanisms that enable aggressive growth of a cancer is the errant cells' ability to divert the system's energy to feed its own growth at the expense of the organism. This same mechanism is at work when concentrations of financial power control the State: they can divert more and more of this energy to themselves. The State's power to concentrate and redistribute the surplus is effectively diverted to serve their private interests.

Weakened by this diversion of the system's limited surplus to increasingly powerful Elites, the economic/political ecosystem is less able to mount an effective response to this growing domination: as the power of the State grows, the power of the Elites in control of the State also grows at the expense of the nation and the State's regulatory immune system.

In theory, the separation of Central State powers into three branches of governance (legislative, judicial and Executive), the protection of a free press and the separation of the State from a potentially dominant church/theocracy are the systemic foundation of self-limitation: these internal mechanisms should theoretically limit the unrestrained growth of State power and of Elites within the State.

The State's rise to complete dominance over the past century across the entire ecosystem is proof that these structural self-limits have failed. The capture of State powers by private Elites proves that regulatory and judicial limits on the political power of private wealth have also failed.

What we have witnessed is the State's own self-regulation being compromised by the stealth mechanisms of false choices, shadow systems of power, and the masking of this cancerous growth by a marketing/public relations complex that serves the narrow interests of the Elites dominating State policy. The free press has been undermined by concentrated private ownership, and the judiciary has been seduced, browbeaten or marginalized into acquiescing in the diversion of State power to serve private interests.

As the State's own immune system has been undermined and starved, the judiciary's power to restore self-limiting mechanisms has weakened into irrelevance: control the financial resources and you control the State. Judiciary rulings have become part of the marketing artifice, the façade that serves the useful illusion that the State is not a cancerous super-organism.

Transparency and dissent have been reduced to useful fictions, simulacra that offer a mist of legitimacy to a State that has neutralized all mechanisms of self-limitation, leaving only self-reinforcing positive feedback inevitably leads to runaway collapse.

There is one other feature of Nature that applies to the State: the advantages and risks of monoculture. As discussed earlier, a monoculture concentrates risk and gain by trading off the hedging offered by diversification. But since Nature cannot separate risk and return, then the heightened chances of a windfall also heighten the harvest's vulnerability to predation by pests should any pest gain the ability to bypass the monoculture's immune response. The planned outsized gain can just as easily become an outsized loss.

This analogy of the Central State as a monoculture carries a number of negative implications. Since the State has expanded to dominate the ecosystem, its collapse would threaten the stability of the entire system. This is one supremely negative consequence of equilibrium being destroyed by the unlimited pursuit of private self-interest partnering with the unlimited power of the State.

Equilibrium has two fundamental sources: diversity that distributes risk and gain over a spectrum of participants, and self-limiting mechanisms that limit any nodes of self-interest from gaining systemic dominance.

We see this threshold in systems such as chimpanzee troops and economic niches: when one troop or enterprise gains enough mass and power to breach the threshold, it can then dominate the other troops or companies in its space by acquisition, erosion of their market share or outright destruction (killing or closure).

This dominance enables predation via monopoly, cartels, the Central State or some combination of the three: in other words, financial tyranny.

By eliminating diversity and self-limiting mechanisms, monoculture is enabled—but so is collapse. Once the counterweights that limit attractors of power are sufficiently weakened, then one attractor can break through the threshold and dominate the ecosystem as a monoculture.

Since a monoculture is exquisitely vulnerable to small instabilities, then energy must be expended to limit instability. These measures increase the vulnerability of the monoculture in two ways: one, they take scarce resources away from other potentially more productive uses, and two, by eliminating whatever residual fluctuations and dissent remain, they greatly increase the vulnerability of the monoculture to whatever fractal force evades suppression.

This diversion of scarce surplus to protect an increasingly vulnerable system is a form of malinvestment that radically weakens the entire system over time by starving productive resources to increasing funding of repression. We can witness this dynamic in police states, where the surplus of the system declines as the State siphons off more and more of the surplus to fund its machinery of suppression. Once the system's costs of suppression exceed its dwindling surplus—dwindling because capital, energy and talent that could have been productive was squandered on repression—then the system implodes.

Paper money and propaganda can be printed in quantity, but these cannot actually increase surplus (wealth) or lower systemic friction. Once friction exceeds surplus, the system freezes up. This is the story of the Soviet Union and other totalitarian regimes and theocracies.

Monocultures can only bring a very limited range of selective traits to bear, and that means that applying those limited traits to every circumstance will necessarily lead to gross mismanagement and inefficiency. This is the cost in trading diversity for windfall.

Since the Central State is a monoculture, it is intrinsically wasteful, inefficient and systemically prone to mismanagement, as it is *a priori* limited in diversity and the resourceful ness that flows from creative instability. The State has the resources to coerce but lacks the systemic features to nurture long-term stability.

Put another way: monocultures introduce systemic instability, and they are vulnerable to the kind of low-intensity fluctuations that act as the "immune system" for the system. By repressing this low-intensity instability of dissent, free-flowing information, experimentation, etc., the State has effectively destroyed the system's ability to maintain long-term stability.

In suppressing low-intensity instability, the State guarantees a non-linear cascade of chaotic volatility from random, seemingly small triggers.

We can now see that the Central State faces an impossible contradiction: to pursue its primary purpose of protecting the membership from predation, it is granted powers that enable it to evade its own self-limiting "immune" functions. Private self-interest—

what we can term attractors of power—gains entrance to the State via bribes to those within seeking to maximize their own private gain. This partnership then gains control over the State's immune functions that were intended to limit private control of State power.

To enhance their own power, these Elites increase the State's reach and power until it dominates the entire political, social and economic ecosystem. Once it is dominant, then it can increase its share of the system's surplus. To protect itself from threats, the State diverts an increasing share of the surplus to repress the very forces of low-intensity instability that act as the system's stabilizing forces.

This sets up an inherently self-destructive feedback in which the State's own actions to protect its self-serving Elites weaken both the State and the ecosystem it dominates. The State's innate mismanagement (a monoculture lacks the traits needed to manage a diverse ecosystem of environments and niches) and inefficiency (diverting surplus to friction rather than productive assets) lead to dwindling systemic surplus, which causes the State to increase its share of the remaining surplus, which is then squanders on repression, friction and the maintenance of its self-serving Elites. The more the State expropriates, the less surplus is left for productive uses, and so the surplus continues to decline.

Once the system's surplus drops to zero or the State's consumption of resources exceeds the surplus, the system seizes up and collapses.

Ironically, expansion of the State and of its suppression machinery leads to the very tyranny the citizenry fear and the systemic collapse the State's Elites have attempted to stave off with repression and propaganda.

Tyranny has a variety of manifestations—theocratic tyranny, financial tyranny, etc.—and are doomed by the self-destructive dynamics of tyranny.

Political Expediency Dominates State Policy

An openly tyrannical State and a crony-capitalist/Central State such as the U.S. share one systemic dynamic: political expediency inevitably comes to dominate the State's policy responses.

This has several causes. One is the nature of systems stripped of low-intensity instability: systemic imbalances remain invisible until it's too late to stabilize the Status Quo, while low-intensity instability (transparency, dissent, etc.) poses a visible threat to the individuals who are benefiting the most from their State-protected Elite status.

The second causal factor is the immediacy of the low-intensity threat and the distance of the systemic threat. To the individuals reaping risk-free gains from inside the State or crony-capitalist cartels, the generalized risk of systemic collapse is abstract, while the threats of exposure of their fraud, collusion, lies, embezzlement, bribes, etc. is entirely pressing.

The quelling of threats posed by low-intensity instabilities and the paying off of restive constituencies take priority over concerns for the resilience of the system at large.

Thus political expediency to maintain the Status Quo without upsetting key constituencies and cartels inevitably drives out longer-term concerns about the risks posed by endless rounds of hasty but expedient policy interventions by the State.

In this sense political expediency is like bad (increasingly worthless) money: it inevitably drives out good money, leaving only bad money in circulation. Within the State, only the bad policies of political expediency are in circulation, as these "quick fixes" and suppressions of instability have driven out thoughtful policies that actually considered potential consequences, both intended and unintended.

A third factor is the personal nature of threats to the State's fiefdoms. While the State and its institutions may view transparency and exposure as threats to the fiefdom's public image, the risk to the individuals within the Elites is much more personal: they might lose their perquisites and power. As a result, individuals in leadership roles within State will be extremely motivated to suppress transparency and pursue politically expedient cover-ups. Only saints—few and far between—would willingly sacrifice their perquisites and power for abstract notions of transparency and public service. Indeed, people with these traits would tend to be self-selected out of leadership roles in State fiefdoms.

For these reasons, the State is predisposed to being dominated by politically expedient policies that only hasten destabilization.

Divergent Interests of Elites Lead to Systemic Instability

As we have seen, as the Central State breaks free of its weak self-limiting machinery, it gathers all the weaknesses of monoculture. It also has another set of weakness that stem from the cycle of convergence and divergence of its various Elites.

When the self-interests of the key Power Elites converge, then their support of the State's expropriation of the nation's resources is near-unanimous; the jockeying for how much of the State's harvest is distributed to each fiefdom is essentially signal noise.

These periods of convergence tend to occur, for self-evident reasons, during times of systemic prosperity, when the State can expropriate an increasing share of the national output without triggering resistance because the system's surplus is expanding rapidly. This expansionary cycle often corresponds to the expansion of credit and the exploitation of a new energy supply, labor source or technology (or all three).

Though participants in this expansion are easily persuaded that it is permanent, such expansion of credit and consumption inevitably leads to overleveraged speculation, over-indebtedness and mal-investment. Once the expansion reaches a statistical point far from the mean—a point of over-reach—then the cycle reverses and credit contracts, causing the repudiation of debt and leverage. This deleveraging of debt leads to an oversupply of assets purchased during the boom and an undersupply of cash buyers, leading to severe and sustained declines in assets and wealth.

As the teeth of this contraction breaks the skin of the economy, the State finds its ability to continue expanding is crimped. In a biological analogy, the cancerous tumor finds the blood supply it has been tapping for its growth is weakening as the host weakens. The tumor, lacking other avenues of expansion, continues growing and kills the host. Fast-growing cancer is after all an aberration that is intrinsically self-destructive.

The Central State has a mechanism to mask its parasitic growth: print money, and use that money to continue paying its private partners and growing army of dependents.

This increase in the supply of money does not of course create new output or surplus; it merely siphons off more output via a reduction in purchasing power known as inflation. The membership finds its purchasing power is declining as the State effectively transfers that arbitraged wealth into its own coffers.

The purchasing power of the State's own funds also declines, and the incomes of the State's Elites is crimped by both inflation and the resistance of citizens as they become aware of this stealth transfer of their income.

At this juncture of systemic unhappiness, the interests of various Power Elites diverge. For example, mercantilist corporations will demand the Central State pursue policies that benefit mercantilism, i.e. "free trade," while other Elites will demand the exact opposite, i.e. protection of domestic industries that benefit them.

Much of this divergence can be traced to the "ratchet effect," the dynamic in which expansion is effortless as everyone likes to consume more, have another assistant, acquire another weapons system, and so on. When the inevitable contraction begins, every bureaucracy, employee and subcontractor that was added during the expansion will resist any reduction with every fiber of their being, as it soon becomes a binary choice: be ejected as friction (i.e. become expendable because you possess less political power than alternative sources of friction) or claw your way to sufficient political power to protect your security and income.

This "life or death" struggle means the Central State cannot contract, as the political pain is too high for its Elites and dependents to bear. As a result, a system burdened with friction, inefficiency and malinvestment continues expanding to the point of implosion.

In an objective view, we can say that the Central State's self-limiting machinery requires an army of saints, impervious to bribes and personal gain. Not only are these saintly multitudes impervious to greed and self-aggrandizement, they also willingly and uncomplainingly sacrifice themselves like army ants when called upon to lose all their income, status and power when the State must contract.

Such people exist in vanishingly small numbers, which is why the Central State cannot lessen its friction, malinvestment and inefficiency.

As the self-interests of these public and private Elites diverge, political unity is fractured and the State is crippled as its various power Elites battle to retain as much of their power as possible. Any gain comes at the expense of an equally powerful Elite or fiefdom, and so it is truly a zero-sum game.

This is one source of what I term profound political disunity.

The Feedback Loop of Profound Political Disunity

At some point, the State's inefficiency, mismanagement and malinvestment reduces the system's surplus to the point that the membership (citizenry) is profoundly dissatisfied as their minimum threshold of security and comfort is breached. At the same time, the unproductive friction within the State becomes so inescapably obvious that propaganda is no longer sufficient to mask it. Resentment grows at the squandering of dwindling resources that are no longer accessible to non-Elites even as the State's fast-rising repression also serves to alienate everyone who has the misfortune to run afoul of the State's everyday tyranny machinery—parking tickets, petty fines, higher taxes and lower quality service, and all the other results of a parasitic self-serving State.

This is another feedback loop of profound political disunity: as the State suppresses rising resistance, the State consumes more of the nation's surplus, leaving less for the citizenry, which then responds by increasing its resistance. As the national economy contracts, so does the State's share, triggering Internecine Conflict Between Protected State Fiefdoms and the State's private-sector partners, the rentier-wealthy and corporate cartels. The State responds by distributing a greater share of its dwindling resources to these unproductive Elites, placing further downward pressure on the economy.

This reduction in State largesse and efficiency in service of entrenched Elites further deepens the citizens' sense of betrayal and injustice, which then strengthen the dissent the State is trying to suppress.

Since income can only sustainably arise from productive investment of capital, energy and labor, the Central State's diversion of scarce resources to fund its fiefdoms and voracious private Elites means that an ever-declining share of the systems' surplus is available for productive investment.

At a certain threshold, a key segment of the productive citizenry "vote with their feet" by opting out of the system entirely: they abandon the system for low-maintenance communities beyond easy reach of repressive State control s, or they close their enterprises and abandon high-stress careers to disappear into the informal cash economy.

These are seemingly small but ultimately devastating blows to the Central State, as pursuing these escapees is costly even as the return is marginal: snagging and prosecuting someone in the cash economy will likely yield little actual financial return, nor provide much of a deterrent, as observers will note that 99 others escaped detection and punishment for every one tracked down by the State's enforcement machinery.

We can discern a Pareto Distribution in the process: once 4% of the productive citizenry opt out of supporting the State, then that withdrawal of critical support will impact the 64% who remain complicit out of deluded self-interest.

In a similar vein, attempting to collect an outrageously mispriced junk-fee parking ticket in an impoverished community will yield little to no cash but generate a wealth of long-burning animosity and even hatred of the State's enforcers.

The decreased stress and increased well-being of those who opt out of the system will not be lost on the increasingly oppressed debt-serfs still clinging to the false promises of the State's system, and that realization feeds a positive feedback of the most knowledgeable members opting out, who then provide an example for everyone below them on the social ladder.

Eventually, only the State's Elites, protected castes and subclasses who depend entirely on the State will support the State's friction and predation. Since these are the least productive segments of the economy, the system soon collapses under its own unproductive weight.

When an "Enemy of the State" Is a Friend to the Nation

Since dissent and transparency are threats to an increasing fragile, unstable Central State, the State views anyone who questions its presentations of "fact" or resists its expansion as "enemies of the State." Since the State has essentially unlimited power to create complex webs of regulation, it can always unearth some violation to threaten, punish or marginalize dissenters. Since it also has essentially unlimited powers of coercion, it can unleash a "shadow" campaign of "black operations" to infiltrate resistance groups, assault members with State-funded thugs and stage "false flag" disruptions that give the State justification to savagely suppress dissenters. Those who claim (out of ignorance or misdirection) that such campaigns are "impossible" in our nominal democracy should study the State's COINTELPRO campaigns of the late 1960s and early 1970s.

The ideal form of dissent to the organs of State repression is an unruly public demonstration, as this gathering offers a concentrated target for the machinery of State suppression: cracking heads, arresting "criminals" and herding them into prison cells is what the State organs are trained to do and what the system is set up to accomplish with great efficiency.

The private-media organs of propaganda are equally delighted with unruly public demonstrations, as the inevitable "broken glass" destruction perfectly suits the labeling of dissent as hooliganism lightly cloaked with political purpose.

The form of resistance that completely evades State detection and suppression is refusing to support our parasitic and predatory system where it counts: debt, the ballot box, consumption and taxation. This resistance includes refusing to take on debt or vote for incumbents and voluntarily lowering expenses and income, i.e. reducing participation in the consumerist-State economy. While it is illegal to not pay taxes, earning less money and thus owing less tax is still legal. It is not yet illegal to consume less of corporate goods and services and refuse to support political incumbents.

The consumerist-State system encourages an adolescent mindset of instant gratification and self-pity, i.e. loudly proclaiming victimhood and passing responsibility to others. This has fostered a widespread and subtle illusion that our consumerist debt-based lifestyle can continue on into the future if only we uprooted the greedy Elites currently in power.

That is the ultimate illusion of the consumerist-State system, for greedy Elites are not the problem, they are merely the symptom of a completely imbalanced, unsustainable system.

The citizen who withholds support of this sociopathological system is a friend of the nation even as he risks being labeled an "enemy of the State" that enforces the pathology.

Chapter Seven: **The Dis-Equilibrium of Community, Market and State**

A truly sustainable nation requires a balance of community, marketplace and State kept in dynamic equilibrium by creative instability. The purpose of this book is to outline the nature of this equilibrium which has been lost to the dominance of the State.

It has been lost to living memory, but not so long ago the average person and community rarely if ever felt the presence of the Central State; the State was limited to a small professional Armed Forces and a court/judiciary and excise tax system that was rarely experienced directly by the citizenry. Life did not depend on Central State dominance, control, intervention or largesse.

The memory of a market that wasn't managed by the Central State has also been lost to both institutional and public memory. It is now the State's implicit and explicit role to intervene constantly in markets to achieve politically expedient results that serve the interests of the State and private Elites that control the State's policies and fiefdoms.

Life without the intervention and largesse of the Central State is now difficult to recall or even imagine: 46 million residents obtain Food Stamps (SNAP) from the State, 57 million draw Social Security benefits, Medicare pays all but a fraction of the healthcare expenses of 47 million, millions more work directly for the Central State or serve in the Armed Forces, and the regulatory agencies of the Central State control or influence virtually every aspect of everyday life and enterprise.

Retirement, healthcare and community charity were once private, voluntary acts; now the State controls most of the distribution of these funds and commands the fealty of those receiving them.

Markets for stocks, bonds and securities are now manipulated as a matter of policy to create a politically expedient perception of the State's sagacious control, and the State's proxy central bank, the Federal Reserve, prints electronic money and buys trillions of dollars of questionable assets to benefit politically favored cartels in banking and housing.

These examples merely scratch the surface of State control. Where once citizens had little if any contact with their limited Central State, now the majority of citizens either draw a direct payment from the

State or are otherwise beholden to the State, which has concentrated what were once diverse, widely distributed investments into enormous bureaucracies controlled solely by the State.

Concentrations of power provide irresistible opportunities for those seeking to turn that power to their private advantage. This single "initial condition" of the expanding State—its increasing concentration of wealth and power—creates a dynamic in which private concentrations of wealth (financial Elites) will have tremendous incentives to influence the State to further their own interests. This dynamic also feeds Elites within the State, which partner with private Elites to divert the national income to their own pockets via the State's immense powers.

For every legitimate control (monitoring and enforcing water quality, for example) performed by the State, there are others that mask private gain behind the auspices of public protection: the agencies tasked with preventing predation by lenders, for example, actually enable predation on a vast scale, as the banks essentially control the regulatory mechanisms of the State via campaign contributions and lobbying.

We now understand the contradiction at the very core of the Central State: to establish and protect freedom of faith, movement, expression, enterprise and association and limit predation by private concentrations of wealth and power, the State is granted sole coercive powers by its citizenry. But that power is inevitably turned to private self-interest by concentrations of wealth, and the State's own feeble self-limiting mechanisms are incapable of thwarting this infiltration or arresting its own expansion. Indeed, the State's regulations inevitably become simulacra conjured to manage perceptions.

With an understanding of natural systems, we can now see that the only way to limit any component of the overall system is an equilibrium established by equally powerful counterweights that enable low-intensity instability to permeate and inform the entire system. In this wider view, the State is simply one subsystem within the entire ecosystem of the nation/society; the other two primary components are community and the marketplace.

The only force that can restrain the State is an informed and active citizenry that acts as the system's "immune system" by generating creative instability within the private society (what I term community) and a transparent, free marketplace.

If the State has co-opted or hollowed out these other key components, then the citizenry are denied the means of expressing and sharing creative instability. The State needn't repress its citizenry directly via a police State if can marginalize or control the marketplace and the private society that enable this expression.

The State's Expansion Comes at the Expense of Community and the Marketplace

The State's vast expansion within the national ecosystem has not occurred in a vacuum; the national ecosystem is not infinite, and so the State's expansion has come at the expense of community (private society) and the marketplace.

Many observers have noted that the Central State—what I term the Savior State—has largely replaced community within the nation's ecosystem. That is, the Central State now dominates the society and the economy, and community and the marketplace operate beneath its shadow.

Some see this withering of community as occurring off-camera, so to speak, for reasons that had nothing to do with the State. The decline of community left an opening that has been filled by the State. This view discounts an active process of encroachment by the Central State that is not benign but rather an uncontrollable expansion of a super-organism at the expense of less centralized, more diverse systems. The same can be said of the marketplace, which is now a State-managed platform for perception management and private predation.

The primary mechanism the State has used to supplant community is bribery—entitlements that demand complicity. When enough of the citizenry are thus bound to support the State's control (lest their personal share of the largesse be threatened), then a citizen-supported tyranny has been established. The productive minority is then coerced to support and defend the unproductive State and its vast class of dependents.

The number of those drawing direct benefits or payments from the State is now roughly equal to the private-sector full-time workforce that ultimately funds the State and its entitlements (115 million each), which are all "pay as you go," that is, funded by current taxes paid by workers and their employers.

To understand the irresistible appeal of the State's bribery, we must first examine the risk and gain offered by the alternatives.

If we examine community from the point of view of risk and gain, we find that community requires a substantial upfront investment of time and energy and offers an uncertain (risky) payout. Community is essentially a self-organizing, decentralized opt-in system of trust: only those who have "paid their dues" with honest effort on behalf of the community are allowed to draw benefits or gains. (The special case is charity, in which a community freely offers surplus to the needy without demanding any exchange of value or labor.)

As anyone involved in community work can attest, sometimes the gain is meager compared to the investment made, and sometimes there is no payoff at all except inner fulfillment. The point is that the gain from an investment in community and social capital is uncertain, especially when compared to a "guaranteed" check from the Savior State.

We can characterize community as a system in which risk and gain are intimately connected. Any gain—which often takes the form of intangible "social capital"—is commensurate with the investment made over time.

The transparent marketplace is also characterized by upfront investment and highly correlated risk and gain. Indeed, risk is ever-present in any open market and can only be hedged, not eradicated.

Prior to the State's encroachment, retirement and medical care were private arrangements based on savings, having children to support one in old age, establishing a bond with the local doctor, and establishing an interlocking network of community support (churches, associations, neighborhood groups, friendships, extended family ties, professional/trade associations, alumni groups, etc.) that could be tapped in times of need or crisis. The investments made to aid others were risky in the sense that there was no guarantee of a return on investment.

This high risk was offset by the relative safety and resiliency of the decentralized, overlapping networks of community and a cash marketplace for goods, labor and savings.

In contrast to community's substantial investment and risky return, the State's guarantee of pensions and healthcare were remarkably painless to fund, being paid by a low payroll tax (especially in the beginning), coupled with a very substantial payoff in the form of a guaranteed cash pension from the age of 62 until death. Not only was this payment far more substantial than the modest sums paid in, it was indexed to rise with inflation, and was presented as completely risk-free.

The same is also true of Medicare, an immensely costly system supported by a payroll tax that is all but invisible to the average wage earner. The payout—by some measures, between $300,000 and $500,000 per person—is risk-free and incredibly substantial, equaling an entire decade of labor for most workers. (The median household income in the U.S. is about $48,000 annually.)

The ready acceptance of dependence on the State is understandable when viewed through a risk-gain analysis: the State programs are zero-risk and require no real sacrifice to "earn" a gargantuan gain.

It was all sleight of hand, of course; no system can collect $10,000 per taxpayer and pay out $300,000 for each taxpayer. The difference was initially made up by a demographic bulge known as the Baby Boom which enabled a "pay as you go" system to sustain itself because there were 10 workers for every beneficiary. As this ratio is now 2 to 1 (57 million Social Security retirees and 115 million workers with full-time jobs as of March 2012) then the unsustainability of the system is finally becoming visible.

The other sleight of hand is money-printing, which devalues the money held by everyone. This expansion of the money supply beyond the actual expansion of goods and services allows the State to confiscate, without any visible mechanism, the wealth of everyone holding the currency via inflation.

Like the marginal taxes that supposedly fund Medicare, moderate inflation does not appear to cost the wage earner much; just as a 1.45% Medicare tax is barely noticeable, so too is a 3% rate of inflation, though it ends up confiscating over 30% of the wage earner's money in the course of a decade.

This decline in real purchasing power is masked by the apparent rise in nominal earnings. For example, a $14,000 annual wage in 1977 equals a $52,000 annual wage in 2012 dollars. Even though the $52,000 wage looks more prosperous, the purchasing power of the $14,000 in 1977 was actually much higher: the wage earner could buy far more goods and services with $14,000 than the worker can buy with $52,000 today, with the one exception of electronics and digital technologies. This reduction in actual earnings is masked with manipulated inflation statistics and the illusion of nominal gains.

There are several noteworthy features of this State encroachment on what were once private arrangements. One is that the State has once again separated risk and gain; the risk of surrendering one's independence and becoming a State dependent is presented as zero, while the gain is visibly substantial. This is precisely the sort of windfall transaction we as a species are primed to seek and embrace.

Yet risk has not vanished simply because the State mandates it; any system that collects $10,000 per person in Medicare taxes and pays out $300,000 per person is doomed to insolvency via default or hyperinflation. So all that has actually happened is the risk has been transferred by the State to the entire economy. This transfer masks the risk, but only until the built-up instability breaks out.

Another way to state this "separate risk from gain" project—and it is the ultimate State project that defines all the State's actions—is that the State deliberately misprices risk to persuade the citizens to surrender their independence and resilient communities.

Along these same lines, we might usefully catalog what was traded by the private citizens for their "risk-free" dependence on the State: their self-reliance, their political independence, their control of their own assets and future, and also their resilient community, which was off-loaded as a low-gain, high-risk system.

In many subtle but very real ways, the citizen who accepts the "easy, risk-free" windfall of State support loses their sense of self and community as potentially powerful providers of security and adaptability. When crisis comes, the dependent citizen now demands the State fix what is troublesome, not just because the citizen has surrendered his autonomy but because he no longer has the confidence or skills to address the problems via his community or the marketplace.

The State, as noted earlier, is not merely the collection of individuals who serve it at any moment in history; it has an ontological imperative to expand its control as a means to lowering its risk and maximizing its gain.

Thus the State seeks to curry the dependence of its citizenry, for dependence produces passivity and obedience, the opposite of the creative instability the State fears as a threat.

In the grand irony mentioned before, the State thus weakens the only source of systemic stability to cement the surface stability of its own control.

From this broader view, we see that the State necessarily views community (that is, all of private society) and the marketplace as obstacles to its dominance, and thus it is driven to undermine, co-opt and control these sources of creative instability.

The forces of financialization view the traditional non-market community as something to be financialized to expand profit. Since financialization is ultimately enforced by the Central State, this monetization of what were once decentralized local institutions into outposts of distant concentrations of capital can also be traced back to the State's replacement of community with its financialized model of predation and control.

There is a profound irony in the State's hollowing out of community. When the State is collapsing under its own weight, then what was shunned as a high-risk, low payout "bad deal"—investing in the community and the transparent local marketplace—will suddenly be revealed as attractive investments.

In other words, in times of windfall, the State's risk-free offer of dependency cannot be bested by natural systems like community and the marketplace; but when times are hard and the State is failing, then the upfront investment and resilience of community and the cash marketplace become attractive alternatives—and eventually, the only alternatives, as the State defaults on its unsustainable promises of no-risk windfalls for all.

The Ontological Connection between Dependence on the State and Consumerism

The doomed disequilibrium between the expansionary State and the community and marketplace has a number of subtle yet profound features, one of which is the connection between dependence on the State and the pathology of consumerism. Both are characterized by the alienation, insecurity, infantilism and dissatisfaction resulting from a surrender of autonomy, community and self-reliance.

While philosophers such as Jean Baudrillard have critiqued consumerism from a Marxist and post-modernist perspective, and critics such as Pierre Bourdieu have examined the tyranny of markets, few (if any, to my knowledge) have traced the connection between a State seeking passive obedience to its dominance in exchange for "risk-free" individual gain and the "risk-free" exchange of consumerist signifiers for personal identity, and how the State's control of markets creates a tyranny of both markets and the spirit. From this point of view, the State and consumerism are one system.

This ontological connection requires its own further development, but I introduce it here in the context of an equilibrium that has been destroyed by the State's mispricing of risk to serve its own dominance over community and the marketplace. To fully understand this destruction, we will have to investigate the ontology of insecurity, identity and community described in Chapter Four.

Before we investigate those subtleties, we must first grasp the grand narrative of State dominance and seek an understanding of sustainable equilibrium by parsing the five types of Capitalism.

The State's Concentration of Power

If we seek a grand narrative of the State's inexorable expansion, we must weave a number of elements together: technology, media, oil and the State's concentration of power.

The starting point is to understand that the State's concentration of power is what sets it apart from the intrinsically diffused, diverse systems of community and marketplace. The State doesn't merely exercise control; it concentrates wealth and power into nodes that are separated from risk which can then be influenced and dominated by private concentrations of wealth.

If we had to identify the enabling factors of State dominance, we would be required to list cheap, abundant petroleum which has fueled the global economy. This vast energy windfall enabled the State to effortlessly expand along with the economy. If the State expanded faster than the economy, who noticed in a sea of rising prosperity?

The American State was especially blessed, as its first 70 years of expansion were fueled by a domestic oil supply which made it the Saudi Arabia of the first half of the 20th century. This tremendous windfall enabled the U.S. and its Allies to win a global war that was fundamentally based on obtaining and consuming oil.

In the aftermath of the war, the U.S. was forced by the rise of the Soviet Bloc into a global expansion which played to its strengths and its ontological imperative. Once the domestic oil supply fell below demand in the 1970s, then the U.S. State added securing overseas oil supplies to containment of the Soviet Empire to its global goals.

The rising cost of oil and the burdens of these two goals temporarily suppressed the State's expansion and led to economic stagnation. The solution was the financialization of the U.S. economy, which leveraged debt into financial assets that then leveraged the renewed expansion of the Central State. This resurgence helped push the tyrannical Soviet Empire into implosion and led to a series of phantom booms in phantom assets.

No State could achieve the dominance of either the Soviet Empire or the American State without advanced technology (compare Napoleon's Empire circa 1805 and the thoroughly technocratic Soviet Empire) and a ubiquitous media attuned to distributing propaganda, either explicitly as in the Soviet model or implicitly in the American model.

A key methodology of State expansion is to never let a crisis go to waste, and every crisis of whatever nature always gives the State an excuse to extend its reach, what author Naomi Klein calls The Shock Doctrine. By concentrating power in every crisis, the State has trained its docile citizenry to expect the State to further expand its power in every crisis.

In the long view, the State's mechanisms to concentrate power boil down to:

1. Separate risk from gain (i.e. institutionalizing opacity, "moral hazard" and unaccountability)

2. Concentrate the gain and divert it to State and private Elites while distributing the risk to the entire system.

3. Reduce an independent citizenry to dependence by bribing them with unsustainable promises of risk-free individual entitlements.

4. Misdirect public awareness via propaganda and politically expedient policy responses that deliberately mask risk.

As these mechanisms transfer risk to the entire system, destabilization is the inevitable result.

The Perverse Consequences of Concentrating Power and Disconnecting Risk from Gain

An entire volume could be filled with the perverse consequences of concentrating power and disconnecting risk from gain.

To fully understand the immense structural damage these mechanisms of tyranny wreak on the nation, we would benefit by returning to the political and social schema of classical Greece.

Let us begin with the idea that the body politic is a reflection and manifestation of the human soul. Every nation's political and economic system reflects that nation's soul. What can we say about the soul of a nation ruled by financial tyranny? Clearly, the soul of America is ill and conflicted; given its obvious dis-ease, perhaps we can draw a diagnosis from another classical concept.

This schema identifies three basic classes in society: an aristocracy, an intelligentsia and the people.

Since the educated wealthy were presumed to be less motivated to loot the public coffers than the poorer citizens, they were entrusted with safeguarding the State and the public good.

The intelligentsia's primary task was to accurately frame the problems and challenges facing society and the body politic.

The citizenry's job was to decide the issues once they had been properly framed and presented.

If we think of the upper class in the U.S. as an informal aristocracy, we find that looting is now their primary goal, regardless of how much wealth and power they have already amassed.

We also find that the quality of leadership emerging from this class has declined to the gutter: self-service, profound ignorance, fecklessness, political cowardice, hubris and a remarkable dexterity with political expediency are now the dominant traits exhibited by the "leadership" class. Their exterior emotion is bombastic confidence (because they believe that "sells") and their internal emotion is fear— fear of losing their slice of the State's immense wealth and power.

The intelligentsia, almost wholly dependent on the State or the financial Elite and its proxies (think tanks, institutes, tenured chairs in universities, etc.), has been domesticized to obedient lapdogs of the Status Quo. This is evidenced by their abject failure to place their own wealth and position at risk by accurately contextualizing the tyranny they serve either implicitly or explicitly; instead of showing courage and intellectual independence, they choose the safety of tempest-in-a-teapot academic arcana or the repetition of cargo-cult myths like Keynesism.

The people have chosen poorly, selecting cardboard aristocrats who rattle sabers and over-promise everything to everybody via a game of mirrors that shunts the costs onto future generations who are as yet too young to eject them from office.

In other words, every segment of American society has failed to perform their minimal duties adequately, as each act solely from the distorted sense of self-service born of financial tyranny. This is the sad result of a system poisoned by self-interest, fraud, artifice, propaganda, suppression and collusion—the forces of tyranny that arise irresistibly from the intrinsically flawed initial conditions of a State without limits.

This is how the "center fails to hold"—another way of saying that creative instability has been stifled by the State and abandoned by the self-serving—and how society fractures into the profound political disunity of warring camps demanding that their share of the spoils remain sacrosanct. This is dissolution, and it is an inevitable consequence of a system that separates risk from gain and expands the unproductive tyranny of the State at the expense of the sources of creative instability: the community and the transparent marketplace.

If there is no threat of dissent to the State and its financial Elites, then the tyranny of exploitation and corruption become the Status Quo until the entire system collapses under its own sclerotic, maladapted, unproductive weight

The Five Types of Capitalism

Another way to understand the current disequilibrium of State, community and marketplace is to tease apart and examine the five types of capitalism—or what is identified as "capitalism" by detractors and apologists alike.

The word capitalism inspires the same sort of high emotion as religion, and indeed, we cannot make sense of the reactions triggered by the word without understanding it as a quasi-religious ideology that is considered gospel by some and anathema by others.

You have probably noticed there has been no recitation here of standard left-right ideologies or equivalent conventions. These ideologically based concepts have lost any explanatory power they might have once had; they no longer make sense of our world in a coherent fashion. As a result, they are akin to the illusory magic invoked by cargo cults that attempt to call up long-lost prosperity that has vanished for reasons the cultists cannot fathom. Lacking any coherent understanding and gripped by a sense of loss, they turn to magical incantations to restore their lost world. Ideologies are artifacts much like cargo cults, emotionally compelling appeals that promise an illusory restoration of a bygone era.

We might fruitfully understand ideology as the preferred emotional tool of the propaganda/ persuasion complex that has been harnessed by the State and the corporate media to convince the citizenry that financial tyranny is not only the best of all possible worlds, it is the only possible world.

Convictions which are unmoored from discourse and unperturbed by facts make fertile ground for exploitation by propagandists. To those who hold capitalism as gospel, the mere invocation of the word is enough to inspire outpourings of enthusiasm for the "magic" of the market's "invisible hand" and the wondrous consequences of single-minded pursuit of self-interest. This offers an irresistible opportunity for assorted scoundrels and frauds to win the approval of this orthodoxy by slipping their exploitation and fraud under the capacious tent of unfettered "capitalism" and "free markets."

To those whose conviction is based on the faith that capitalism is the foul root of all our troubles and the State our Savior in all matters, the mere attachment of the word "capitalism" to any position is enough to arouse their opposition. The ease of manipulating this orthodoxy is equally irresistible to propagandists, and "capitalism" has thus ceased to be signifier of a coherent system and instead become a favored tool of the persuasion complex.

Thus we might start by stripping capitalism down to its initial conditions:

1. Capital is placed at risk (invested) for an uncertain gain (profit).
2. Capital fluidly seeks the highest available profit.
3. Open markets discover the price of goods, services, securities, currency, debt and risk.
4. Innovation offers competitive advantages in open markets.

These are the initial conditions of classical capitalism. The other essential dynamics are less wholesome:

1. The single best way to dramatically lower risk and increase profit is to eradicate competition by whatever means are available and create either a monopoly or a cartel that controls supply and price. In monopolies and cartels, the risk has been shifted from those investing the capital to those purchasing the good or service. The free flow of information that is competition is replaced by asymmetric information: only the cartel members know supply and price are fixed to the benefit of capital.

2. The next best way to lower risk and increase gain is to eliminate transparency so price cannot be discovered and debt and risk can be mispriced. Put another way, information becomes asymmetric as the value of that information is diverted to those who control the information.

Competition can be strangled or eradicated in a number of ways, but since the rise of the modern Central State, the lowest risk method has been to persuade the State to grant an outright monopoly to private capital (for example, the East India Company), approve a cartel, or erect barriers to competition via regulation.

Once these special privileges have been granted—establishing a cartel or monopoly, eliminating transparency and thus the market's ability to price risk, and shunting risk to the public—then the cartel is no longer accountable to the community, it is only accountable to the Elite within the State that enforces its special privileges.

3. The third best way to lower risk and increase gain is to locate or create (and then protect) a windfall that can be exploited: a store of value that can be extracted or a supply of productive assets that can be sequestered for monopoly exploitation such as a captive labor pool.

Once again the most direct pathway to enforcing control over a windfall is to persuade (via application of concentrated wealth) the State to do the enforcing for you.

Thus if mine workers go on strike, then the State sends in troops to "restore order," the public relations term for "restoring monopoly and the dominance of capital." Members of the Savior State cargo cult are constantly promoting the State as a "solution" to all ailments, yet they fall strangely silent whenever the State uses its growing power to grant special privileges to capital and enforce those privileges.

Controlling capital and lending via the banking sector is another excellent way to choke off competition and establish essentially risk-free cartels: if competitors are denied capital, they will be unable to scale up to challenge existing corporations.

There are also myriad ways to eliminate transparency and create a low-risk, highly profitable asymmetry of information. An investment bank might structure a derivative in such a complex fashion that only the originators can parse out the consequences of price action on the derivative's value. Worthless assets can be presented as valuable when risk is mispriced due to deliberate misinformation.

Legislators can bury a favor to a generous financial benefactor within complex legislation that few outside the process will understand. Accounting chicanery can be hidden in pro forma financial statements and obscure footnotes. The low quality of a product can be hidden behind a glossy surface where it is invisible to consumers, and so on.

One of my favorite examples of the value of asymmetric information can be traced back to the beginnings of Capitalism in the

15th century, when it became commonplace to hedge the risk of trading voyages from Europe to the Far East by selling shares of the cargo (or options on the shares). If the ship sank en route and the cargo was a complete loss, the risk was spread among many investors. If the cargo arrived safely, the gain to the owners was reduced as the return was shared with those who took on some of the risk of potential loss, i.e. those who put capital at risk by buying a share of the cargo.

Quite naturally, if a ship became overdue then the market repriced the odds that the ship had been lost at sea, and the price of a share of the cargo plummeted. Traders in Amsterdam paid scouts to scan the coast in France; if the overdue ship was sighted, then a fast messenger was dispatched to alert the traders, who then bought the shares/options for low prices, knowing they would skyrocket in value once the ship reached Amsterdam.

The market does not operate in a vacuum; the State and the community/society are dynamically linked to the marketplace. This is why Capitalism in its classical form did not arise everywhere, nor is it equally successful in every society.

For the present analysis I have broken all that is passed off as Modern Capitalism into five phenotypes. I have left so-called "primitive" capitalism of barter and trade off the list, as our focus is the interaction of the modern State, community and marketplace.

1. Extractive
2. Exploitative
3. Enterprise
4. Marketing
5. Corporate/State

Extractive capitalism is based on the gain reaped by the extraction of a "found" asset in the environment such as a metals mine or a rich fishery. Once the resource is depleted, capital moves on, seeking another higher-yielding investment.

Exploitative capitalism is based on the monopoly control of labor and other productive assets such as land. A classic example is a feudal estate or a plantation with slave or indentured labor.

We should note that since capital is definitely being put at risk (even slave plantations went bankrupt on occasion) and innovation pays significant dividends, then these exploitative economic models have key characteristics of capitalism, even as they lack others. Though they may not have open markets for labor or local competition, their final products (metal ore, fish, sugar, tobacco, etc.) may have been traded in a larger open market and been exposed to competition. These basic distinctions should sensitize us to the complexity of deciding just what "capitalism" means and identifying which phenotypes are dominant or present in any particular situation.

Enterprise capitalism is the variety that inspires the rousing paeans from those glorifying the "magic" of markets: an open ecology that enables new enterprise, rewards capital invested early in the enterprise where the leverage of innovation and competitive advantage is greatest, and heaps the greatest gains on innovations in products, services, technology and the other means of production.

Enterprise capitalism can only flourish in environments that are not dominated by cartels, monopolies or the State, all of which smother enterprise capitalism in the crib as a potentially disruptive threat to their low-risk, highly profitable skimming operation.

Marketing capitalism is based on the stimulation of previously non-existent (and generally superfluous) needs, wants and impulses. This is the consumerist ideology that is generally seen as the irreplaceable foundation of the global economy—there is never enough of anything except insecurity to be sated with a new product, service or status signifier. Marketing capitalism requires ubiquitous access to credit as the fuel for instant gratification and the pursuit of becoming a different person by consuming differently.

Corporate/State capitalism is the institutionalization of crony capitalism in partnership with the State. According to the famous dictum of Italian dictator Mussolini, the marriage of corporation and the State is the beating heart of fascism.

Modern economies generally combine elements of all five types, and discerning each strand's relationship to society and State is difficult enough in the best of circumstances. But the propaganda/ marketing complex obscures the unsavory features of the economy that are used to concentrate wealth and power lest the debt-serfs catch on. While the forces of persuasion are coy about the shadow systems that enrich the Elites, they are ceaseless in their promotion of those that seem accessible to everyone.

We can cut through the complexity by asking two questions:

1. What is the relationship, in terms of accountability and dominance, between the State, the marketplace and the community?

2. What deliberate policies, shadow or explicit, are being deployed to misprice risk and debt?

If we answer these two questions, then we can ascertain the essential causal relationships (i.e. the initial conditions) that define any financial/economic ecosystem.

The Asymmetric Advantages of Capital

If we examine capital, community and the State as organisms in a dynamic financial ecosystem, the first thing we note is that capital is mobile and fluid while the State and community are fixed to one location. Mobility offers an enormous advantage, and this initial condition explains much of capital's dominance over the State and community and over labor, which is mobile only at the margins. That is, a small percentage of labor is highly mobile and can move about the planet like capital in search of the highest return, a somewhat larger but still modest percentage of labor has limited mobility within a community or nation, and the vast majority of labor is unable or unwilling to move far enough to dramatically lower their risk and improve their gain.

Capital has another overwhelming advantage over community and nominally democratic States: it does not need to influence the entire community or State to gain special privileges that cement its profitability; it only needs to bring its wealth to bear on small Elites within the State that have the power to grant special privileges.

In an analogy, capital need not buy a tugboat to turn the ship of State to its advantage; it need only persuade the individuals on the bridge to do its bidding.

Capital also has an intrinsic advantage in its access to credit. The State can of course borrow money by selling bonds, but in democracies this is a quasi-public process and the proceeds become part of the unwieldy State budget. Private capital can borrow money and buy the key Elite's compliance much more easily and with little to no visibility.

Community has a similar ability to sell special-purpose bonds, but once again this money is diffused in a quasi-public special-purpose budget.

In other words, the vector of influence flows in one direction, from capital to the State and community. Capital can easily raise the relatively modest sum of money needed to persuade a handful of individuals within a State to grant it special privileges, but neither the State nor the community can raise this kind of money and apply it in sufficient concentration to persuade the Elites that control capital to do their bidding.

This highlights yet another advantage of capital: its controlling Elites are only accountable to the owners of the capital and the lenders who have extended credit to capital; their allegiance to the community and State is intrinsically contingent, as capital will flow fluidly to higher return elsewhere, leaving the State and community behind. This fundamental truth cannot increase capital's persuasive powers, so capital employs the persuasion complex to promote a happy-story fantasy of "caring about the community we serve."

Should capital's profits sag below those obtainable elsewhere, then this purported allegiance to the community will be revealed as illusory, as capital will slip fluidly away. The community itself has some influence on capital, of course, but it also only flows in one direction: if the community attempts to impose restrictions on capital that crimp its return, then capital will either bypass the community by purchasing its Elites or it will move elsewhere.

Each of the three systems—capital, community and the State—have different imperatives: capital must earn a positive return or it will contract. It must also earn a return similar to those earned by its competitors, or its owners will abandon it for higher return elsewhere, leaving it at a disadvantage in terms of access to credit and influence over the State.

The State's imperative, as we have seen, is straightforward: expand by whatever means are available until it controls the entire ecosystem. The imperative of the Elites within the State is to maximize their gain while they hold the reins of power. Community has a simpler but more challenging imperative: wedded in most cases to a particular locale, community must sustain itself in an environment where capital and the State hold the vast majority of the wealth and power.

In terms of accountability, once capital brings its concentrated wealth to bear on the key Elites within the State that have the power to grant special privileges, then it becomes accountable only to that Elite; the community has lost all meaningful feedback to capital except the diffused feedback of voters and consumers.

Thus accountability is also a vector that flows only one direction; the State is nominally accountable to the community (voters and citizens), but capital is not accountable to either the State or community except on the margins, i.e. the pressure exerted by boycotts, strikes, voter rebellions and other dissent against the domination of capital and its captured State Elites.

But capital, having purchased special privileges and protection from the State, can always call upon the State to suppress public dissent.

We now see that these three organisms, capital, community and the State, are arranged in a hierarchical pyramid, with capital at the apex dominating the Elites within the State, who then control the State which then dominates community and market.

This explains why, beneath the glossy surface of globalization, the exploitative plantation economy remains the model of global "growth": capital locates a low-risk, high-gain opportunity; it buys special privileges from the local Elites, and proceeds to extract whatever value is available as a windfall. Once the windfall (cheap labor, resources, etc.) has been depleted, capital leaves the ravaged community behind for greener pastures. The local Elites who thought their power was permanent discover that their wealth was contingent on capital; when the risks rose or the gains fell, they were jettisoned as needless baggage, just like the workers and citizens they exploited from their position of power in the State.

The only way to restore equilibrium to the ecosystem is to restore community and the market at the top dominating the State which then dominates capital.

Interestingly, but not coincidentally, the only form of capitalism that can thrive when capital is limited by a State that is itself limited by the community and market is the healthy, sustainable form, that of enterprise.

Credit as a Vector of Power

Credit plays a special role in the dominance of capital and State, as access to credit enables the borrower to concentrate wealth and power. This can be illustrated by a simple example of a dynamic which has played out many times over the ages. If capital has $10,000 in cash, the amount of special privileges it can purchase from the Elites in the community or State is essentially zero. If, however, capital can leverage that sum 25-to-1 via credit, then the resulting $250,000 can buy considerable special privileges in the local community or State.

Once a privilege has been secured, then wealth will flow to capital like a spring, for as we have seen, risk is lowered and gain increased once competition and transparency have been replaced by the privileges of crony capitalism.

Credit is thus a vector of power projection in the hands of capital.

In the hands of the State, credit enables the State to bribe constituencies and wage costly war to secure resources.

In the hands of the citizen, credit enables a vast expansion of consumption.

This highlights the fundamental asymmetry between credit extended to consumers and credit extended to capital or the State: when credit is used for consumption, then it doesn't concentrate power, it relinquishes it to the owner of the credit: the consumer becomes a debt-serf, beholden to those who issue the credit.

How is it that credit is an instrument of power projection for capital but a vector of servitude for citizen-consumers?

The answer can only be found by examining the consumer ideology and the marketing complex that created it and sustains it.

Debt-Serfdom as the Result of a Consumerist State Economy

My opening statement may strike you as a non-sequitur, but it is central to understanding our current state of self-destructive dis-equilibrium: the State is incapable of love.

To understand the import of this "obvious" statement, we must return to the initial conditions of human nature laid out in Chapter Four:

humans ontologically need not just to establish an identity within the world and themselves; they must constantly renew that identity. Their external identity must be reaffirmed with productive connections to others and their internal identity must be renewed with coherent belief structures that establish meaning and their place in the world.

The need to constantly renew identity and meaning is the key to understanding human cultures, societies and economies.

As we have seen, the State's ontological imperative is relentless expansion that crowds out both community and transparent markets. Since the community is the natural source of identity and meaning, then the hollowing out of community by the State and its corporate partners leaves citizens only two sources of identity and meaning: the State and the consumerist ideology that serves the State/capital partnership.

As previously noted, there is a profound connection between financial dependence on the State and the consumerist ideology; in an ontological sense, they are two sides of the same coin. Our understanding of this connection can be enriched by an analysis of *cui bono*—to whose benefit?—and risk/gain.

We might start with the profound spiritual and psychological poverty of the citizen who is dependent on the State for either his sustenance (broadly speaking, "welfare" or entitlements) or his privileges (broadly speaking, "corporate welfare"). Rather than drawing upon a decentralized network of community-based relationships (the local marketplace, neighborhood, extended family, professional and trade associations, religious organizations, community-based financial associations, etc.) for work, social status and meaning, the State dependent has no personal connections at all with the impersonal State which seeks only one thing: a passive, complicit citizenry that has been stripped of the will or even the concept of dissent.

As noted previously, the dependent agreed to surrender his autonomy and independence because the State presented itself as "risk-free," and thus the payment granted by the State is also perceived as "risk-free."

But as noted many times, risk cannot be eliminated; it can only be temporarily shifted onto others, and so the State shifts risk from itself to the entire system. Thus the State-dominated system is not at all the "risk-free" structure promised the dependent, but in fact the opposite: a system that is doomed to destabilization.

We can understand this dynamic another way: what the citizen is gaining is distinctly but narrowly meaningful—a payment or privilege. What the citizen is giving up—autonomy, independent thought and action, and the potential for dissent—is not just diffused and less meaningful, but a burden, as all these attributes requires responsibility and effort.

Accepting dependence on the State is "convenient" while autonomy, independent thought and action are difficult.

In other words, a cash payment is a "windfall" in the sense that there is no apparent risk to dependence on the State. Not only is there no apparent risk, there is also no need for investing substantial time or energy to secure this gain.

What the citizen who surrenders his autonomy and independence to the State does not realize is that he is also trading his authenticity and identity, for authenticity, like trust, can only be earned; the State, incapable of love, is incapable of granting authenticity.

Once shorn of a positive identity or the means to establish and renew it, the State dependent soon finds his mind and soul clouded with resentments, imagined and real: someone else manipulated the system for a larger benefit; some State minion denied a deserved benefit, and so on. Eventually this resentment—which we can properly understand as the anger that naturally arises from the loss of identity—spreads to everyone who has more than the dependent.

The psychology of dependence is the psychology of resentment and envy; the citizen who has surrendered his identity and soul for "windfall" benefits from the State envies those who still have their autonomy.

Even more destructive, the citizen who relinquishes his identity for State dependency also loses his self-reliance, which quickly withers in disuse. The only "skills" that can be brought to bear on the State's system of granting benefits are lying, fraud and gaming the system—the very "skills" that would quickly get the practitioner ejected from the community and shunned as a malefic force.

This same exchange of identity and meaning for a "risk-free" benefit is also the heart of the credit-consumer economy: credit is extended to "buy" social status that would otherwise require major investments of time and energy in the community or marketplace.

Credit-based consumption appears to be a "windfall" to the naïve citizen: not only is no investment required to obtain an identity-enhancing status identifier, but with credit the acquisition of a "new identity" is instantaneous, enabling every child's dream of instant gratification.

In this sense, credit and consumerism both infantilize the citizen, drawing out the worst traits of adolescent demands for all the benefits of adulthood but without any of the work or responsibility.

In deferring payment and making future payments modest in size, consumerism explicitly fosters the illusion that the immediate gains of gratification are vast while the costs are minimal.

There is no awareness in this seduction that "modest payments" on credit are a form of gradual enslavement, nor is there any recognition of the brevity of the gratification. Each purchase acts to renew the illusion that the person is larger than their own life; but since identity and meaning must be constantly renewed, then this places the consumer on an endless treadmill: if you make status identifiers the foundation of your identity, then you must constantly buy more to renew that contingent sense of self. The ownership alone does not renew; it is the act of purchasing, of being seen making the purchase, of opening the box and reveling in its meaning that renews identity.

Thus ownership can never be enough; more identifiers must be acquired lest the consumer's "store-bought" identity depreciate. Once identity is no longer renewed by an overlay of actions, skills, relationships, associations and internal effort, then it is effectively a monoculture, with all the innate vulnerabilities and potential for collapse that we have outlined in previous chapters.

This treadmill of endless consumption to renew an inauthentic identity leads most consumers into financial ruin. Those with typical incomes keep acquiring debt until servicing their accumulated debt (including their home mortgage, auto loans, etc.) dominates their finances and thus their life. At this point they have become debt-serfs, indentured to Capital and working solely to make minimum payments on their debts.

The wealthy, unfulfilled by mere "aspirational" spending, step on an escalator of expectations that lead to either outright squandering of their fortune or the slow erasure of their capital as malinvestment in consumer identifiers diverts capital from productive returns.

In other words, the consumer has traded his liberty and identity for a temporal boost in social status that renders him a debt-serf, indentured to capital.

A vast expansion of credit for consumption benefits the State enormously, as some of the profits flowing to capital from this orgy of debt are diverted to State coffers. Any contraction of debt is a catastrophe for the State, as not only do tax revenues decline precipitously, so do the private profits flowing directly to the State's Elites.

If private capital collapses, then the State simply transfers the borrowing to its own ledger, and the hapless citizen finds himself indentured to public credit: the State explicitly promises bondholders that its citizens will repay its debts with interest.

The fraud, of course, is the nominally democratic representation has been captured by capital, so the people are indentured to debt servitude by a State they no longer control. In this sense, the State and capital are truly one, as both indenture the citizen to servitude in service of debt that enriches capital and the State Elites.

In a perverse fashion, this expansion of State revenues from the expansion of debt servitude gives the State sufficient funds to buy the complicity of its vast armies of dependents. As long as the State can borrow enough to fund their payments, State dependents will support the State.

The establishment of identity in the community is arduous and time-consuming; one must build trust slowly by showing up when promised and making an effort that actually yields results.

Consumerism—what we might call the quasi-religion of convenience—holds out the bright promise of bypassing this difficult process by simply buying signifiers on credit that painlessly transform the consumer into a higher-status person. This is the implicit promise of consumerism: you can become a different and much "larger" person simply by consuming differently.

Consumption, especially the instant-gratification type enabled by credit, offers a "low-risk" way around this steep investment and risky outcome: simply by possessing signifiers, the dreamy goal of enhanced status can be reached with essentially no investment or immediate cost. Indeed, the promise of purchase on credit is that the "pain" of paying for the consumption is like the State's modest tax to fund entitlements: it is insignificant compared to the outsized gain in status.

This consumerist exchange is radically different in terms of initial conditions than community-based identity and security. When an individual strives to increase his material security and social status, the entire community benefits from his investment of caring and work, even if his intended goal was self-glorification or personal fulfillment.

When the individual consumes a good or service to construct a new, more grandiose status, then the gain flows only to the distant concentrations of capital that enabled the consumption and the capital that extended the credit; the community gains nothing, while the State harvests a sliver of tax revenue from the transaction.

In this way, consumerism reduces the complex experience of identity, social status and material security to a shriveled, private transaction between an isolated individual and distant concentrations of capital (and it is always distant, for capital is constantly roaming the globe seeking higher returns).

The consumer purchases "membership" in a "tribe" of fellow consumers seeking instant gratification and higher status, and this faux membership is heavily reinforced with the cheap facsimiles of community offered by social media: by buying a brand, tone "joins" the faux "community" of other consumers who fleetingly extracted a dose of fulfillment from the purchase.

But the tragic irony of consumption as the means of establishing identity and meaning is that is ontologically incapable of providing those essentials. What it does provide in infinite profusion is facsimiles of identity and meaning, at the terrible cost of debt-serfdom and the spiritual poverty of an isolated consumer whose life is devoted to servicing debt.

Thus we can say that just as the State is incapable of love, so too are the distant concentrations of capital that operate the consumerist economy incapable of love.

In a consumerist world dominated by the financial tyranny of capital, then the citizen has sacrificed everything of profound value—community, identity, autonomy, meaning and security—for the empty baubles of dependence on the State and debt-serfdom to capital.

Nothing suits the State's desire for passive citizens better than debt-serfdom, as the debt-serfs, exhausted and anxious, have neither the time nor energy to dissent. In a pathological symmetry to the classical Greek polis, the populace breaks down into three subgroups, all in service of the State and capital: the State and Financial Elites and their Upper-Caste class of technocrats and apparatchiks; the debt-serfs whose labor enriches capital and the State, and the vast army of passive State dependents.

The domination of consumerism is just another example of the State's mispricing and masking of risk. Just as the State masks the risks of dependence when citizens surrender their autonomy for entitlements, it also masks the risks of debt- servitude to distant concentrations of capital.

If we consider the initial conditions described here, we conclude that a pyramid of capital and State dominating a hollowed-out community and a populace of isolated, alienated consumers leads to financial tyranny, an expansionist State and a citizenry reduced to debt-serfdom.

To re-order the pyramid and place community at the top where it can limit both the State and capital, then the citizenry have only the diffused tools of dissent and resistance.

For the individual, these tools offer an authentic identity, sense of place and meaning; in aggregate, they offer a way to restore equilibrium to the entire ecosystem of culture, society and economy.

Chapter Eight: The Nature of Liberation

Liberation is the goal of resistance and revolution, and so we must carefully define what we mean by "liberation."

In the shared imagination of revolution, toppling tyranny liberates oppressed people; liberation is the relief and freedom experienced when the yoke of dictatorship is thrown off. In this sense liberation is the absence of oppression; its other characteristics are left undefined.

In the adolescent mindset fostered by the consumerist-State, liberation means freedom from responsibility and consequence, as this is the ultimate adolescent fantasy: freedom and consumption without consequence.

In spiritual traditions, liberation is an inner state achieved by freeing oneself from worldly attachments and desires.

Though these conceptions of liberation are quite different, they share the idea that liberation is a destination or end-state.

In my view, the necessary conditions for liberation are an end-state but liberation itself is a state of being, a process rather than a destination. We can understand the distinction by comparing the Bill of Rights, which establishes the civil liberties that underpin the pursuit of happiness with the actual pursuit of happiness. The first is the end-state of a political order devoted to safeguarding liberty; the second is a messy, dynamic individual process that continues through all of life.

Without a political foundation, then liberation, even the spiritual variety, is contingent on the whims of tyranny, for the State can loot the monastery and oppress individuals at will.

What is Liberation?

As noted above, liberation tends to be defined by what chains have been cut, rather than by the attributes of that liberation. If we define liberation as a goal that is reached when shackles fall away, then our definition is based on negative space, i.e. by an absence rather than positive descriptors. Can we define anything fully by absence alone? Clearly we cannot. Thus liberation is not merely the absence of oppression but a dynamic process with a variety of often-conflicting attributes.

For example, cheering crowds that gather to celebrate the end of a political tyranny are experiencing the euphoria of new-found freedom, but the next day brings a question: what do we do with that freedom? If we do nothing different than we did under tyranny, might not new Elites arise to fill the power vacuum left by the toppled regime? If we find ourselves beholden to financial Elites via heavy debts, then how much freedom did we actually gain in the breaking of political shackles?

If liberation is fundamentally a process, then it follows that we renew liberation on a daily basis by our actions and thoughts. In this sense, liberation is akin to identity. Identity is not static; it must be established and renewed with actions, social connections and an inner map of the world that makes sense of our experience.

If the now-toppled regime generously funded its supporters, then all those who have lost their funding and security will not welcome liberation. As we observed in our discussions of risk, gain and conservation, most people prefer the safety of the known over the risks of the unknown and the security of dependence over the risk of independence. Erich Fromm called this ontological preference "escape from freedom," as people escape the burdens and risks of responsibility and choice for the security of authoritarianism and a rigid social hierarchy.

When the insecurity and risk of freedom are traded for the safety (what is perceived as a low-risk windfall) offered by an authoritarian political and social order, then security is equated with dependence. Those seeking dependence on an authoritarian State will define "liberation" as an escape from responsibility and risk.

Those who have chafed under tyranny will readily pursue their newfound freedoms of faith, movement, exchange, expression, enterprise and association.

Though spiritual liberation is explicitly apolitical, that is, the nature of the current political regime is of little consequence to the seeker, it is self-evident that human spiritual potential and freedom are both constricted by tyranny. This is why various Protestant sects fled the social constraints of 17th century Britain for the explicit freedom of religion offered by the wide-open (and risky) colonies in America.

A third group of people experience political and social liberation as an opportunity to expand their religious community and openly express their faith. These people will be less interested in the mechanics of the replacement political order, as their focus is on spiritual expansion and freedom.

A fourth set of people will seek to exploit the power vacuum to expand their own wealth and power at the expense of others. As we have described, the standard way to accomplish this parasitic predation in nominal democracies is to transfer risk to others while diverting gain to a few hands.

Even in this very preliminary sketch, we see how fundamentally different concepts of liberation will lead to conflicting views of the ideal social and political order.

In my view, the primary lesson to be drawn from this is the need for a decentralized, transparent and dynamic ecology of choice and responsibility in which individuals and groups are protected from parasitic exploitation and predation. If communities of like-minded people can make their own arrangements without transferring risk to others or depriving others of freedom, then this is the most advantageous and fair social and political order possible.

Liberation from Financial Tyranny

Since we inhabit a corporeal world that is intertwined with the abstract world of finance, there is necessarily a financial aspect to liberation, even of the spiritual sort. This can easily be illustrated by these questions: If we are enslaved via exponential debt to a financial tyranny, how free are we, even if our civil liberties are intact? How much of our destiny do we actually control if our political choices are false ones arranged to further the power of financial Elites? Even if we are personally debt-free, how free are we if the Central State has indebted us as taxpayers with its exponential expansion of Central State debt?

Borrowing a concept from historian Giovanni Arrighi, we can fruitfully conceptualize the global economy as a three-floor structure where the market machinery of profit-making occupies the bottom floor. This is the economy as most people understand it: global supply chains, manufacturing, research and development, global trade and currency flows, technological innovations, product cycles, marketing campaigns and so on.

Above this level of production and commerce is the machinery of finance, which few people outside of the Upper Caste that toils here understand. This is the abstract world of pure finance in which financial instruments generate "real money" that then dominates the first floor world of commerce. The machinery on this second level is largely debt and leverage-based: derivatives of credit such as credit default swaps, derivatives of real estate debt such as mortgage-backed securities, currency swaps and carry trades and various abstractions of sovereign and corporate bonds. This level is where the enduring profits of global capital are generated.

The third floor is even more rarified, for this is the level where political power and capital partner to control the lower two floors and the political realm of governments and alliances. This is where oligarchies, cartels and monopolies are forged and protected, where risk is off-loaded onto the citizenry and gargantuan gains are diverted into the hands of various Elites. This is where crises are managed and exploited to cement the control of plutocratic Elites, and where the intellectual foundations of the Status Quo are distilled and passed down for marketing to the masses as ideology, political parties, and so on—the machinery of false choice and propaganda.

Once we understand this structure, then we realize that freedom of enterprise is limited by the plutocracy (rule of the wealthy) to a dim corner of the first floor. To truly be free, we must be free of the financial tyranny of debt and leverage manufactured on the second floor and controlled by the shadow systems of the third floor. Once we grasp this, we understand social and political liberation is still only partial liberation; only when we are free of the servitude imposed by the second and third levels can we truly be free to pursue the freedoms of faith, movement, expression, enterprise and association.

The financial tyranny of the third level is subtle, for it expropriates wealth behind facades that are purposefully designed to obscure and confuse (by using limbic words such as "capitalism" and "democracy") and by transferring risk and debt to the citizenry via Central State debt

(debt resulting from runaway deficit spending), loan guarantees issued to private banks and the pernicious mechanisms of inflation (gradual theft of purchasing power from every holder of the currency).

Since the nation is nominally a democracy, the Central State's enforcement of capital's privileges is legitimized by false-choice elections in which all the candidates are "party members," i.e. members of the political Elites who serve capital.

Since the nation nominally operates under "free market capitalism," then private debt is voluntary, though this is also a false choice as debt is now indispensable for the vast majority of citizens who seek security within the Status Quo. The Status Quo offers two alternatives to taking on immense loads of debt—poverty or being born into great wealth— and the system incentivizes debt. For example, interest paid on debt is tax deductible, but repayment of principal must be paid with after-tax income. The Status Quo is so designed to reinforce debt that few households can resist leveraging most of their income into debt, i.e. becoming debt-serfs. The notion of "voluntary" becomes suspect when the incentives are all on the side of leveraged debt.

We can generalize non-Elite reactions to this cloaked financial tyranny into three basic categories: compliance, aggression and detachment. Those who believe they stand to gain from the Status Quo will comply, those who see opportunity to expand their own wealth and power will aggressively seek to join the Upper Caste that serves the Elites, while the third group who gains little from the Status Quo and who declines to expand their own power at the expense of others will opt out or detach themselves from the system.

Since the Central State cannot fulfill its financial promises (the only options are hyper-inflation or default), all those who believe the Status Quo will serve their self-interests will be disappointed. This is likely to spark emotions of betrayal and resentment, which will likely be directed at those seeking to expand their own wealth and power via membership in the Upper Caste serving the Plutocracy.

The most productive segments of the economy on the first floor will increasingly be taxed to support capital-State hegemony, and their incentives to remain in the system will decline drastically. As they opt out or detach themselves from dependence on the State and capital, then the State will enter the death-spiral financial crisis described in Chapter One.

After this financial collapse, a new arrangement, that is, a new social, political and economic order will arise. This is not to say that the Central State will cease to exist; but since its financial foundations will be in ruins, then a new financial arrangement will arise. At that juncture, a political "reset" will be possible that forcibly decentralizes concentrations of capital and political power.

There are many vulnerable populations that have come to depend on the Central State, and they will have to be sustained by new localized, decentralized arrangements. The community, eroded by the Central State, will be free to reassert its adaptive, cooperative collaborative genius once the shackles of capital-State domination have been broken.

If we follow these threads to their conclusion, we see that liberation can only be fully realized in the real world if the financial tyranny of the Central State and concentrated capital is broken up into a decentralized, diverse ecosystem and its sociopathological drive to aggregate capital and political power into plutocracy is severely limited.

Liberation can mean many things to many people, but it means little if the populace has been driven into financial servitude by concentrated capital and an expansionist Central State.

We can characterize one key feature of liberation in this way: there is no shortcut to liberation, any more than there is a shortcut to mastering a difficult skill or building an enterprise.

The Destruction of Money and the Servitude of Debt

As noted in Chapter One, there is a key difference between the two options the Central State has to resolve the crisis of its exponential expanding debts and obligations: high inflation destroys the purchasing power (value) of all money, while default destroys only debt and debt-based assets.

To understand this in practical terms, we can start by reiterating that printing money does not create wealth, it only creates the illusion of wealth. Printing money to pay debt is a shortcut, and since there is no shortcut to creating productive goods and services, then there is a consequence to this illusory "solution" and that consequence is inflation or the depreciation of money's purchasing power.

Default or the renunciation of debt is the honest resolution to over-indebtedness, as it is a direct statement that the obligation cannot be met. Those who risked capital for gain by loaning the money or by buying the debt suffer the loss: risk and gain/loss are causally connected.

The Central State can transfer the cost of exponentially expanding debt to the citizenry in two ways: it can steal their purchasing power via inflation or it can burden them with high taxes to pay the interest on expanding public debt. If the State can load the citizenry with essentially unlimited debt, then servicing that expanding debt becomes a form of servitude and tyranny.

If the Central State can transfer the risk and loss of exponentially expanding debt to the citizenry, then the citizens' purchasing power and wealth is always contingent on the State's whims—or more correctly, on the whims of the plutocratic Elites that rule the State.

If we follow this to its logical conclusion, we see that liberation is impossible if the Central State can transfer the risk and cost of expanding debt to the citizenry.

Is there any way to restrain the State's power to depreciate the value of its currency or transfer private losses to the public?

There is one way, and only one way, to limit the State's power to depreciate its currency to near-zero and that is to base the money on an asset that cannot be printed or borrowed into existence, an asset that does not depend on a counterparty, i.e. a promise to pay issued by some entity. Historically, the most common example of such an asset is gold.

The mechanism to limit the State's power to destroy money is known as the "discipline of sound money," as gold-backed money cannot be printed or electronically created at will. There are various other proposals for "sound money" and it is beyond the scope of this book to analyze them. It is enough to understand the very simple principle that "sound money" only provides discipline if the State or central bank cannot print it in unlimited sums.

The only way to limit the State's power to transfer private risk and debt to the public is to limit its power to borrow money via selling bonds backed by taxes extracted from the citizenry.

Eliminating the Central State's ability to borrow essentially unlimited sums leveraged by taxation is anathema to the intellectual foundations of the Status Quo, the central tenet of which is that the State needs to borrow essentially unlimited sums of money to "help" the citizens or wage war. The idea that such expenditures could be raised directly via increased taxation approved by elected representatives is anathema because that is not a painless shortcut.

The implicit assumption here is that the citizenry are adolescents who will heartily approve apparently painless shortcuts and disapprove of adult solutions that require facing facts and making difficult tradeoffs.

Borrowing money always appears to be a low-risk windfall, the classic "something for nothing," and as we are programmed to seek low-risk windfalls, then we will naturally find debt extremely attractive, especially if the interest is deferred to the distant future or is paid by others.

But since there is no shortcut, then there is a consequence to granting the State the right to borrow unlimited sums of money: political Elites can transfer the debts of financial Elites onto the public ledger at will. This is precisely what happened on a grand scale in the 2008-2012 financial crises.

If we understand that the power to print and borrow money in unlimited quantities gives the State the power to steal from all holders of its currency and transfer debt from private hands to the public, then we must conclude that financial liberation requires sound money that cannot be destroyed at will by the Central bank and State and a State that is unable to borrow money as a means of concentrating gain in private hands while transferring the risk and loss to the citizenry.

Like the *Titanic* sinking, a Central State that cannot print or borrow money at will is seen as impossible. Freeing ourselves from rationalizations for the Status Quo is the first step of liberation.

Liberation from Debt, the Central State and Concentrated Capital

As we have seen, expanding debt becomes a form of tyranny, and freedom in a political system that offers up only false choices is illusory, as either choice empowers the same Status Quo Elites.

This suggests a two-fold pursuit of liberation: public support of a limited Central State that is unable to impoverish its citizens at will via high inflation (printing money) or expanding debt (unlimited borrowing) , and private financial independence from the State and the concentrations of capital that control the State's finances.

Since reforming a system of false choices is impossible—the option of fundamental transformation is never offered, as that would threaten the Status Quo—then this public pathway boils down to voting for whatever marginalized third option is available, if any, and challenging the intellectual foundations of the unsustainable Status Quo with public expression of the forces of low-intensity instability that create long-term adaptability and stability (skepticism, inquiry, dissent, etc.).

The goal of this public dissent is to lay the intellectual groundwork for a "reset" political order with a limited Central State that has been shorn of the powers to print and borrow money but which is empowered to limit plutocratic concentrations of capital and other forms of predation, parasitism and exploitation.

Such a reset is "impossible" until the exponential-expansion-of-debt financial order implodes.

I need to stipulate here that financial independence from the Central State and plutocratic capital means very simply that the household does not rely on a transfer payment, pension or salary from these institutions as the primary source of income.

We are all dependent on a functioning State and financial system to conduct everyday life, but this is qualitatively different from depending on the State for monthly payments and on the global financial system for financial security. When I speak of independence from the State and plutocratic capital, I refer to financial dependency, not a reliance on the infrastructure provided by the State and financial system.

In the broadest sense, the social contract offered by the State is that the citizenry will pay taxes to the State which will use those funds to maintain an infrastructure of equivalent means to the taxes paid. In this sense we are all dependent on the State to maintain roadways, rule of law, an independent judiciary, department of public health to combat pandemics, law enforcement, environment protection, trash removal, and so on. Our obligation as citizens is in the biblical phrase, to render unto Caesar that which is Caesar's, i.e. pay taxes in accordance with regulations approved by our elected representatives.

In a similar way, having an account at a local credit union is depending on the financial system to accurately account for our money and enable digital transfers and payments.

Dependence on distant concentrations of capital does not mean everyday banking; it refers instead to the global system of extreme leverage and assets entrusted to the management of Wall Street firms in stock mutual funds, overseas funds, bond funds, mortgage-backed securities, derivatives, and other financial instruments.

As previously noted, financial dependence on the Central State lead to complicity: those drawing "bread and circuses" or "corporate welfare" from the State will naturally support the Status Quo, even when they understand it is unsustainable. This is a form of moral hazard, meaning those who depend on the State assume their dependence carries near-zero risk (that is, the checks will always arrive and have the same purchasing power they have today), and therefore they make different choices than those who are exposed to transparent risk in the real world.

As we have shown, the risk of the State's finances imploding has only been masked temporarily by massive money-printing and borrowing, and so those who believe their dependence on the State is risk-free will eventually discover that the Status Quo's security is illusory. Put another way, their definition of self-interest will be revealed as delusional.

In a similar fashion, dependence on expanding debt is equally unsustainable. Eventually depreciation outstrips new investment and interest payments outstrip increases in income and the debt is repudiated via default and insolvency.

If we follow these two lines of thought, we conclude that liberation requires freeing ourselves from financial dependence on the Central State, debt and the concentrations of capital that profit from leveraged debt. Recall that capital uses these immense profits to expand their power by buying control of State policy and regulation.

In other words, if we accept that risk cannot be eliminated, it can only be masked or transferred, then our behavior will be completely different from those who believe the Central State's debt and money will maintain their present-day value. Those who believe the State's financial order is sustainable will see no reason to establish financial independence, while those that do will see financial independence as the minimum requisite for liberation.

Financial independence from the Central State is not an abstraction; it is a practical way to radically reduce your risk as the unsustainable succumbs to gravity. Depending on the State financially is like clinging to the *Titanic*; five minutes after the encounter with the iceberg this looks like a low-risk strategy, but two hours and thirty minutes later as the great ship eases into its final descent to a watery grave then the folly of that assessment is revealed, but too late to be of any value.

By the time you're thirsty, it's too late to dig a well.

Another way of understanding financial independence from the State and Wall Street is that this independence is a hedge against the fiscal implosion of the State and its plutocracy. In our *Titanic* example, a raft you assemble on your own is a hedge against the great ship sinking; if it doesn't sink, then your labor assembling the raft has no yield. But if you understand that there is no way the ship cannot sink, then the risk shifts from wasting effort building a raft to drowning in ice-cold seawater.

This leads us to ask if entrusting our financial wealth to distant concentrations of capital (i.e. Wall Street) isn't just as risky as depending on the State. If the highly leveraged global financial system's stability and security are illusory, then which forms of wealth are more secure, funds held by Wall Street or assets and income streams we control directly in our own community?

Since concentrations of capital have partnered with the State to guarantee their gain while transferring risk to the citizenry, then isn't depending on distant capital akin to trusting the feudal lord to grant his debt-serfs financial security? To finance capital, debt-serfdom is security: we pay them interest for life and in return we get to consume corporate brands without the sacrifice of saving.

Liberation has two financial aspects. One is that a financialized economy necessarily leads to immensely profitable concentrations of capital that naturally protect their power by buying control of the Central State's regulatory and policy machinery, i.e. a plutocracy. This monoculture limits political freedom by offering only false choices, all of which support the Status Quo, and by repressing or marginalizing the forces of low-intensity instability that enable systemic stability.

Secondly, the consumerist-State economy incentivizes leverage and debt which then lead to debt-serfdom, where most of the citizen's earnings are devoted to debt service and taxes.

Liberation from the servitude of debt begins with freeing ourselves from the consumerist-State mindset, and this also frees us from the cruel chains of social defeat.

We can summarize the conditions of liberation in any number of ways, but here is one summary:

1. Indebtedness is not in our self-interest as it creates servitude and works against our goal of financial independence from the Central State and finance capital. We reject debt-serfdom.

2. We free ourselves of the consumerist-State mindset and the social defeat it generates.

3. Political reform within the Status Quo is an illusion; liberation is financial independence from both the Central State and finance capital.

4. Liberation flows from the forces of low-intensity instability we bring to our own lives: dissent, innovation, experimentation, competition, transparency, meritocracy, accountability, consequence and the free exchange of feedback and information.

5. Liberation is freely expressing the freedoms of faith, movement, exchange, expression, enterprise and association.

Resistance as Liberation

If liberation is more than just the absence of overt oppression, then independence from destructive systems is liberation, and resistance to an unsustainable Status Quo is itself a form of liberation. The oppressive tyranny we have outlined is not overtly political, as the U.S. and other advanced economies remain nominally democratic; it is a financial tyranny that has infiltrated and subjugated the political and social orders. Since this conquest has been achieved by suppressing the forces of dynamic stability (feedback and the other forces of low-intensity instability) such that the Status Quo is now dependent on systemic fraud and the endless expansion of leveraged credit for its survival, then the collapse of the financial Status Quo is inevitable.

Just as this "quiet coup" (to use Simon Johnson's phrase) was politically voluntary—nobody forced the political class to cede institutional control to capital at gunpoint—our participation is also voluntary: nobody is forcing us to take on massive debt or vote for plutocratic incumbents at gunpoint.

Thus the first step of liberation is to free ourselves of the internalized notion that becoming indebted to financial Elites serves our self-interest or the interests of the nation. We can generalize this further by stating that liberation explicitly means financial independence from crony-capitalist concentrations of capital—what I have termed debt-serfdom.

Our analysis has described how the consumerist worldview exploits our innate need for social affirmation by internalizing a distorted sense of self-interest that renews identity via credit-based consumption.

The second step of liberation is to free ourselves of this internalized sociopathology and assert our identity in real social connections rather than the phantom connections of consumerism. In other words, we must liberate ourselves from the terrible yoke of social defeat.

We have identified that the ontological imperative of the Central State, now fully financialized and dependent on ever-expanding debt for its own survival, is continual expansion of its reach and control. As the State becomes increasingly brittle and unstable (the supernova model of expansion and collapse), it pursues politically expedient bribes of its restive army of dependents even as its various Elites splinter into warring factions.

As a result, the third step of liberation is to free ourselves of dependence on the doomed Central State and the centralized, financialized economy it controls and forge instead a pathway of social and financial resilience based on decentralized self-reliance.

Since the political Elites that nominally rule the Central State profit from the forces of financialization, they are incapable of identifying the interests of the nation, or placing those interests ahead of their own.

The fourth step of liberation is to free ourselves of the illusion that the political class of either party is capable of authentic leadership, as that would require destroying the power of the plutocracy that funds the political class. Since the Elites are only capable of pursuing their own narrow self-interests, then leadership falls to the citizens who must lead by example rather than power.

Once we understand these four steps of liberation, we also realize this is the agenda of resistance: an internal liberation from unsustainable sociopathological social control myths and the forging of a positive, sustainable social order via coherently directed actions in the real, lived-in world.

Liberation and the Pursuit of Happiness

Liberation has a positive connotation, but it is somewhat abstract; if asked for their goal in life, most people would answer fulfillment or happiness. The American Declaration of Independence recognized the enduring centrality of human happiness by including it in the inalienable rights to be secured by revolution: life, liberty and the pursuit of happiness. (The Virginia Declaration of Rights and other listings of sovereign rights included the right to acquire and possess property.)

To make liberation practical, then, we must connect it to the pursuit of happiness. In keeping with our analytic order, we start by identifying the initial conditions that enable the pursuit of happiness and those that inhibit it. Though we think of happiness as a private pursuit, in aggregate the pursuit of happiness constitutes a public happiness, and thus it is central to the political and social order. As author Garry Wills observed, public happiness is the test and justification of any government. If individual and community happiness is made difficult by constraints imposed or controlled by the State, then that State must be judged a failure.

We can discern the rough outlines of human fulfillment and happiness in the dynamic model outlined in Chapter Four, as well as the systemic sources of human misery, alienation and despair.

When we have a secure standing in a stable, trustworthy group, an internally coherent worldview that makes sense of our experience, meaningful ways to contribute, earn the essentials of life, renew a positive identity, and opportunities for movement, marriage, association and enterprise, then the foundations for happiness and fulfillment are in place.

Conversely, when we are denied any of these conditions, then disappointment, frustration and despair are the inevitable results. If a society excels in distributing social defeat but is parsimonious with positive social standing, then the majority of its citizens will be alienated, distressed, anxious, depressed and prone to drug abuse and despair.

We can also see why human happiness and fulfillment are relatively uncommon experiences: if any one of these conditions is denied, then fulfillment is thwarted. For example, if we have a way to earn a living, but no freedom of enterprise and limited access to potential mates, fulfillment is correspondingly restricted. If we have no trustworthy group, or no way to establish and renew a positive identity within the group, then the human spirit defaults to loneliness, depression and a negative self-identity.

In other words, we can also discern the sources of humanity's creativity and its capacity, perhaps even aptitude, for self-destruction. When we are denied a positive outlet for our innate hunger for expression, choice, renewal, meaning and identity, then we descend into the only available alternative, self-destruction or the destruction of others.

This understanding runs counter to the assumptions underpinning most developed world economies, where having an abundance of money ("prosperity and wealth") is seen as the one essential key to happiness and fulfillment.

No wonder so many of those who achieve this coveted state of financial abundance find instead dissatisfaction, depression, alienation and emptiness. The reason is simple: money can buy the essentials, and perhaps open wider opportunities for mating, but it does not provide an

internally coherent worldview, purpose, a trustworthy group or
meaningful ways to renew one's identity. It provides superficial
placeholders for these needs, but this substitution only creates an
equally hollow facsimile of fulfillment.

As an example, a recent sociological study compared wealthy Hong
Kong residents' sense of fulfillment and contentment with those of the
immigrant maids who served the moneyed Elites. The study found the
maids were much happier than their wealthy masters, who were often
suicidal and depressed. The maids, on the other hand, had a
trustworthy group—other maids they met on their one day off—and the
coherent internal structure of purpose provided by their support of
their families back home.

The "American Dream" (as well as the "Chinese Dream") presumes
the opposite would be true, and this explains why reaching monetary
abundance is not the promised fount of fulfillment: it fails to recognize
the other necessary conditions of human happiness and fulfillment. It is
a monoculture of the spirit, as brittle and prone to collapse as any other
monoculture.

Isn't an abundance of money the same as financial independence,
one of the goals of liberation? The confusion is natural in a financialized
system that values mobile capital as the ultimate form of wealth and
security. To explain the difference between an abundance of money
and independence, consider a household of modest needs that lives on
productive land it owns outright (debt-free) and that has invested
heavily in social capital and its community. It is financially independent
of global concentrations of capital and the Central State, though it
continues to depend on utilities and other necessities.

By contrast, the owner of a luxury condominium with an abundance
of money in financial assets may find that the money depreciates along
with the financialized State. If the elevators stop working because no
one will accept worthless currency in payment, then the vulnerability of
this "abundance" will be fully revealed.

Financial independence means liberation from debt and on
financialized debt-based payments from the Central State. Such
independence is less a function of great wealth and more a function of
self-reliance, resilience and the attainment of the other conditions of
fulfillment and happiness: work you care about, people you care about

and who care about you, opportunities to positively renew social identity, etc.

With this understanding, we can discern the qualities of societies and economies which promote fundamental human fulfillment and those that thwart it.

The ideal political/economic system enables the free and open exchange of goods and services, at values agreed upon by participants, and enables freedom of movement, enterprise, expression and association. It protects individuals, small groups and "the commons" shared by all from the predation and exploitation of larger, more aggressive groups, and punishes aggressors and transgressors by ostracism and by limiting their ability to wreak havoc on others.

A parasitical, exploitative political/economic system uses pervasive mass-media persuasion to wring asymmetric gains from participants via social control myths, manipulation of data, illusory choices and ever-expanding debt. This central management of public perception and use of "shadow" systems are the hallmarks of the modern Central State and its neofeudal aristocracies, oligarchies and theocracies.

A predatory tyranny wrings asymmetrical gains from participants by coercion, force and threats, and by severely restricting freedom of faith, movement, exchange, expression, enterprise and association. Theocratic tyrannies also restrict mating/marriage options via caste or other cultural constraints. All tyrannies limit social and economic mobility, either explicitly or implicitly.

Once we understand the mechanisms deployed by predatory political/economic systems, then we see what must be resisted: opacity, extreme concentrations of capital and political power, centrally directed propaganda and perception management, and all restrictions, political or cultural, on freedom of faith, movement, exchange, expression, enterprise and association. We also see what must be institutionalized and protected: transparency, limits on extreme concentrations of wealth and power, and decentralized means of persuasion.

One key way the current system protects itself from resistance is to convince participants that liberation is an apolitical, individual act of self-fulfillment that is entirely independent of the social/economic order. Blinded by the marketing/media machine, alienated individuals seeking self-fulfillment in the conventional Status Quo dutifully serve the interests of the Elites.

This is the triumph of delusional self-interest: that single-minded pursuit of self-interest magically aggregates into public happiness and a positive social order. In reality, the concept that happiness is achieved by the single-minded pursuit of self-interest leads not to a happy populace but to a distracted, alienated populace that is easily herded by Elites into obedient consumption and debt-serfdom.

As noted above, the essential transaction of debt-serfdom is the serf voluntarily exchanges his purchasing power and wealth for an illusory notion of self-interest that serves neither his own interests nor public happiness but mightily enriches and empowers the aristocratic Elites.

The Political Nature of Liberation

The purpose of understanding the social, political and economic foundations of liberation is to be prepared to establish a positive replacement when the current financialized order collapses. To do this, we must understand the causal connection between liberation and political order.

In our carefully cultivated atmosphere of apolitical individuality, it is absolute heresy to state that human fulfillment is ontologically, that is, intrinsically and necessarily, political. It is a core tenet of the Status Quo that individual fulfillment is apolitical as politics is public and fulfillment is private. This derealization of public happiness purposefully breaks the causal connection between individual alienation and the political order so the atomized individual doesn't connect his own distress and unhappiness with the sociopathologies of the consumerist-State social order.

Once this derealization is complete, the isolated "consumer" no longer looks at the social order as a potential contributor to his alienation but instead looks to religion, psychotherapy or medications as private, internal solutions to the sociopathology he inhabits.

This derealization is possible because the human condition is intrinsically insecure as we must dynamically juggle our internal purpose and meaning with our need for social affirmation and renewal of identity. Thus it is an easy "sell" to convince individuals that their unhappiness stems from their own personal failures rather than from an Elite-dominated sociopathological social order.

Once atomized, isolated individuals accept that their alienation and unhappiness are the sole result of their private circumstances, then the aristocracy can rest easy, knowing its *droit de seigneur* dominance will go unquestioned and unchallenged.

The key to understanding this dialectic of private and social distress is to recognize that individual identity and the social order are dynamic ecosystems in their own right, and each interacts with the other. Separating individual identity from the social order is akin to separating pollinating insects from flowering plants: each can be studied separately, but their symbiosis and interconnectedness is the key dynamic in the system.

Another way of describing this dynamic is to note that public happiness is not just the aggregation of individual happiness; it is a reflection of the social and political order's success in enabling what used to be called the common good, i.e. the common interest, one expression of which is the potential for individual fulfillment.

The spiritual and psychological traditions of religion and psychotherapy serve as coping mechanisms for individuals as they navigate the difficulties and challenges of human existence; intended to provide insight and solace for the voyage through life, these traditions were not designed, so to speak, to recognize or analyze pathological social and political orders. They are apolitical because they address problems from the point of view of faith and inner understanding.

All this is to say that the apolitical nature of spiritual and psychoanalytic traditions should not be viewed as a weakness, but rather as the difference between possessing sight in a narrow band of the electromagnetic spectrum and being able to see a broader spectrum.

Though it is not intended to do so, this blindness to the spiritual emptiness of the consumerist-State system and to the chronic psychological trauma of social defeat it generates directly aids the aristocracy. It does so in two ways: one by confirming the exceedingly convenient ethos that "it's all in your head" and "the system enables success, so any failure is your fault alone," and secondly by channeling alienation into a safely apolitical network of pressure relief valves: counseling, therapy, motivational speakers, and so on, all focused on "fixing" the flaws of individuals that are purportedly solely responsible for their social defeat.

When any of these systems does recognize the pathological, self-defeating nature of the Status Quo, then it is only to dismiss it with a resigned shrug: there is nothing we can do about the sociopathological system we inhabit, so fix what you do control, i.e. your own perspective.

This ignores the causal connection between political and financial orders and human fulfillment: if a system is sparing with social success and lavish in distributing social defeat, then the claim that "it's solely the individual's fault" is not just self-evidently false but a clever misdirection.

The ideal way to avoid skeptical inquiry is remain invisible, and the aristocracy benefits greatly from the invisibility of the causal connection between political and financial orders and a populace of alienated, isolated, distressed individuals.

That we have no field exclusively devoted to understanding sociopathologies is not surprising once we understand the politics of experience of those benefitting from their elevated status in the existing order. How many mortals would place their own status, prosperity and perquisites at risk by undermining the intellectual foundations of the Upper Caste to which they belong? History shows that among thousands of people with direct knowledge of sociopathologies that endanger the nation, it is rare that even a single individual has the courage to risk his/her status and wealth for the common good.

Social orders that excel in creating and distributing social defeat will necessarily be populated with unhappy, depressed, anxious and frustrated people. Social orders that generate positive social ecologies that support positive identities will be populated with secure individuals who contribute to the common interest as part of renewing their identity and seeking their own individual fulfillment.

Individual experiences do not arise in a vacuum; they arise from specific genetic propensities and families and from the institutions and worldview of specific financial and social orders. Once we understand this causal connection between social defeat and powerlessness and the

Status Quo, then the pathological nature of the consumerist-State plutocracy is revealed.

Once we understand this, then we also realize that every act and every internal intellectual construct is intrinsically political: it either enables or supports the Status Quo or it resists it.

This realization itself irrevocably undermines the Status Quo, as the key social control myth of the consumerist-State plutocracy is that individual's problems—debt-servitude, isolation, alienation, social defeat and failure—are either "all in your head" or "solely the result of your own weaknesses." But sociopathology exists in both the head of anyone who has internalized the social control myth and in the real world; the financialized, debt-dependent economy is not a figment of imagination that we can will away or transform with an attitude adjustment. Debt-serfdom is the dominant mode of the real world, as most households spend the majority of their productive effort servicing private debt and paying taxes that service public debt.

Social/financial/political orders that fail to support the common interest, including individual fulfillment, must be deemed failures. The financialized consumerist-State Status Quo has failed to support the common good, as its sole purpose and imperative is pursuit of self-interest at the expense of the common interest. Financialization is the penultimate iteration of the myopically self-serving culture of "hustle" that sees fraud, embezzlement, collusion, lying, despoliation of the landscape, debauchery of credit, bribery and corruption as acceptable tools to maximize personal profit, power and control, which can then be leveraged into further expanding wealth and power.

Once again we can profitably turn to the model of monoculture to understand why this obsessive pursuit of financial self-interest is intrinsically self-destructive, and why financialized systems are doomed to over-reach and collapse.

I know this description of the current social order's dynamic of distributing social defeat in the guise of self-interest is difficult to grasp for a number of reasons, most importantly that it is unfamiliar and runs heretically counter to the conventional American ethos that the single-minded pursuit of financial self-interest magically serves the common interest. An entire volume could be written and perhaps should be written to describe how financialization does not just undermine the economy; it undermines and pathologizes the political and social orders as well.

How do we design a political/economic order which enables and protects core freedoms and the common interest from intrinsically parasitic concentrations of power, persuasion and predation?

The first step is to realize that complex systems are generated by a small number of initial conditions and dynamics. Once we understand those conditions and dynamics, we can reset the initial state of the system.

Liberation Is a Coherently Planned Process

One of the most difficult aspects of liberation for those emerging from the shadows of pathological plutocracy to grasp is that the goal is not to reform the system or reach an inner state of perfect insight but a planned process of financial and intellectual liberation from the Status Quo's pathological social control myths and debt-serfdom.

In the conventional view of liberation, failure to reform a corrupt and oppressive regime is proof of powerlessness; that is, power is measured by the influence exerted on the power structure. In this view, power flows from every act of resistance, no matter how small or seemingly apolitical, and from the pursuit of coherently directed actions in the real, lived-in world and in our internalized understanding of the world.

This liberation via resistance can be expressed thusly:

"I no longer care if the power centers of our society—the distant, fortified castles of our financial feudal system—are changed by my actions, for I am liberated by the act of resistance. I am no longer complicit in perpetuating fraudulent feudalism and the pathology of concentrated power. I no longer covet signifiers of membership in the Upper Caste that serves the plutocracy. I am liberated from self-destructive consumerist-State financialization and the delusion that debt servitude and obedience to sociopathological Elites serve my self-interests."

What does this mean in real life? Refusing to consume a needless signifier of status is both a political and a financial act, for saving that money creates capital that can be invested in income streams that increase your household's income, resilience, independence and self-reliance. Refusing to expand debt removes the future interest payments from the wealth of concentrated capital; in refusing to give your money to financial Elites, you are no longer complicit in their purchase of political influence and power.

The immense sums that would have been diverted from your future income to interest payments can be conserved as capital to be invested in yourself and your own enterprises.

If a household consciously chooses to lower its income to live more simply and legally pay fewer taxes, then it is diminishing its support of the debt-dependent expansionist Central State and pathological consumerism.

In the mindset of the consumerist-State economy, purchasing something feels empowering because the act of consuming is experienced as renewing identity. But since that identity is ontologically inauthentic, the sense of euphoric renewal is short-lived, and soon defaults to the base state of insecurity and social defeat.

In the coherently directed actions of liberation, then every act of resistance also renews identity. Since the action is grounded in understanding rather than in social control myths, it is authentic and thus establishes and renews an authentic identity that resonates in ways that are far beyond the reach of consumption.

In the act of consuming, the only feature that continues on after the initial euphoria fades is the debt taken on to make the purchase. In the act of resistance, the action creates a power that is literally unknown to those still shackled in consumerism and dependence on the Central State.

Since the consumer is only empowered by buying and display of signifiers, the balance of their lives is experienced as powerless: that is, a chronic state of social defeat. The citizen is empowered by resistance, and since liberation is coherently directed actions, i.e. planned, then the resister's sense of liberation and power grow with each act of resistance.

Actions which are conventionally dismissed as apolitical are actually intensely political. The act of riding a bicycle is intrinsically political because it breaks the chain of private money flowing to those Elites that benefit from our dependence on fossil fuels and foreign entanglements based on securing fossil fuels.

As I noted in my book *Survival+* and on my weblog, oftwominds.com, a healthy homecooked meal is a revolutionary act on a number of fronts: by buying and/or growing real food and preparing it at home, the citizen is resisting the Status Quo marketing that encourages consumption of unhealthy packaged and fast food at a corporate-owned front that diverts money out of the community to distant concentrations of capital that deploy the stupendous profits to buy political power. This is either fascism (the corporation and State are one) or plutocracy (rule of the wealthy), and in either case risk or debt is transferred to the citizenry so gain, wealth and power can be concentrated in the hands of the few.

By preparing food at home, real-world, pragmatic skills are honed, and surplus is created that can be shared with extended family and friends. A meal taken together without the derangement of digital distraction is also a revolutionary act, as this breaks the chain of consumerist social control myths and disabling of coherent thought that arise from immersion in digital media.

Though you will never hear this truth acknowledged publicly, the "healthcare industries" profit greatly from the chronic ill-health of consumers, for managing chronic disease is immensely profitable just as selling junk food is immensely profitable. A healthy populace is dismally unprofitable, the equivalent (not coincidentally) of the low profitability of fresh produce. As a side-effect, ill-health makes people more dependent on the Central State and less likely to challenge the State.

This reality has been so effectively derealized that the conventional view will reject the truth that chronic ill-health arising from a sedentary media-centric lifestyle and unhealthy corporate food is incentivized in the Status Quo because it is highly profitable. Not coincidentally, chronic ill-health leads to dependence, resignation and weakness. A digitally deranged, malnourished and chronically ill populace poses little threat to the plutocratic Central State, and so in terms of maintaining power that is the ideal populace.

This is not to say that undermining the mental and physical health of the populace is an intentional goal, but the reality is the Status Quo profits from debt-serfdom and chronic ill-health, both of which are destructive to the citizenry. The self-interest of the corporate and State Elites does not magically benefit the non-Elites; rather, it sickens them and yokes them into servitude. Poor mental and physical health and debt-serfdom are not coincidental, but rather manifestations of the same forces.

These are a few examples of thousands of potential daily acts of liberation that are not only resistance; they are establishing and renewing an alternative identity that is no longer dependent on the Central State, consumerism or the social control myths of the marketing/media complex.

Stress and the Suppression of Self-Control, Planning and Resistance

As noted above, resistance and the establishment of a healthy identity are two sides of the same coin: the pursuit of coherently directed actions in the lived-in world and in our internalized understanding of the world.

Individuals reflect the social order and public good of the societies they inhabit. As noted above, social orders that excel in creating social defeat will necessarily be populated with unhappy and anxious people. Social orders that generate positive social ecologies that support positive identities will be populated with secure individuals who contribute to the common interest as an integral part of their own individual fulfillment. They have no desire to pursue fraud, looting, exploitation and predation, all of which they correctly identify as evil.

The physiology of stress illuminates many of the dynamics we see manifesting in the poor mental and physical health of the American populace and in the passivity we see in the political and financial realms.

Research has found that every-day stress can close down our rational "command center" that normally keeps subconscious primal impulses of aggression, hunger, sexual drive, etc. sublimated to the tasks at hand. The neural circuitry of our "command center" (located in the neocortex) suppresses these impulses in order to concentrate our attention on consciously organized activity.

When stress disrupts the default hierarchy of the brain, primal impulses are unleashed as our higher mental functions of self-control become paralyzed. Not only do we experience disorientation and "brain freeze," but potentially destructive impulses that were safely held in check escape our conscious control and we become capable of actions that we would never allow ourselves in less stressful circumstances. Once our "command center" loses control, we are prone to harmful behavior that we later regret.

This shutting down of conscious control to unleash primal instinct explains the highly charged "fight or flight" response we feel when suddenly confronted with potential danger, and the value of this reaction in a hunter-gatherer environment is clear. More importantly, it illuminates how we lose the ability to analyze circumstances rationally when we are "stressed out." Once our rational analytic abilities are shut down, we are prone to making a series of ill-informed and rash decisions.

This has the potential to create a destructive positive feedback loop: as we become more stressed, our rational decision-making and self-control both rapidly degrade. This degradation leads to impulsive actions that generate negative results that increase our stress, further degrading our already-impaired rational processes. This feedback loop quickly leads to "losing it completely," i.e. complete breakdown.

If we consider human development over the past 20,000 years of transition from hunter-gatherer groups to modern life, it seems self-evident that stress was likely to be resolved relatively quickly in the hunter-gatherer lifestyle. In terms of human conflict, everyone was known to everyone else in the small nomadic groups, and conflicts had to be resolved quickly simply because the group survival depended on a peaceful and prompt resolution. Most external threats could be fended off with vigilance and an organized defense or left behind by a few hours of fast walking.

Contrast the hunter-gatherer environment where our stress-self-control feedback offered selective advantages with the modern urban life and work environment, where stress is more or less constant and our ability to resolve stressful situations is often limited.

This helps explain the increasing prevalence of people "losing it" in public when they encounter everyday frustrations: their self-control has been ground down by stress, exposing their raw primal impulses. Many of the clinical features of post-traumatic stress disorder (PTSD) are increasingly visible in everyday American life, and an understanding of how chronic stress erodes rational analysis and self-control helps explain the spectrum of responses to stress.

We intuitively understand how short-term stress triggers "fight or flight" alertness and we have all experienced how high levels of stress make it difficult to concentrate. But long-term, unrelieved stress creates a host of other disorders, some of which have been grouped into post-traumatic stress disorder but others of which have yet to be fully explored or understood.

There is a growing body of evidence that chronic, unremitting stress has a number of subtle and destructive consequences to both mental and physical health. In addition to the common-sense connection between chronic stress and hypertension, evidence is mounting that obesity and other so-called "lifestyle" diseases are causally linked to stress-related conditions such as inadequate sleep and chronic inflammation.

Western medicine traditionally divides physical and mental health, but it is self-evident (as Eastern traditions have long held) that the mind and body are one. The physical consequences of mental stress make this abundantly clear, as the powerful hormones that we experience as "mental stress" erode the immune system's responsiveness.

Behaviorally, stress fuels addictive disorders by breaking down the self-control that inhibits destructive bingeing, impulse buying, unsafe sex and drug/alcohol abuse.

Though few are ready to declare it supported by clinical studies, it seems self-evident that chronic low-grade stress significantly degrades our ability to rationally analyze situations and perseveringly pursue long-range plans. This stands to reason, for if stress shuts down self-control and the ability to concentrate in the short-term, then chronic stress must similarly suppress rational analysis and coherent, self-directed planning.

The consequences of chronic stress are multiplied by our reliance (or perhaps more accurately, our addiction) to digital media and communication, what I have characterized as digital distraction. Clinically, these manifestations have recently been termed Attention

Deficit Trait or ADT, a broader, more inclusive term than the more
familiar Attention Deficit Disorder.

ADT manifests as distractibility, inner frenzy, impatience and
difficulty in setting priorities, time management and making informed
decisions. As the positive feedback loop described earlier takes hold,
previously competent people become harried underachievers who
berate themselves for their inexplicable loss of competence.

ADT, unlike post-traumatic stress disorders triggered by a single
event, arise not from a single crisis but from a chain of events that in
less stressful times would be considered "a bad week" but in chronic
stress are experienced as an unending series of emergencies. The
response—to try harder to keep up and successfully manage the
crises—only increases the stress load and sense of failure as the ability
to rationally analyze and pursue plans degrades with each perceived
emergency. Making matters worse, the conventional American
"solution" to being overwhelmed is to avoid expressing these difficulties
lest this be interpreted as complaining or an equivalent personal failure.

This is the consequence of pathological chronic stress being
derealized and normalized: an accurate description of the condition is
dismissed as whining and the truth-teller is instructed to "buck up,"
keep his head down and his nose to the grindstone.

These mechanisms help explain why people who experience chronic
stress are prone to acting erratically and impulsively, and why they find
it so difficult to stick with a coherent plan of action. With the rational
mind and self-control centers permanently suppressed, we are prone to
"zombie-like" passivity, in effect "sleepwalking" though life. This
dynamic may help explain Americans' remarkable political passivity as
their civil liberties are curtailed and their financial insecurity increases.

If we step out of the derealized, delusional mindset promoted by
the Central State and the marketing/media machine, we can see that
the sociopathological nature of the Status Quo—the ontological
insecurity and social defeat fostered by consumerism, the financial
feudalism enforced by the Central State and the extreme concentrations
of wealth and political power amassed by the plutocracy—are all
sources of chronic stress that cannot be resolved with psychotherapy,
motivational speakers or spiritual insight. These are real dynamics in
the real world, and we experience them as chronic stress that erodes

our ability to analyze these very dynamics and understand the sociopathological system we inhabit that serves the self-interests of the few to the detriment of the many.

The stresses created by these financial and political pathologies are not abstract; rather, they lead to the self-destructive behaviors that are now ubiquitous in America: impulsiveness, addiction, abuse of drugs and alcohol (often attempts to self-medicate stress and social defeat), obesity, impoverished sense of self, low level of fitness and vitality, inability to concentrate or complete coherently organized tasks (ADT), high levels of distraction and passivity and a loss of resilience and self-reliance.

This is not to say that all disorders arise solely from social and political orders; a percentage of the human population is genetically vulnerable to mental disorders, and life itself is filled with challenges and unwelcome surprises that create stress. The question being explored here is: since it is self-evident that the financial, social and political order we inhabit influences our mental and physical well-being, what are the long-term consequences to individuals living in a sociopathological system of financial feudalism and aristocracy, an autocratic, predatory expansive Central State that enforces extremes of wealth and power and an unparalleled corporate marketing/media propaganda machine?

Anyone who claims these pathological monocultures have negligible effect on individuals' well-being is either fixed in derealized denial or is a well-paid shill for the Status Quo.

The net effect of chronic stress and ADT is the ability to implement long-term, coherently organized positive plans—all attributes of liberation—is severely impaired. This explains why liberation is so difficult to understand and why it is even more difficult to sustainably pursue in a pathological system designed, as it were, to disrupt our capacity for rational analysis, self-control and coherent, self-directed action.

We have four ways to counter the destructive consequences of this sociopathologically generated stress:

1) Develop positive physical and mental responses to stress via discipline and practice (for example, yoga, martial arts, meditation/prayer, walking, bicycling, etc.)

2) Withdraw from sociopathological systems and influences such as the mainstream media

3) Pursue a healthy, non-pathological "reset" system to replace the current Status Quo when it implodes in financial insolvency and political instability

4) Remain focused on coherently organized plans of resistance and liberation. The simpler and more positive the plan, the more likely it is we can stay focused on it in increasingly stressful circumstances.

As I stated in the introduction, revolution begins in your internal understanding and reaches fruition in your coherently directed actions in the lived-in world. What is the basis of our coherently directed actions? Simply stated, any coherent plan aims to introduce and conserve the forces of low-intensity instability (LII) into one's life, household, community and nation. These forces of adaptability (innovation, experimentation, competition, transparency, dissent, feedback, variation, volatility, meritocracy, accountability, consequence, risk, failure, accurate communication of facts and the free exchange of information) are scale-invariant, meaning that they create resilience and stability in individuals, households, communities, enterprises and nations.

Forces that limit or suppress adaptability—concentrations of wealth and power and monocultures—create brittleness that lead to inevitable collapse via the supernova or the stick/slip model. In either case, the rising systemic instability is well-masked by illusory "guarantees" and facades of stability and power.

We have seen that liberation is not a goal that must be reached but a process that establishes and sustains a new identity and sense of self-purpose and worth. Author David Pink (among others) identified these three traits as our core motivators: autonomy, mastery, and purpose.

Autonomy is the opposite of dependence on the Central State and financialization.

Mastery is the acquisition of useful skills and the replacement of an insecure consumerist identity with a productive, self-reliant secure identity that holds a valued place in the household and community.

Our purpose is to leave dependence, insecurity and social defeat behind and find liberation through autonomy from the expansive Central State and the financialized feudalism it enforces. Breaking the chains of consumerism, debt-serfdom, the authoritarian Central State and its financial tyranny is liberation, but to the forces attempting to impose the Status Quo this autonomy is viewed as resistance.

Liberation and resistance are two sides of the same coin. The process of liberation is also the process of resisting tyranny, dependence, ill-health, chronic stress and State/media propaganda. Resistance is voluntary and legal. It oppresses no one and suppresses no facts or information. It is the process of liberty, adaptability, stability, autonomy, transparency, enterprise, health, self-expression, fulfillment and decentralization.

Chapter Nine: The Meaning and Purpose of Resistance

Before we proceed with the practicalities of resistance, it would be beneficial to catch our breath, so to speak, and briefly review the core narrative of this book.

The impending implosion of the financial Status Quo and the Central State is the causal consequence of the system's initial conditions and ontological imperatives. As noted, the ontological imperative of both finance capital and the State is expansion of control and reach. In the financial realm, this manifests as financialization of the global economy and an expansionist, authoritarian Savior State increasingly dependent on debt and leverage for its survival.

The 19th century industrial and financial revolutions seemed to prove that ever-increasing centralization—of State control and concentrations of capital—was the key driver of expanding prosperity and stability.

But like all systems, centralization follows an S-curve. Centralization reached its apogee of utility decades ago, and has now entered its decline phase where increasing centralization—central banks, central states, central planning, global banking—no longer pays dividends but actively destabilizes the systems it seeks to control.

We have been trained by the enormous success of the centralization model to see top-down centralized "solutions" as the only possible response to the system's rising instability. Ironically, in seeking centralized answers we only increase systemic instability.

Centralization's analog in Nature is monoculture. Monocultures are intrinsically brittle, slow to adapt and vulnerable to sudden instability/collapse. By eliminating the low-intensity instability of diversity and decentralization, monocultures lack the very forces that create long-term stability.

For example, consider the consequences of our centrally-managed Status Quo's fiscal and monetary contradictions. To hold its ground as the over-indebted economy contracts, the Central State must borrow roughly 10% of the nation's entire output (GDP) every year (currently $1.5 trillion). As the real economy shrinks and tax revenues decline, this gargantuan State borrowing will only increase. If it stops borrowing this vast sum, then the Savior State will be unable to service its exploding debt and meet its obligations to its 100 million dependents (57 million recipients of Social Security, 46 million recipients of food stamps, etc.).

But if it continues to borrow these vast sums, then eventually the cost of servicing of all this debt (interest payments) crowds out other spending, and the profound political disunity described earlier reaches criticality. The third option is for the State or its proxy central bank, the Federal Reserve, to "print money" to meet its obligations, which are now so monumental that such an expansion of the money supply would depreciate the money to near-worthlessness (i.e. hyper-inflation). This destruction of the currency and financial wealth via inflation will also cause the Status Quo to collapse.

Thus there is no sustainable path for the expansive Savior State: if it keeps borrowing on such a monumental scale, the debt service will eventually destabilize the financial and political orders. If the State stops borrowing these astounding sums, then it will be unable to meet its obligations to its 100 million dependents and its parasitic financial aristocracy, and that will trigger the same destabilization. If it expands the money supply to meet its obligations, then the nation's currency will be depreciated to near-zero and the Status Quo will be destabilized.

Regardless of what path the State and central bank take to "save the Status Quo," they will end up destroying the very system they are attempting to save. The reason is that increasing centralization of wealth and power and the suppression of low-intensity instability as a "threat" doom any system to collapse. If you remove the forces of stability as a "threat to the Status Quo," then the only forces left are those of instability: increasing centralization ruled by concentrations of wealth and power.

Those without a systemic understanding miss the key elements of this inevitability; no system can be "reformed" if its initial conditions and core dynamics remain unchanged.

The only way to change a system is to change the initial conditions and the core dynamics.

This truth has a number of important consequences.

One is that nothing can stop the systemic destabilization of the expansive Savior State and its partner in oppression, the financial plutocracy. We can believe in an eternal State, we can mourn its coming collapse, we can be angry about it, we can feel betrayed, we can be afraid—none of these emotional responses will alter the destabilization of the expansive State. We might as well spend our last hours on the deck of *Titanic* raging against the iceberg.

We have some basic choices. We can live in denial until it's too late to modify our circumstances, that is, cling to the warm interior of the *Titanic* as its bow sinks ever lower into the icy Atlantic. This is the passive complicity the State has reinforced (i.e. selected for) with its displacement of community and self-reliance via its relentless expansion of control and dependency.

We can recognize the unsustainability of the State and its financial tyranny, but do nothing because "the banks are too powerful" and our actions inconsequential.

This too is passive complicity, and it is precisely the surrender the State and financial tyranny desire as it lowers the risk and cost of maintaining their domination.

Or we can choose to pursue a goal of radically re-ordering the political order and eliminating the tyranny of debt and financialization by promoting a new set of initial conditions and system dynamics, what I term a system reset.

This requires that we choose a life of resistance and liberation rather than docilely accept complicity in a pathologically parasitic and ultimately evil financial tyranny enabled and imposed by the Expansionist State.

Many citizens declare their belief that the financial Elites are "too powerful" to ever be taken down. This belief ignores the fact that the financial aristocracy, being entirely dependent on the State for their protection from competition, risk and transparency, will collapse along with the State they control.

The view that "there's nothing I can do against such powerful forces" completely misunderstands the meaning and purpose of resistance, and the intrinsically political nature of apparently apolitical actions.

Just as interactions between the fundamental particles of Nature express several forces at all times (strong and weak force, electromagnetic force and gravitation) so every action has a political aspect, whether we intend it or not and regardless of whether we sense it or not. Though the forces of gravitation are too weak to detect between everyday objects, gravitation has limitless reach. In a similar fashion, individual acts that appear powerless are in aggregate extremely powerful, and exert their force regardless of distance.

For example, every dollar you spend is a "vote" for or against the forces of financial tyranny and the debt-serfdom of isolated, alienated, insecure, atomized consumerism. Every step you take toward arrangements that are resiliently diverse and decentralized and not dependent on the State's funding is a "vote" for a new set of initial conditions and dynamics. Every effort to liquidate debt and move away from a pathological, soulless consumerist definition of identity and self-worth is a decisive rejection of debt-serfdom and the tyranny of social defeat.

Once a revolutionary understanding is reached, then the value of resistance is not measured by its results in the external world, but by the power it releases within the individual who is freed from passivity and complicity. Each act of resistance is a renewal of an autonomous identity that is independent of the financial aristocracy, the State and their financial tyranny. This establishment of an authentic, community-based identity based on independence from debt-serfdom and State dependency is a revolutionary act that liberates the citizen from the tyranny of social defeat.

Once a citizen embraces a life of resistance and liberation that renews his/her internal and external independence from the pathological Status Quo, then he/she is already free. To discount this embrace of resistance and liberation because it doesn't directly bring down the financial tyranny is to completely misunderstand the nature of liberation and the dependence of that financial tyranny on our passive participation.

There are two aspects to this liberation. If one is free of debt and thus debt servitude, then one is no longer beholden to the forces of financial tyranny. If one renews one's sense of self from non-consumerist sources, then one is free from the media/marketing complex and the insecurity of consumerism. If one no longer depends on the State for sustenance, then one is free of the State.

The citizen who is no longer dependent or in debt servitude is already free; he needs nothing from the financial tyranny or the State, and he no longer cares if they are "reformed" or not.

The most profound leadership is by example, and so those who free themselves of debt-servitude, complicity, dependence and consumerism will influence those wishing to be free. The authentic will always wield a power that the inauthentic cannot imagine.

In terms of the Pareto Distribution, once 4% of the citizenry refuse to participate in consumerist debt-serfdom and State-imposed financial tyranny, then their actions and understanding will exert outsized influence on the 64% who are as yet obediently complicit.

The act of resistance need not have any visible effect at all; the internal consequence is profound and revolutionary. Once resistance and liberation have been embraced, then the financial tyranny has already lost its power to exploit and control. Once resistance and liberation have been embraced, every act is an explicitly political act of resistance against this tyranny.

In our discussion of initial conditions in Chapter Four, we described the essential nature of a coherent belief system that "makes sense of the world" and also makes sense of the individual's place in that world.

Consumerism and the State are both monocultures which actively seek to reduce the ecosystem to a single relationship: isolated citizens in thrall to the State, and isolated consumers in thrall to distant concentrations of corporate capital and the media/marketing complex it controls.

The relationship of the consumer to capital and the dependent to the State are both hollow, inauthentic, artificial; neither can possibly nurture nor renew an authentic self and identity, or establish a coherent internal world of meaning. Acceptance of an authoritarian expansionist State and debt-based consumerism yields an extreme of pathological inner poverty; diversity is replaced by monoculture, and the shriveled self is vulnerable to disorientation, derangement and ill-health.

One of the key dynamics in this inner poverty is the reduction of individual actions to apolitical powerlessness, when in reality every act is deeply and intrinsically political and thus powerful.

This realization is a key feature of revolutionary understanding: what we are told is meaningless and apolitical is in reality deeply political and powerful, not in terms of its immediate impact on centralized power but in forging our own identity, autonomy and purpose.

To repeat the basic credo of liberation:

"I no longer care if the power centers of our society—the distant, fortified castles of our financial feudal system—are changed by my actions, for I am liberated by the act of resistance. I am no longer complicit in perpetuating fraudulent feudalism and the pathology of concentrated power. I no longer covet signifiers of membership in the Upper Caste that serves the plutocracy. I am liberated from self-destructive consumerist-State financialization and the delusion that debt servitude and obedience to sociopathological Elites serve my self-interests."

As an example, nothing is more apolitical than food, according to the Status Quo. Yet this is entirely backward; nothing is more political than food, for it either sustains us and our freedom or it indentures us to disease and dependence on the Savior State's immensely profitable sickcare system, i.e. the abomination known as "healthcare" that profits from chronic disease, not health.

From the Status Quo perspective, the citizen who bicycles to work is either a "health nut" or some outlier who perversely refuses the obvious convenience and comfort of the auto. From the point of view of one who has experienced an inner revolution of understanding, then the simple machinery of the bicycle has freed the citizen from dependence on the oil complex and its enforcer, the State, and also from the sickcare system and its enforcer, the State.

In the consumerist mindset, riding a bicycle to work is an apolitical "personal choice" that is meaningless on the larger stage. To the citizen with a revolutionary understanding, every bicycle ride is an overtly political act of resistance against the concentrations of capital that maintain their power over the State via dependence on oil, auto-centricity, and sickcare.

To the unaware citizen burdened with multiple chronic diseases brought on by a corporate-supplied diet of packaged food and fast food and a sedentary life based on the worship of "convenience," then buying frozen pizza and fast-food are apolitical, "personal choice" actions. To the citizen with a revolutionary understanding, then these are the actions of the indentured, and the refusal to consume packaged "food" that no caring consumer would feed their dog lest it sicken and die is a deeply and overtly political act of resistance.

There are no apolitical "personal choice" acts; there are only profoundly political acts of resistance or complicity.

How can an act be apolitical to one person and deeply political to another? How we view an act depends on our inner account of how the world works and our place in it. If we watch a person perform a ritual in a religion unknown to us, the physical actions may seem meaningless to us, even as they are profoundly meaningful to the believer performing the ritual.

The consumerist mindset sees individual acts as meaningless except as "personal choices" in the marketplace of objects, beliefs and ideas. Objects and acts have meaning only as identifiers of status. Stripped of political import, every transaction is reduced to a "purchase" between a seller and an individual consumer. Thus we "buy into" a belief or intellectual framework; even our beliefs become transactions of "consumption."

The key dynamic in the reduction of active, engaged citizens to passive consumers is the acceptance of apolitical powerlessness, that is, the belief that the individual is powerless against the forces of the Central State and financial power centers. Nothing could be further from the truth: each individual has the power to change the world by changing their understanding of the power structures that dominate the political economy and by withdrawing their support of financialized feudalism.

It is instructive to follow the money stream created when a consumer buys an electronic gadget for $100 on credit. The manufacture of the gadget might cost $30, the distant concentration of capital (the corporation that markets the device) maintains gross margins of between 30% and 40%, and the wholesale and retail channels might receive 30% of the final sale price.

Since Asian subcontractors work on slim profit margins of around 3%, then only $1 of the $30 cost goes to the manufacturer as profit. Most of the input costs are capital (fabrication equipment), energy and materials, so the workers in the factory receive a tiny slice of the manufacturing expense. Many U.S.-based global corporations actually own their factories in China, so even the paltry profit from manufacturing the device flows to corporate headquarters.

If the consumer bought the item in a "bricks and mortar" retailer, a razor-thin percentage of the total cost flows to the retail workers, and a modest sum goes to local financial Elites or real estate corporations who own the land and building.

Corporate profits are about 10% of the entire gross national product, so at least $10 of the $100 is net profit to the corporation that produces and markets the gadget. Another 20% to 30% so flows to corporate headquarters for overhead, interest on debt, etc. and a tiny percentage ends up in the consumer's own community as wages and transaction taxes that go to the local government. Most of the major expenses such as rent are simply transfers from one concentration of capital to another, and essentially none ends up in the local community.

The truly phenomenal profits, however, are earned by the bank issuing the credit card. At the point of purchase, the bank skims a $3 fee—roughly equal to the entire wages and profits earned by the manufacturer. If the consumer pays down the purchase over time, then the bank stands to earn as much as $50 or even the entire purchase price of $100 in interest. Since electronic transaction costs are low, the primary expense the bank incurs is loss write-downs in their portfolio as some percentage of debt-serfs default on their credit card debt.

Even after these expenses, the bank has earned far more from the initial $100 purchase than everyone else in the supply chain put together. The workers who fabricated the gadget earned $1, the manufacturing subcontractor earned $1, the retail clerks earned $1, the corporations that marketed the gadget earned $10, and the bank earned $40 or more.

This example illustrates the immense profitability of credit and consumerism. The terrible irony is that the consumer who pays the bank $50 in interest to own a $100 device is enabling his own servitude, not just financially as a debt-serf, but politically, as the banks need only spend a thin slice of their immense profits to buy political power via campaign contributions and lobbying.

This same preponderance of profit and power characterizes the entire financialized economy: the home "owner" pays roughly double the purchase price of the home in interest alone, a profit that dwarfs every other financial aspect of home ownership.

The "consumer" loses thrice: his own limited surplus income is diverted to the banks and distant concentrations of capital, his own community receives a trivial share of the purchase, and the banks which reap low-cost windfall profits from the use of State-backed credit then buy control of the machinery of governance.

In return, the consumer indentures himself to the bank which issued the credit, all in exchange for a temporal status provided by the gadget—a renewal that fades far faster than the debt taken on to buy the device.

If we understand this dynamic between credit, consumerism and an immensely profitable banking aristocracy that dominates the economy and State, then we understand the futility of "reforming" the economy and State with additional regulations. The only way to change the dynamic is to stop diverting income to debt service, that is, stop using credit for consumption.

Any "reform" will be quickly bypassed or watered down by bank lobbyists and politicians who are controlled by the financial plutocracy. The only action that will have any real consequence is millions of passive consumers restoring their identity as citizens and producers by renouncing debt and debt-serfdom.

If every household in America refused to use credit cards and either paid off or renounced all household debt (mortgages, student loans, etc.), and refused to take on any debt thenceforth, the banking cartel would starve to extinction. With no cash flow and no profits, the banking cartel's grasp on political power would soon evaporate.

The same can be said of the packaged food cartel, the fast-food cartel and the sickcare cartels: our individual participation and passive acceptance of debt-serfdom, digital distraction and consumerism gives these cartels their political power. If we remove our participation, we liberate ourselves from both the cartels' grasp and their political power.

The State cannot force us to take on debt; we indenture ourselves of our own will. The State cannot force us to consume unhealthy food that sickens us; we do so of our own free will. The State cannot force us to remain sedentary; we do so of our own free will. The State cannot force us to earn an income high enough that roughly half flows to the State as taxes; we could choose to earn considerably less and devote a smaller share of our labor to the Expansive State.

If we understand this systemically, we must conclude that the supposed powerlessness of the individual is pure propaganda. Were households to resist debt-serfdom by renouncing debt and consumerism, the banking cartel and the State would both lose power and leverage over the citizenry.

If households resisted the subtle servitude of chronic ill-health by renouncing packaged and fast-food and sedentary "consumption" of corporate media, the food, sickcare and media cartels would cease to be so profitable and would lose their political leverage over the State.

If households and enterprises freed themselves from financial dependence on the State, they would cease looking to the authoritarian expansive State for "answers," and the State's impending financial destabilization would have less impact on their well-being and security.

In demanding the State "reform" to the point that our dependence on it will remain low-risk is to grant the State all the power. The only way to liberate ourselves from State domination is to no longer rely on the State acting in one way or another; other than in very limited and specific conditions such as national defense (not Empire) and the protection of our environmental commons, the State ceases to be relevant.

Thus if the State goes through the "management perception" charade of "regulating" the banking cartel, we no longer care; we owe the banking cartel nothing and they have no power over us.

If the State trims entitlements or modifies the parameters of corporate welfare, if we have renounced dependence on the State then we no longer care whose stake is expanded or trimmed.

If we have cut the cost-basis of our household to the point that we can live securely on a modest income, then the State's "tax the rich" response to dwindling tax revenues will not impair our well-being.

Once we renounce debt, consumerism, financialization and dependence on the Expansive State, then we no longer need the State or any other entity to grant us liberation—we have liberated ourselves. We no longer need a particular government policy to be adopted or adapted; we have liberated ourselves from all State control except in matters of infrastructure, public health, law enforcement and conscription to fight the State's overseas wars.

Since liberation does not require the breaking of any laws, the State has no leverage over the liberated under the rule of law; it must completely renounce the rule of law to oppress the law-abiding.

In surveying the basic forms of resistance available to us, we must also keep in mind that resistance serves not just to undermine financial tyranny, but to establish the system that will eventually replace the current tyranny. The "reset" State must have a very different imperative than the current one, which is to expand until it controls every niche of the national ecosystem so it can protect monopoly, plutocracy, corruption and financial tyranny.

The Reset State has a much different internal imperative than the expansive State: to protect the citizenry and the nation's commons from the predation and exploitation of financial tyranny, criminals, concentrations of wealth and political power—and the Central State itself. Citizens will then be free to make their own arrangements in their own communities and enterprises.

The Many Pathways of Destabilization

The dissolution of empires from excessive indebtedness and the depreciation of currency are common occurrences in history; what is unsustainable destabilizes and collapses. Though we know the financialized economy and State are unsustainable, we cannot know when the supernova will implode or the system will destabilize. The façade of stability may stand for years before suddenly crumbling.

We also cannot know what new arrangement will restabilize the system after the current Status Quo fails. Some observers suggest that the dissolution of the Soviet Union offers a useful example, while others point to the Roman Empire as an insightful model of devolution. Financialization and centralization have reached new heights in 21st century America, and though we know the unsustainable will destabilize, we don't know precisely how the events will unfold or how the citizenry will respond.

I have chosen not to discuss resource S-curves (fossil fuel, fresh water, uranium, soil, etc.) that have been cogently described as "peak everything," as it is tangential to the narrative here. Many people have difficulty accepting that the truly critical resources are tracing S-curves that have plateaued or begun their decline into depletion regardless of what new troves are discovered or tapped. Where we are on the S-curve can be endlessly debated, but the point is that geopolitical issues can turn nominal abundance into scarcity with remarkable alacrity.

The intersection of these narratives is that consumerism is fundamentally based on cheap abundant energy—to mine, refine, manufacture and ship goods around the globe. If either energy or trade flows were seriously disrupted, that has the potential to trigger the destabilization of the financialized debt-leverage sand castle.

There are many other potential triggers of destabilization, for example, the global Internet being taken down or disrupted. The financialized, over-indebted sand castle does not need much disruption to collapse in a heap, as a key feature of highly centralized monocultures is their lack of resiliency and vulnerability to cascades of instability.

The brittleness and fragility of the pathological, financialized Status Quo is not only a key reason it is unsustainable, it is an imperative that the "re-set" economy and State must avoid by embracing decentralization and the forces of low-intensity instability (LII)—everything that is being suppressed by the Status Quo as a "threat" to their expansion and control.

Hubris itself is fully capable of destabilizing a brittle system.

The point here is that though we cannot know the precise timing or pathway of destabilization, diversifying and decentralizing our income and social capital and embracing the forces of low-intensity instability (LII) will provide individuals, households and communities the resilience, stability and adaptability that the centralized, financialized Status Quo lacks.

The Spectrum of Freedom/Resistance

I anticipate many people stating that it is "impossible" to live without ever-expanding debt in America, that without debt it is "impossible" to own a house, obtain a university education, and so on. What they actually mean is that it is inconvenient to buy a house or obtain an education without credit, but it is far from impossible. As noted in Chapter Five, the majority of housing and education expenditure is actually non-essential consumption and thus is not an investment.

This purported impossibility of living a life of prosperity and well-being without expansive debt is terribly ironic, for it is precisely the dependence on expansive debt that leads to the debt-servitude that precludes both prosperity and well-being.

The inability to see a debt-free life as an option is both a failure of imagination and a lack of familiarity with the many possibilities of radically reducing dependence on debt for consumption and identity. As previous noted, going into debt to fund consumption is experienced as a windfall, as the costs are shunted into the distant future while the gain is enjoyed in the present.

Thus expanding debt is the essence of convenience: consumption can proceed immediately while the costs are safely pushed into the future. Only the future arrives with the first billing of interest, and what has been traded away for instant gratification turns out to be freedom from financial tyranny.

This is similar to the confusion between shopping and consumerism that I explicated in Chapter Five.
Basing one's identity on consumption creates an inauthentic and fragile sense of self that is vulnerable to social defeat, and sacrificing capital accumulation (savings) to fund debt-based consumption leads to lifelong servitude. That is the essence of consumerism.

Browsing the bazaar for fun without buying anything is simple entertainment; impulsively buying things on credit that you can easily live without is consumerism. Saving up cash to replace an essential item is pragmatic replacement; foregoing saving to buy status-enhancing identifiers with debt is consumerism.

Consumerism destroys the freedoms offered by zero debt and having capital to invest in oneself and one's enterprises and indentures the consumer to a pathological insecurity.

If a person bases 1% of their identity on status identifiers—their address, the brand of auto they drive, the brand of shoes they wear, etc.—and 99% of their identity on pursuing their own enterprises and sharing home-made meals with friends every week, then the attraction of consumerist debt servitude will be near-zero. Which is more likely to lead to health and prosperity, this arrangement or consumerist debt-servitude?

There are no absolutes in this spectrum, for the flexibility, diversity and adaptability created by the forces of low-intensity instability are the very essence of liberation and resistance.

We can think of liberation and resistance as a sliding scale of trade-offs and sacrifices. Securing freedom from financial tyranny can take many forms, most of which are small steps taken daily, weekly and monthly.

The essence of saving (capital accumulation) and financial security is an understanding of the future gain secured by sacrifice and the risk posed by debt-servitude. As previously noted, the ability to make and follow coherent long-range plans is the essence of liberation.

For example, we have been conditioned to believe that a 30-year mortgage is the foundation of home ownership. In many countries, mortgages are offered for 5 or at most 10 years. This was the norm in the U.S. in the early 20th century. The debtor is expected to make whatever trade-offs and sacrifices are necessary to pay the mortgage off in a few years. Many immigrants to the U.S. obtain a mortgage but pay it off in a few years by sacrificing consumption and pooling household incomes.

If buying or building a home that is not merely a form of consumption requires some debt, then the debt could be sized to what can be paid off in full within five years. Ideally, the property has the potential to create an income stream that diversifies the household income, for diversity offers stability and resilience.

If a field of study offers some pragmatic return, then the pursuit of that field in the workplace can be pursued in parallel with a university diploma, and the income from work can pay for most or all of the costs of education. This is widely considered "impossible" but once again impossibility is being confused with inconvenience or difficulty. This option was recently described by author Zac Bissonnette in the book "Debt-Free U: How I Paid for an Outstanding College Education without Loans, Scholarships, or Mooching off My Parents."

Diversifying risk and income is the foundation of sustainable financial security and well-being. As previously noted, financial independence from the Central State and the financialization aristocracy is a form of hedging against the destabilization of the State and the financial system it enforces. The key building blocks of resilience, self-reliance, independence and security are decentralization and the many forces of low-intensity instability. Embracing these forces is the foundation of resistance and liberation from financial servitude.

Principle Pathways of Resistance

Though these are self-evident by now, at the risk of redundancy here are the principle pathways of resistance.

1. Support the decentralized, non-market economy. The core ideology of consumerism and financialization is that non-market assets and experiences have no status or financial value. This includes social capital, meals with friends, projects done cooperatively with friends, home gardens and thousands of other decentralized activities that cannot be financialized into centralized market transactions. Identity and social status are established in the non-market economy by collaboration, sharing, conviviality and generosity.

Decentralized generally means localized; farmers markets are examples of local market economies where the transactions are in cash (so banks can't skim transactions fees) and the money stays in the local economy rather than flowing to some distant concentration of capital.

If you start valuing non-market assets and experiences as the most important markers of high status, you are resisting both financialization and consumerism.

Top-down centralized "solutions" imposed by the Central State are the problem, not the solution, as they further the concentration of wealth and power into unstable monocultures. Stop looking to overly complex "reforms" and centralized solutions to unsustainable systems and start exploring decentralized, localized solutions that bypass both the Central State and its financial aristocracy.

2. Stop participating in financialization. Financialization is the insidious imperative of the financial aristocracy that seeks to turn every interaction into a financial transaction that can be charged a fee and all assets into financialized instruments that can be sold for immensely profitable transaction fees.

As the finances of local governments implode under the weight of their protected fiefdoms, many are heeding the siren song of financialization as a temporary (and inevitably disastrous) "fix" to their structural insolvency. For example, the revenue stream from parking meters is financialized into an asset that is sold to a private corporation. When parking fees double, the residents of the city have no recourse via democracy or petition, as the meters in their city are now "owned" by a distant concentration of capital that can double late fees, charge outrageous transaction costs, etc., at will.

This is how financialization inevitably transitions into financial tyranny.

The erosion of America's middle class financial security has several structural causes, but chief among them was the financialization of the housing market. This led to a bubble of credit and housing valuations and the widespread extraction of equity for consumption—the classic "windfall" that financialization always produces in its first toxic blush. Mortgage debt doubled from $5 trillion to $10 trillion in the bubble, and now America's indentured homeowners "own" negative equity of $4 trillion.   That is, the difference between the market value of the homes they ostensibly "own" and the mortgages they took on to buy the homes is negative $4 trillion.

3. Redefine self-interest to exclude debt-servitude and dependence on consumerism and the Central State. Unless you are long retired and have no other option, minimize reliance on the State. Reliance on the State weakens the correlation between sustained effort and gain, so the work ethic and entrepreneurism both atrophy as they no longer offer competitive advantages in a system where bread and circuses are guaranteed by the State.

4. Act on your awareness that the nature of prosperity and financial security is changing. Dependence on centralized concentrations of power (Wall Street and the Central State) is now an extremely risky wager that what is demonstrably unsustainable will magically become sustainable at some distant point in time via pixie dust or the intervention of aliens from Alpha Centuri. Security flows from resilience, self-reliance, decentralized, diversified sources of income and abundant social capital.

5. Stop supporting distant concentrations of capital that subvert democracy by using their gargantuan profits to buy the machinery of State governance and regulation. For example, stop watching broadcast programming owned by the six global media corporations that control the vast majority of the media/marketing complex.

Stop eroding your health and sending your money to corporate headquarters for distribution to the financial aristocracy—stop frequenting corporate fast-food restaurants and stop buying unhealthy packaged foods from corporate agribusiness.

Close your accounts with Wall Street investment firms and the five "too big to fail" banks that dominate the mortgage, credit and debt markets in the U.S. If you need such an account to transact your business, then maintain low balances so the banks cannot "sweep" your capital for their own use every day.

6. Stop supporting the debt-and-leverage based financial aristocracy. Liquidate all debt as soon as possible, take on no new debt except for short periods of time, explore localized or "crowd-sourced" private-capital loans that exclude the banks and limit the number of financial transactions that enrich the banks and Wall Street.

7. Transfer your assets out of Wall Street and into local enterprises or assets that do not enrich and empower Wall Street.

8. Refuse to participate in consumerist status identifiers and the social defeat they create. Stop admiring and respecting those displaying status signifiers; start thinking of them as pathetic prisoners of a pathological mindset. Stop judging people as "lower value" based on their lack of status signifiers. Free your own mind from the toxic sociopathology of consumerism and social defeat. Stop watching commercial television, block advertisements on the web, and minimize your exposure to marketing and consumerist propaganda.

9. Vote in every election with an eye on rewarding honesty and truth and punishing empty promises. Unless the incumbent has renounced corporate contributions, unsustainable debt, financial tyranny and Central State encroachment of civil liberties, then vote against the incumbent, for they are just another lackey of the State-plutocracy partnership. Avoid voting for either the Demopublican or Republicrat branches of the plutocracy; vote for an independent or third party candidate.

Remember that resistance isn't just about refusing to participate in pathological plutocracy; it's about establishing a sustainable alternative to the unsustainable State-plutocracy partnership. When people say that voting for a third-party candidate is "wasting your vote," reply that voting for either of the plutocrat parties is the real waste of a vote because their "leadership" is dooming the nation to destabilization and insolvency. As independents pick up more and more "wasted" votes, they shift from being "marginalized" to becoming powerful voices of honesty and transparency.

10. Stop supporting inflationary policies such as "money creation" by the Federal Reserve and Federal deficit borrowing; act on your knowledge that inflation is theft and that the Federal Reserve is a private consortium of banks that is the enabler and protector of the parasitic financial aristocracy.

11. Become healthy, active and fit. Refuse to consume unhealthy junk and packaged food, refuse to squander much of your time in sedentary "consumption" of corporate entertainment and digital distraction, and devote your energy and time to mastery, new skills, developing social capital and friendships, projects you "own" and enterprises that benefit your true self-interest. Refuse to follow the marketing/media siren song into chronic ill-health, addiction and social defeat.

12. Embrace self-directed coherent plans and construct a resilient, diverse inner ecology of identity and meaning. Build a social ecology of positive, active, collaborative, non-pathological people of like minds and spirits. Be powerful via resistance, not powerless via complicity.

It's easy to confuse faith and political ideology. We resist changing our understanding, as we experience this transition as instability and insecurity. But changing our minds does not require changing our faith; rather, the firmness of our faith—in our Creator, in truth, in prayer, in our ability to help others and prevail—is the bedrock that gives us the discipline and resolve to confront the brutal and unwelcome facts of our circumstances and make coherent plans accordingly.

Chapter Ten: **The Limited, Protective State**

We have seen how the current political structure is a pyramid, with financial and political Elites dominating the State which then dominates the national ecosystem of communities and open markets. The only way to escape financial and political tyranny is to restore the balance of power between communities, transparent markets and the Central State so neither private nor State Elites can dominate the entire national ecosystem.

As noted in the Introduction, we cannot know when the Central State and financial system will destabilize, we only know they will destabilize. We cannot know which of the State's fast-rising debts and obligations will be renounced or written down; we only know the debts and obligations will be renounced in one fashion or another.

Once the State and financial aristocracy's debt-dependent empires destabilize and collapse, the citizenry will have a golden opportunity to "reset" the Central State to an updated version of the Founding Fathers' intent, a limited State devoted to establishing and protecting the core freedoms of faith, movement, exchange, expression, enterprise and association.

The forces of greed, monopoly and tyranny will always try to suppress the forces of low-intensity instability—transparency, innovation, volatility, dissent, experimentation, competition, transparency, meritocracy, accountability, consequence, accurate communication of facts and the free exchange of information—as these preclude the separation of risk and gain and the opacity that Elites require to expand their wealth and control. The forces of low-intensity instability lend dynamic stability to any system and their suppression leads to systemic collapse, so the reset State must not be allowed to suppress these decentralizing forces.

As noted earlier, the sole purpose of this limited but powerful State is to protect the citizenry from external aggression and predation and exploitation by criminal organizations and extreme concentrations of wealth and power.

In the current Status Quo, the State's imperative is to expand its reach and control into every niche of the national ecosystem. In granting the State coercive powers, we must also set strict limits on its expansion.

Though we cannot know the precise technologies that will be available to the citizenry when the State and financial order destabilize, it is self-evident that the World Wide Web enables a level of transparency and direct democracy that was simply not possible in the 1780s when the core Constitution was drafted. In updating the Constitution, we should be mindful of the positive role technologically enabled transparency can play in limiting the corrupting opacity sought by Elites, and the potential for direct citizen engagement and democracy in matters of governance and regulation.

There are only two systemic limits on the State's expansion:

1. An active, engaged citizenry that demands transparency and accountability in all State functions.

2. A limit on the State and its central bank (if any) from printing or creating money.

If the State can print or create money from thin air, then it will do so to fund its expansion until the currency's value has been depreciated to near-zero. Therefore the State must be denied the power to create money; the national currency must be based on the discipline imposed by a tangible asset (for example, gold) or by the time-honored precepts of "sound money," that is, a limited money supply that only expands in parallel with the expansion of production of goods and services.

Creating money out of thin air is simply theft by hidden means. If the money supply expands while the output of real goods and services remains stagnant, then that rise in money supply steals purchasing power from everyone holding the currency.

Leverage must also be limited. For example, if 50% of all loans outstanding must be held in real money (for example, gold or tangible-asset-backed notes), then that reserve requirement doesn't allow the sort of leverage (26-to-1) that has corrupted the current banking system.

There must be no central bank, as a central bank is intrinsically the financial aristocracy's enabler and enforcer. If a central bank has the power to print money, then it will debase the currency to favor its banking cronies and the State's fiefdoms. The only way to limit the debasement of the nation's money and limit the financial aristocracy's political power is to outlaw central banks.

The banking cartel gained power, like all cartels, by consolidating smaller rivals and eliminating competition and risk. The only way to limit the power of the banking cartel is to outlaw consolidation and cartels. As of today, five "too big to fail" banks control most of the mortgage and banking industry. The most direct way to limit the political power of cartels is to limit banks' reach and capital. Thus commercial banking must be separated from investment banking, and the nation should be served by 500 moderate-sized banks that are banned from consolidating into five dominant ones.

A simple rule that limits any financial corporation or entity to no more than 10% of the local market and 5% of the national market within its industry will effectively eliminate monopoly and make assembling a politically dominant national monopoly impossible.

Apologists for monopoly will protest that this forced diversity is "inefficient." Tyranny and monopoly may be superficially "efficient," but then monocultures and tyrannies are systemically unstable and prone to collapse—so there is a hidden systemic cost to the "efficiency" of tyranny and monopoly. Once monopoly is established, then prices rise and the profits create a positive feedback loop: the more profit concentrates in an Elite, the more political power that Elite can purchase.

We should note that democracy is itself inherently "inefficient," as transparency and dissent impose costs along with stability and resilience, just as diverse ecosystems are superficially "inefficient" compared to monocultures. Competition and all the other forces of low-intensity instability impose a "cost" but the gain is systemic stability and adaptability.

There must be risk, i.e. a threat of loss, in any system, especially the Central State. Thus the ideal State is unable to separate risk from gain, and the citizenry must be empowered by rule of law to dismiss its officeholders, both elected and unelected, for corruption, fraud, blocking transparency or incompetence.

No State can remain uncorrupted unless equality under the law for all individuals is rigidly enforced. No State can remain uncorrupted if powerful financial entities such as corporations are granted the same rights as citizens. No State can remain uncorrupted if property rights are not inviolate. No State can remained uncorrupted if money is allowed to influence elections and the machinery of governance.

Thus the only way to keep concentrations of capital from influencing and capturing the State is to prohibit all money from electoral and governance processes. The only systemic way to do this is to ban all private campaign funding of cash, goods or services and have a system of publicly financed elections.

As always, public finance is like democracy and competitive capitalism, "imperfect" and "inefficient," just as financial tyranny and monopoly are "efficient."

The other highway to financial tyranny is lobbying, and so the reset State must forbid lobbyists from receiving any compensation and must forbid the contributions of cash, goods or services to any State employee or contractor. Lobbying by private citizens and corporate employees will be allowed as free speech, but they must pay their own expenses, and cannot give any form of value (cash, gifts, etc.) to any individual employed or paid by the State.

To prohibit "revolving door" corruption between State employees and State contractors, then anyone leaving State service cannot take employment with any State contractor for 15 years, and the same is true for employees of State contractors. Only after the passing of half a career (15 years) can an individual slip through the revolving door between the State and its suppliers.

It is necessary to emphasize that complex systems arise from a small number of initial conditions, core dynamics and imperatives, and so each initial condition must simply and directly establish the imperative of the system.

The Reset State's sole imperative must be to protect itself and the citizenry from predation, exploitation, and the corruption of concentrated wealth and power. Nuance, complexity and exception are the stuff of tyranny; the laws must be simple, direct and inviolable:

1. No private funding of elections

2. No paid lobbying; private unpaid lobbying by individuals and corporate officers is protected freedom of speech

3. No gifts or money can pass from lobbyists to State employees or contractors

4. No State employee can take employment with a State contractor for 15 years, and vice versa.

It is important to choose initial conditions which enable only those dynamics and imperatives that define the State's sole purpose: to protect the citizenry (and thus itself, as the system's immune system) from predation, exploitation, corruption and financial tyranny.

The State must not be allowed to expand into a Savior State. The State's mandate and budget must be aggressively circumscribed to its one core task: limiting predation and protecting the citizens from external threats and domestic concentrations of wealth and power.

In designing the Reset State, we must always keep in mind that the State exists solely to defend the nation from external aggression and to limit the influence of criminals and concentrations of wealth and power. Beyond these tasks, the State exists only to enable the citizens to arrange their lives and enterprises as they see fit, what the Declaration of Independence summarized as the right to life, liberty and the pursuit of happiness.

The State's task as the nation's "immune system" is to seek out and destroy criminal networks, fraud, embezzlement and corruption; its task is not to "manage" the economy but to let the citizenry and their local governments and enterprises make their own arrangements, only intervening to limit concentrations of wealth and power from pursuing exploitation, predation and corruption.

The Reset State doesn't borrow money to fund itself; it collects tax revenues, pays its expenses in cash and provides the citizenry with a transparent accounting of its expenditures and actions.

The ultimate goal of resistance is to restore the limited yet powerfully protective State that was long ago swallowed up by the expansive debt-dependent Savior State.

The guiding principle of this small, limited, powerfully protective State is transparency in all things, for with transparency comes accountability, a free exchange of information and ideas, and dissent. In terms of system dynamics, the Reset State must be continuously exposed to risk, innovation, dissent, competition, variation, experimentation, transparency, meritocracy, feedback, accountability, consequence, accurate communication of facts and the free exchange of information --all aspects of the forces of low-intensity instability that lend dynamic stability to any system.

Human happiness and fulfillment are only possible in a political/economic system specifically, consciously designed to sustain freedom of faith, movement, expression, enterprise and association. Thus the Reset State enables the free and open exchange of goods and services, at values agreed upon by participants, and enables freedom of faith, movement, expression, enterprise and association. It protects individuals, small groups and the commons shared by all (environmental, intellectual, communication channels such as the Internet) from the predation and exploitation of larger groups and concentrations of wealth, and punishes aggressors and transgressors by isolation and ostracism.

Transparency, accountability and the power of dissent all depend on an engaged citizenry. Just as the State acts as an "immune system" protecting the nation from monopoly and the corruption of private Elites, the citizenry must act as the "immune system" of the State itself. Without an engaged citizenry, then no system can remain uncorrupted and stable, as the forces that create stability are the forces of engagement, transparency and dissent. If the State Elites never face the risk of losing their privilege and power, then there is no feedback of accountability to resist their eventual corruption by private-sector Elites.

The "perfect State" is an imperfect, dynamic state, rigid only in its protection of dissent, civil liberties, transparency, risk, accountability and citizen engagement. As a result, it intrinsically possesses the flexibility, resilience and adaptability of a diverse, decentralized ecosystem. Thus our goal is a system that insists on decentralization, dissent and transparency in all things.

The U.S. is blessed with the sound initial conditions of the Constitution. But as the debt-dependent expansionist Savior State and the current financial tyranny have shown, the present Constitution failed to limit the powers of the State or their capture by private concentrations of wealth and power.

When the Savior State and its financial aristocracy implode in insolvency, the citizenry will have a golden opportunity to "re-install" the Constitution as the initial conditions of a small, limited State devoted solely to the noble task of protecting itself and the nation's citizens from external aggression, political oppression, and the predation, exploitation and corruption imposed by sociopathological concentrations of wealth and power.

Charles Hugh Smith
Berkeley, California USA
March 2012

15043053R00122

Made in the USA
Lexington, KY
06 May 2012